ALL &
HOLD
DEAR

OTHER BOOKS BY JENNIE HANSEN

Run Away Home

Journey Home

Coming Home

When Tomorrow Comes

Macady

Some Sweet Day

ALL I HOLD DEAR

a novel

Jennie Hansen

Covenant Communications, Inc.

Cover images ® 1999 PhotoDisc, Inc.

"Book of Mormon Stories" by Elizabeth Fetzer Bates
© The Church of Jesus Christ of Latter-day Saints
Used by Permission

Published by Covenant Communications, Inc.
American Fork, Utah

Printed in the United States of America
First Printing: April 1999

06 05 04 03 02 01 00 99   10 9 8 7 6 5 4 3 2 1

ISBN 1-57734-477-4

This book is dedicated with deepest love to my father, Jed Smith. Along with giving me an appreciation for mountains, streams, and all of God's creations, he taught me the gospel. He also shared with me his love for a good story, and taught me to work hard and to dream big dreams. Thank you, Daddy.

ONE

Icy prickles ran up the back of his neck, warning him he was being followed. His eyes went to the rearview mirror searching for any sign of his pursuer. Nothing but a wall of white met his eyes. Still he knew. Whoever was following had moved closer.

A slight loss of traction and a tug to the right reminded him to keep his attention focused on the twisting mountain road. The road was paved, but it wasn't maintained like the freeway he'd left an hour ago, and it had been some time since he'd passed another vehicle. If he had an accident or became stranded, he was on his own.

The big four-wheel-drive Grand Cherokee Jeep he drove wasn't immune to icy roads, but it improved the odds he'd make it. Carefully he steered into the skid and his breath resumed a more normal cadence as he felt the tires once more grip the pavement. The higher he climbed, the heavier the snowfall became. Soon it would be accumulating on the road and he'd have to stop to put on chains.

Once more his eyes darted nervously to his side mirror. The gloom of dusk had given way to night, making travel on the mountain impossible without lights. Still nothing behind him, but they were out there. The absence of traffic warned him the locals were expecting heavy snow and were staying put.

He couldn't say how he knew he was being followed. Perhaps it was paranoia, brought on by torture and starvation during the long months of his mistaken incarceration in South America—that was how the shrink back in Dallas had explained it—but he couldn't shake the feeling. Someone was out there and whoever he was, that someone had hovered nearby, playing some kind of waiting game while he'd been recuperating in the hospital. And when he'd checked himself out and begun his journey north, he'd felt a sinister presence following. Since the snow began falling an hour ago, he'd sensed his relentless shadow drawing closer.

He hadn't once caught a glimpse of anyone following, and he'd tried several times, to shake or expose whoever was behind him, without any luck, but the feeling persisted. He couldn't even say how he knew he was being followed. He just knew. He laughed mirthlessly at his own expense. He didn't know how he could be so sure someone who meant him harm was following him when he certainly didn't know much else. Not even his name.

The shrink back at the hospital had told him he was Nicholas Mascaro, but the name didn't feel right. The only name that really stuck in his head was Sam. He didn't know if that was his own name or the name of the person he had to find. He wished he had more than a shadowy impression that he had to find someone. Some force deep inside himself wouldn't let him rest or even try to trace his own past until he found this mysterious person.

His grip tightened on the steering wheel as he strained to see between the intermittent swipes of the windshield wipers, and the urgency gnawing at the back of his mind grew sharper. He sensed time was running out. He had to be there. He wasn't even sure exactly where he had to be and he didn't have a clue why, but from the moment he'd awakened in that hospital in Dallas, some powerful premonition had warned him he wasn't safe and that he had to reach Colorado. Once he reached Colorado, something had drawn him on. He'd stopped at a truck stop to pick up a road map, and the moment his eyes found a tiny dot high in the Rockies, he'd known his destination was a wide spot in the road called Isadora, named for some prospector's mule. He didn't know how he knew the story of the town's name, but he did.

He couldn't have lived in Isadora unless the shrink had lied to him, and he couldn't see any reason why he would have done that. Supposedly he had grown up on his grandfather's farm in Vermont. As far as he knew, he'd never been to Colorado.

By the time he reached the summit, the snow had obliterated the road. He could only divine where to drive by following the wide space devoid of trees that lay between two towering banks of snow which had been pushed there by state road crews after the last storm. He'd have to stop soon to chain his tires. The all-season tires on his Cherokee were good, but not good enough to begin the downward journey without the extra traction of chains.

At the top, the plowed area widened, allowing him space to pull over. Before leaving the vehicle, he pulled the hood of his heavy sweatshirt over his head and zipped up the windbreaker he wore over the shirt. He'd wanted to purchase a heavy parka before he began this trip, but the store in Texas didn't carry anything heavier than the lined windbreaker, and his reluctance to stop any longer than necessary to purchase gas and food had prevented him from seeking out a clothing store as he drove north. Before reaching for the door handle, he flexed his fingers inside the leather driving gloves he'd purchased back at the truck stop along with the chains and a coil of thin nylon rope.

The wind stole his breath as he stepped into the storm. Some ingrained habit had him scanning the slope of the mountain he had so recently traversed. Visibility was poor and he could see little else but snow and the dark shapes of trees, but *he* was still out there, still coming closer.

Quickly he spread out the chains and though he didn't consciously remember performing the task before, that portion of his brain that continued to elude him took over and swiftly completed the task. Before stepping back inside the utility, he once again scanned the road behind him.

The tiniest flash of light caught his eye and his heartbeat accelerated. He watched the faint prick of light appear and disappear as the driver of an unseen vehicle maneuvered his way up the steep switchbacks. Indecision swept through him. He could get back in his car and continue on, hoping to evade his pursuer once he reached a lower elevation, or he could conceal himself and wait until the other vehicle reached the summit. Surprise would be on his side and he'd know at last who was persistently trailing him.

Red showed briefly, then again. The driver of the approaching car was applying his brakes at increasingly frequent intervals. A quick mental recap of the road told him as he watched through the snowy whiteness that the other driver was approaching a particularly bad curve. It was difficult to tell much from the glimpses he caught of moving lights, but he suspected that neither the driver nor the vehicle were prepared for the Colorado Rockies in a snowstorm.

Even as the thought ran through his mind that the other vehicle was moving too fast for the conditions, he saw the red flush of brake lights magnified by the snow, then watched as the lights wavered back and forth before forming a graceful arc plummeting down the mountainside.

For several seconds he stared uncomprehending at the spot where the light had disappeared. Slowly silence settled around him. Even the roar of the wind-driven snow took on a hush. He was alone. For the first time in a very long time no one was watching him. Pursuit had ended with that arc of light.

He climbed back in the Cherokee with every intention of continuing his journey, but as he shifted gears he knew he couldn't do it. On the off-chance that someone had survived the crash, he had to go back down the mountain. Maybe, just maybe, he consoled himself, he'd recognize his pursuer and discover why he was being followed.

Slowly he backed and turned until he could begin to retrace his route. As he edged his way carefully down the steep descent, he considered the possibility he might be walking into a trap. He wondered what it was inside him that wouldn't allow him to take advantage of this short reprieve and simply disappear over the mountain. He didn't question how he knew that his pursuit had only been temporarily interrupted. The rapid swipe of wiper blades mocked the inner voice that told him he couldn't leave without making certain the occupant of that car wasn't suffering and in need of help.

When he reached the curve where the other vehicle had left the road, he parked and peered over the side where a shattered guardrail testified that he hadn't imagined the car's hapless flight. He didn't waste time wondering what to do, but quickly returned to his Jeep for the spool of nylon cord he'd purchased along with groceries and chains early this morning. Securing one end of the cord to the trailer hitch on his bumper and wrapping the other end around his waist and one shoulder to form a kind of harness, he began the laborious trip down the steep mountainside.

The snow was light and powdery, like Utah snow; otherwise he would have been soaked to the skin before he traveled twenty feet. Fleetingly he wondered how he knew about Utah snow. He dismissed the question; there were too many things a Vermont schoolboy who grew up to become a Dallas businessman couldn't explain.

Even powder turns wet in time and he could feel cold and wetness along his legs as he struggled through the knee-deep snow. More than once he stumbled over unseen rocks and shrubs and fell to his knees. Sometimes he rolled or skidded a considerable distance before regaining his feet. Each time, he struggled to become upright again and resume his trek down the mountainside.

He nearly tripped over the wreckage before he actually saw it. Raising one hand he wiped the snow from his face and eyelashes and stared at the twisted white sedan lying tilted to one side and tightly wedged between two tall spruces. Inanely he noticed the tires first, top-of-the-line touring tires, excellent for speed, but not meant for climbing the Rockies in a Colorado blizzard.

A caution that seemed to be instinctive had him moving slowly along the side of the vehicle as he approached the driver's crumpled door. The glass was gone from the window and he peered inside. At first the vehicle appeared to be empty and it took several seconds to recognize the snow-mounded shape lying across the seat and partially tucked beneath the dash as a human form.

Opening the door proved impossible, so he reached through the broken window to brush away the snow obscuring the man's face. The face meant nothing to him. Removing a glove, he moved his fingers along the side of the man's neck, searching for a pulse he knew he wouldn't find.

Withdrawing his head from the car window, he stood with both hands braced against the side of the wreck. What now? he questioned. Had this man been following him? How could he be certain?

There was only one answer and he grimaced in distaste; he'd have to search the body and the vehicle. He felt like a vulture as he circled the trees and car to approach from the lower side. Brushing snow from the mangled license plate he confirmed that the car had come from Texas, though he couldn't decipher all of the numbers.

He'd noticed the windows were both missing from the passenger side and the caved-in roof left a little more clearance on that side than over the driver's seat. He dropped to his knees, and after considerable struggle he pulled his six-foot frame through the narrow opening.

Gasping for breath, either from exertion or high altitude, he needed several minutes to orient himself to the task at hand. At least the blowing snow was less forceful inside the wreck, though it continued to sift a dusting of powder throughout the interior of the car.

With meticulous care he brushed snow from the body in the front seat and checked each pocket. He noted without surprise that the dead man had bled very little. Either his more serious injuries had been internal or the cold had inhibited the blood flow. He found a wallet with plenty of cash, but no identification. A small cell phone on the man's belt had been crushed beyond any possibility of salvaging. Next he turned to the glove compartment that had popped open due to the force with which the car had struck some object in its tumble down the mountain.

His hand closed around cold steel in its search for registration papers. Slowly he withdrew the gun and recognized its familiar weight and shape. Somewhere in his own murky past he'd had more than a passing familiarity with a semi-automatic Smith & Wesson like this one. Automatically he checked the load and removed one cartridge before tucking the gun in the back of his belt, beneath his jacket. Even if the gun were accidentally fired, the hammer would first strike an empty chamber.

Continuing his search, he placed a plastic box of shells and a sheaf of papers in his jacket pocket. He'd read the papers later. Even though the falling snow provided a kind of light, he couldn't see well enough to read. The gun and the driver's lack of I.D. verified his hunch that this man had been following him, but it wasn't conclusive evidence. He turned his head to where keys dangled from the ignition, but he knew an attempt to open the trunk would be futile. He'd already noticed how tightly the rear end of the car was lodged against one of the spruces, completely pinning the crushed trunk closed. Now that he was no longer moving, cold seeped through his wet clothes, reminding him he'd better get back to his own vehicle and get warm.

Sudden pain struck the back of his head. Convulsively his hands gripped the mangled dashboard and his body stiffened, expecting a second blow. When it didn't come, he slowly relaxed and looked around. Grimacing, he recognized his mistake. He'd been too hasty in his attempt to extricate his head and shoulders from the cramped space where he'd been conducting his search, and he'd bumped his head against an overhead piece of steel.

Lowering his head, he once more began to move backward. As he told his hands to release their death grip on the dashboard, something in the back of his mind began to scream an alert. His eyes flew to his hands. His left hand was gripping more than a twisted dashboard. Carefully he brushed away the remaining snow covering the object. He recognized it at once. No amount of wishful thinking could convince him the strange box with a small readout screen and several dials was a simple laptop or even a fuzzbuster. He had his answer; he was being followed all right, and he'd never spotted the car because it could stay miles behind and easily follow him with a tracking device like this one. In a flash of memory, he could see himself using a similar device on a fast-moving speed boat. A man with long black hair stood at the helm. Then, as quickly as the memory came, it was gone.

Cold sweat broke out down his back. Now he knew for sure someone was following him, but he still had no idea why. Panic surged through him. He had to get out; he had to get away; he had to reach Isadora. But first . . . he reached behind him and withdrew the gun. The accident had probably disabled the tracking device, but two or three sharp blows made certain it would tell no more tales.

By the time he worked his way out of the wreckage and recoiled the end of the nylon cord around himself, he knew there was no need to try to cover his tracks. The wind had increased to an eerie howl and the snow swirled in dizzying waves. The storm would hide any evidence he'd been there. It might be days before someone discovered the broken guardrail and searched the slope below. The car would remain invisible from the road until spring.

The cord wasn't as helpful as a climbing rope would have been, but it kept him moving in the right direction and prevented his sliding back down the mountain as he stumbled steadily upward. Fatigue and cold took their toll, and he speculated whether adrenaline had the same power as antifreeze to keep a moving object from freezing. A hysterical laugh broke free and that sobered him enough to keep him climbing for several more minutes.

When he finally bumped into the guardrail, he stood stupidly trying to remember something for several seconds before he connected the rail with the Cherokee and stumbled forward the remaining few steps. His hands wouldn't work properly, and it took several agonizing minutes to open the door and collapse inside.

His teeth chattered and his movements were slow and clumsy as he fumbled to wrap himself in the car blanket he'd left on the back seat. He should remove his wet clothes and get into something dry, but his awkward fingers were beyond struggling with zippers and buttons. He just wanted to sleep, but an angry voice in the back of his head shouted he'd come too far to stop now. Sleep was death.

He had to reach Isadora; he had to find Sam. With a groan he pulled himself to a sitting position and fumbled with the key. It took several tries before the engine roared to life. Slumping forward, he pressed his aching head against the steering wheel until life-giving warmth revived him enough to make him realize he couldn't just sit there. He had to keep moving; he had to get away.

Before shifting into gear, he pulled a small brown bottle from a bag on the seat. One of the painkillers would take care of his headache, but he hesitated in the act of reaching for the thermos bottle that sat between the seats. He'd experienced this same reluctance before, almost as though he were violating some taboo. His hands shook as he poured coffee into the lid and brought the cup to his mouth. He swallowed the tablet, drained the cup, and shuddered. He didn't like the taste any better now than he had when they'd brought a cup of the hot brew to him in the hospital, but at least it was warm and perhaps the caffeine would help him fight off the lethargy that threatened to lull him to sleep.

Even with chains, the return trip to the summit was slow and arduous. Twice he had to back up to gain a running start to force the Jeep through monstrous drifts. The descent on the other side passed in a haze. He was only vaguely aware of driving through rolling foothills and crossing wide meadows.

Toward morning the snow began to subside and in the distance he could see a few lights indicating a small town. He anticipated getting breakfast and a room where he could sleep for a few hours before going on. He didn't know how much time he had. Common sense told him that whoever had invested in a sophisticated tracking device to follow him hadn't acted alone. Someone else was out there, and when he found his tracker had disappeared, he'd take up the chase.

Two things happened at once. A road appeared to the right and his foggy mind made a connection it should have made hours ago. The only way that the tracking device could have followed him all the way from Texas was if a signaling device was attached to his own vehicle. He didn't doubt for a minute someone else would pick up the signal and resume the chase. Without consciously planning his action, he swerved to the right. He could see steep mountains in that direction. He'd find an isolated area and go over the Cherokee with a fine-tooth comb until he found that device, then he'd destroy it. If he couldn't find the transmitter, he'd have to abandon the truck.

Thirty miles up the sadly deteriorating road, the choice was made for him when the engine sputtered and died. As he grabbed for the emergency brake to keep from rolling backward down the steep mountain road and off the side, he berated himself for his own folly. He should have continued on to the small town he'd seen just before dawn and bought gas. How could something so important have completely slipped his mind?

Closing his eyes, he shook his head and wondered if he might be insane. It wasn't the first time he'd questioned his mental condition. Two weeks ago he'd awakened in a private room in a Dallas hospital with almost no memory of who he was and how he'd gotten there. He'd been plagued by horrifying dreams that made no sense. Vague memories of a jungle cell and indescribable pain haunted his waking hours. There was also something he mustn't tell anyone. A doctor had assured him that physically he was fine, though he was seriously malnourished. The good doctor had continued to provide him with bits and pieces of his life, though nothing but the agonizing months he'd spent in a foreign jail felt real. The doctor had given him a prescription for pain medication for his persistent headaches and encouraged him to talk about a past he couldn't remember.

Someone from Washington—he never had gotten it straight whether the man was C.I.A., military, or some kind of lawyer—had told him his imprisonment had been a mistake and his rescue was an accident. He'd been on a business trip to South America when guerrillas in the war-torn country had mistaken him for a gunrunner who had double-crossed them. They'd held him until government soldiers had stormed the insurgents' stronghold, freed him, and turned him over to the U.S. consulate. Some American politician had flown him back to Texas aboard his private jet.

The government man had told him to put it all behind him, return to his condo and his healthy bank account, and get on with his life. Only he couldn't do it. His unreliable mind warned him not to confide in anyone, that he was still in danger, and urged him to flee.

Crazy or not, he couldn't continue to sit here and wait for the snow to bury him. He opened his eyes and felt something strange as he surveyed the mountainous splendor all around him. He had no idea where he might be, but he'd been here before. The mountain peaks, even shrouded in white and trailing lingering clouds, were the first familiar sight he'd recognized since he'd awakened in the hospital. He knew, too, that a small cabin lay nestled in a side canyon approximately six miles further up the road. Excitement gripped him and his mind filled with purpose.

He reached behind him for his duffle bag, then decided not to take it with him. The hike would be difficult in knee-high snow, and the bag would be too much to carry. Instead he unzipped the bag and drew out two pairs of heavy socks and an old pair of sweat pants someone had loaned him while he'd been in the hospital. Without removing the jeans that had dried and stiffened against his legs, he pulled the sweat pants over them. He removed his running shoes and replaced his damp pair of socks with new ones, then struggled back into the shoes. Reaching into his bag once more, he grabbed a couple of t-shirts, a sweater, and a fresh hooded sweatshirt. After donning them, he rezipped his jacket, then hesitated before reaching for the small brown plastic bottle. He shoved it into his jacket pocket with the box of shells and the papers he'd taken from the wreck. He drained the last of the coffee and shoved an apple and a package of cookies into the other pocket of his windbreaker.

Taking a deep breath, he opened his door, then reaching sideways, he released the emergency brake. As the Jeep Cherokee began rolling backward, he jumped to the ground. At first it moved sluggishly and he wondered if the deep snow would force it to a halt, but slowly it gained momentum. When the Jeep reached a curve a hundred yards away, unlike the road, it failed to turn. In seconds it left the road, appeared to teeter at the edge of the cliff, then tumbled over the edge. When the sound of tearing metal pounding against rocks far below caught his ears, he turned his back and began walking.

TWO

Courtney stirred her cereal listlessly, then reached for the stack of mail beside her plate. Most were Christmas cards, but a rich creamy envelope caught her attention and she winced. Without even opening it, she knew it was a wedding invitation and the last thing she wanted to do was attend a wedding. She couldn't bear to be happy today for whichever of her friends was announcing marriage plans. Her own wedding should have been today.

She closed her eyes briefly. She wouldn't cry. She'd shed enough tears over Greg in the past two months to fill an ocean. She was through crying. A broken engagement wasn't the end of the world, even if it did feel like it.

Turning the envelope over and over in her hands, curiosity began to sink in and she wondered who had sent it. Most of her friends had been married for years. Penny Jensen, her best friend all through school, had married two months after they graduated from high school and now had four children. All of the girls she'd gone to school with had been married before their five-year class reunion. A few had been married twice in that time. Courtney couldn't even bring to mind any of her former college roommates who were still single. Two of the other teachers at the high school were single, but as far as she knew, neither one was dating anyone special.

Idly she slid a fingernail beneath the seal and lifted out the embossed invitation. A familiar face met her unbelieving eyes; Greg and some blonde, who looked as though she were posing for a tooth-paste commercial, smiled brilliantly at each other. Courtney must have made some kind of cry because even before her mind registered the sound of her father scraping back his chair, he was beside her.

"What is it, honey?" He pulled her to her feet and wrapped his arms around her.

She couldn't speak. Instead, deep shudders wracked her body as she struggled to catch her breath.

"That skunk! And today of all days! He ought to be shot!" Her mother had spotted the invitation. In seconds her cheek pressed against Courtney's and she whispered consoling words punctuated with tart pronouncements concerning Greg's character while Courtney dissolved in tears.

"Now, Mom, who are you planning to shoot?" Jake asked in a teasing voice. Courtney hadn't heard Jake and his wife, along with Luke, enter the room, and she struggled to control her sobs. She didn't want to have to explain to her brothers. But it was too late; she heard Luke explode in a torrent of words she'd never heard either of her brothers use before. He, too, had caught sight of the invitation.

"Shooting's too good for him," Luke muttered.

"He's getting something far worse than shooting," Jake's wife, Lillian, drawled. "He's marrying John Brewster's daughter, Becky."

"What?!" Courtney screamed. "Let me see that invitation." She tore herself from her father's sheltering embrace and grabbed the offending scrap of paper from Luke's hand. It was true. Greg was marrying Becky Brewster. Her mind could hardly assimilate the news; she used to babysit the Brewster's spoiled little darling. Doing some quick mental arithmetic, she arrived at seventeen, maybe eighteen. Greg's bride was twelve years younger than her own twenty-nine—and thirteen years younger than Greg. Had the Brewsters lost their minds? How could they let Becky marry so young? Why were they even allowing her to date a man so much older than herself?

She already knew the answers to her questions. The Brewsters had never denied their baby anything she wanted. And if Becky had decided she wanted Greg, neither Greg nor her parents would get far trying to change her mind. Courtney also knew Greg. When she had made the painful decision to end their engagement, he hadn't accepted their broken engagement with any degree of grace. He'd immediately struck out at her with hateful words and vowed she'd regret her foolish choice. She feared his sudden engagement to Becky had its basis more in retaliation against her than real caring for Becky.

She also knew money and position were important to Greg and that the Brewsters were considered one of the wealthiest families in the state with their considerable land and business holdings. They had close ties to the state house and to Colorado's powerful senior senator. Greg had had financial dealings with the Brewsters during the time she'd known him.

She'd met Greg eighteen months ago when he'd come to the ranch with an offer to buy two hundred acres of ranch land for a developer who wished to put summer homes on the land. The Grant ranch was a large tract of land in one of the state's most scenic areas, a fact which had fascinated her former fiancé. As a realtor and property manager, Greg had known the Grant ranch was valued in seven or eight figures. Even after her father refused the offer, Greg didn't understand that although a third of the ranch would be hers some day, the value of the land and stock were not the same as cash assets. Income from a working ranch fell far short of the one-time price tag a developer placed on it.

"Um, uh, I better get back to Amy. She's not feeling well this morning." Luke patted his sister's shoulder awkwardly and started toward the door. Both of Courtney's brothers had built homes on the ranch they operated in partnership with their father. "Let me know if you need me to kick that guy into the next county." Disguising his pity for his big sister behind little-brother flippancy, Luke rushed out the door. Luke and Amy's first child was due in a couple of weeks, and the closer her due date came, the more nervous Luke became. He found excuses to check on his wife a dozen times a day.

Her other brother, Jake, stood with his arm around his wife's shoulder, and Courtney sensed that their whispered conversation concerned her. A wave of bleak loneliness washed over her. Everyone in the whole world seemed to be part of a pair except her. Years ago when they were growing up, she'd never once considered her girl-shy younger brothers would marry before she did. Though she'd loved college and enjoyed her job teaching at the high school, marriage and a family had always been her vision of the future. She'd had boyfriends, but somehow had never developed a serious relationship until Greg. Now she wondered if she'd fallen in love with him simply because she wanted marriage and a family so badly, and eligible bachelors near her age were few and far between in this rural area.

And though she loved both of her sisters-in-law, her brothers' happy marriages added to her own sense of incompleteness. Even her parents stood close together, her mother's hand resting on her husband's arm, as they watched her with identical concerned expressions. Instead of giving her the comfort and support she knew they intended, their united front emphasized her solitary role in life.

An advertisement from the radio seeped into her consciousness, enumerating difficult situations that were still not as difficult as losing weight. "It's harder than . . ."

"Yes," Courtney's heart responded to the Weight Watchers' commercial coming from the radio to which she'd previously been oblivious. Some things were much too hard. And being the only single in a household of couples was one of those things. Facing all her married friends' sympathy as they opened their invitations to Greg's wedding was another. She couldn't face one more Christmas or one more New Year's Eve as the only single in a world made up of pairs. Despite the painful choice she'd made two months ago, she refused to marry just to be part of a couple. She'd wouldn't sacrifice her membership in the Church or her dream of a temple marriage, even for a man she loved.

"Court," her mother spoke decisively as though reading her mind. "You need to get away for a little while. A vacation would do you good. You could go away for a couple of weeks, then still be home for Christmas."

"Mom, I can't find a substitute on such short notice. Besides where would I go?"

"I'll sub for you." Lillian spoke up from beside Jake. "I'm already on the district's substitute list."

"But you said you didn't want to teach this year."

"You know I only said that because I thought I'd be too busy being a mom by now."

"Oh, Lillian . . ." Courtney's heart went out to her sister-in-law. The whole family had been devastated by Lillian's miscarriage last summer.

"It'll do me good to have something to do besides scrub my kitchen floor and follow Jake around."

"I'm not complaining." Jake gave his wife a gentle squeeze. "I like having you tag around after me."

"Sure you do." She jabbed him in the ribs with her elbow. "That's why you make me sit in the truck while you feed the stock, or check on the kittens while you inoculate sick steers. Seriously," she stepped closer to Courtney. "I think your mother is right. It would do you good to go away for a few weeks, and it would do me good to get back in a classroom."

"This would be a good time to fly to Florida or even Hawaii," her father endorsed the plan.

"I'll get right on the phone and make reservations," her mother added, brightening.

"I don't know . . ." But suddenly she did know. She did need to get away, but she wouldn't be going to some beach resort filled with honeymooners. Being alone could only be bearable if she were truly alone. To paraphrase the Duchess of York, nothing could be harder than being the only single in a world of couples. She needed to be alone, really alone, and she knew just the place.

When Dad had formed a partnership with Jake and Luke, he'd retained a third of the property for himself and stipulated in his will that Courtney would inherit his share and that her brothers would have first right of refusal if she chose to sell. One of their first acts as partners had been to acquire a small neighboring ranch that joined the far northern end of the Grant ranch, partly in anticipation of generating enough income to support three households and partly to keep the land from going to a developer. A small house came with the property, and the three men had decided to maintain it as an occasional retreat and a place to stay while working stock or checking fences on that distant end of the ranch. She'd go there.

As she expected, her family tried to dissuade her from going to the remote homestead on her own, and when she refused to change her mind, Jake offered to drive her there. She refused his offer, but accepted her mother's assistance in packing the small trailer she planned to tow behind her snowmobile.

"Take the cell phone with you." Jake pressed the instrument into her hand.

"The reception isn't any good in the canyon," Courtney protested. "Let Luke keep it, so Amy can call him if she has problems. You know how nervous they both are since you and Lillian lost your baby."

"I'll go to town and buy another one," he grumbled. Reluctantly she tucked the phone into the small compartment in front of the seat of her snowmobile.

"You'd better be on your way," her father interrupted as he surveyed the sky with the experienced eye of a longtime outdoors man. "There'll be snow later today, but if you leave now you should have plenty of time to make it to the homestead before it starts."

"Call when you get there," her mother urged.

"Thanks, Dad." She kissed his cheek and turned to straddle her snowmobile. "Don't worry," she called to her mother. "If you don't hear from me, it will be because the phone signal doesn't reach the canyon. I'll be fine."

* * *

The snow rose to mid-thigh as he moved up the narrow road, and his breath came in short painful gasps. He'd covered less than a mile when the unplowed road came to a sudden end in a fifteen-foot-high bank of snow. If he hadn't run out of gas, he wouldn't have made it farther than this anyway, he acknowledged as he contemplated the snow bank.

His eyes traveled the surrounding mountain slopes as he wondered if he'd been wrong about the cabin. He didn't think so, and he still felt that sense of familiarity. He remembered a logging road, and a hazy picture came to mind. It was summer and he had reveled in the cool gloom beneath the towering spruces. He had ridden a trail bike up the winding trail, occasionally ducking to avoid the slap of a pine bough as he wove his way around exposed roots, rocks, and hummocks of grass. There had been another small motorbike; sometimes it trailed behind him and sometimes it was parallel in the other deep groove left by logging trucks. The picture faded. He had to find that logging road.

To the west the trees were thinner, and it seemed the right direction to go. Surely a road or trail of some kind existed beneath the snow, since a consistent expanse between the huge firs lured him onward. The trail hadn't been used for a long time, he surmised by the number of small trees crowding the narrow space.

Movement was slow and tortuous in the heavy snow, and it was well past midday when he finally left the trees behind to cross a rocky windswept stretch. Here the wind screamed across a flat barren hillside and little snow clung to the ground, revealing for the first time that his instincts were right. He truly was following a long-abandoned road. In a brief flash of memory, he saw an old pickup truck, more rust than peeling paint, lurching across this rocky high point of the road.

His lungs ached and his head pounded. He wasn't accustomed to the high thin air and his legs had become numb long ago. He could feel a wall of blackness closing in on him. He had to rest. Yet rest brought its own brand of fear. Rest was the treacherous route to hypothermia and an endless sleep.

Bracing himself between two massive boulders, he sought a minute's respite from the wind. Delving one hand into his pocket, he brought out a handful of cookies. Slowly munching on them, he struggled to breathe and prepare himself to move on. He considered swallowing one of the pain pills he'd stuck in his pocket. No, he couldn't do that. Without the pain to keep him awake, he might sit down in a snow drift and never wake up again.

Before stepping away from the shelter of the rocks, he glanced at the sky. Billowing white had changed to pewter gray; it wouldn't be long until snow began to fall once more. Whoever took up the chase would waste time ascertaining whether or not his body was in his wrecked Jeep Cherokee, and between the wind and snow there would be no trail to follow from where he'd ditched it.

Lowering his head, he trudged on, plowing his way through snow that varied from knee to waist deep. He thought about snow-shoes and wondered if he'd know how to use them if he had them. He thought he would, but some instinct or buried memory told him cross-country skis would be his first choice. Entering the pines, he sensed he was moving downward again, and he was grateful for the protection from the wind the huge trees provided.

Large flakes of snow fluttered before him and a renewed urgency coaxed him to greater speed as his exhausted body struggled to obey his mind's command. Suddenly the fat, lazy flakes were gone and in their place came driving shards of ice. Earth and sky melded into sameness. He stumbled on, not knowing whether he was moving forward or retracing the route he'd already followed.

* * *

It was mid-afternoon when Courtney crossed the last of the three huge valleys that made up the Grant ranch and stopped at the mouth of the canyon to dutifully report she'd reached that point. Static made the cellular phone practically useless; two miles inside the canyon it would be completely useless. Wind swept down from the north and she knew she'd have to hurry if she hoped to beat the storm.

Snow began to fall as she approached the homestead cabin. She made short work of hauling her groceries and belongings inside, then quickly started a fire in both the fireplace and the cookstove. By that time, the snow wiped out visibility between the cabin and the trees.

Though it was only two o'clock in the afternoon, the storm made the house seem dark and gloomy despite the roaring fires, so she lit several lanterns and scattered them about the house. When that was done she surveyed her surroundings with an eye toward picking her next task. Whichever of her brothers' wives had been here last had left everything tidy and in its place. She only needed to sweep, dust, and make her bed up with clean flannel sheets.

The house was small, just two bedrooms and one common room that doubled as a living room and kitchen, plus a small loft. She took off her coat and tackled the sweeping first. As she swept near the fire-place she admired the massive stone structure and envisioned sitting before it with a bowl of hot chili for her dinner, and later before going to bed, she'd curl up in the rocking chair and watch the flames dance as she sipped a mug of hot chocolate and read.

When a vision of Greg seated across from her in the old recliner drifted before her, she angrily put away the broom and stormed into the kitchen. In minutes she had beef for the chili sizzling on the stove, and her hands were fully occupied with kneading bread dough much more vigorously than necessary.

With dinner started she drifted back to her cleaning chores. She put the flannel sheets on the bed in the larger bedroom, then reached for a can of Pledge. She tried to hum Christmas carols as she worked, but she didn't feel like making pleasant music. And she certainly didn't feel much Christmas spirit!

Her hands stilled on the battered wood of an old piano and she remembered Greg playing the haunting strains of "Für Elise" on her mother's gleaming black grand piano. She shook her head. No matter what she did, memories of Greg intruded.

They'd dated for eight months and during that time they'd shared many wonderful experiences. He'd made her feel beautiful and loved. She'd enjoyed his keen mind and quick grasp of political realities. They shared a love for the old literary and musical classics, and if he valued money and social position more than she did, he'd never made them a big issue. He earned a more than adequate income and was liked and admired by everyone she knew. They had really only disagreed about one thing and that was the Church.

Her life had revolved around the Church for as long as she could remember, while he didn't consider religion important. When he'd asked her to marry him she hadn't hesitated to accept, believing a man as fine as Greg would surely see the light and be converted as soon as he had an opportunity to study the gospel. She'd blissfully proceeded with plans for a white Christmas wedding.

In the four months they were engaged, she'd persistently introduced gospel points into their conversation and invited him to attend church services with her. He'd adamantly refused to have anything to do with the Church, and the night she'd asked him to take the missionary lessons, he'd blown up.

"Stop harping about religion!" he'd exploded. "I don't believe any of that bull, and after we're married I don't want to see you wasting any more of your time on it either. Sunday is a realtor's biggest day. Any Sundays we're not showing properties or attending receptions, we'll be skiing or boating or doing something fun."

Shocked, she'd stared at him speechless.

"Aw, honey." He'd put his arm around her and tried to pull her closer. "You can't expect me to make all of the concessions. I went along with your archaic ideas about not sleeping together until after we're married, I agreed to no champagne at our wedding, and I'll even go to your brothers' kids' christenings if you want me to, but that's it."

Courtney shook her head to clear away the memories. She'd been foolish and naive, but in one blinding flash she'd seen where her life was headed. She'd had to choose between her faith and the man she loved. She'd prayed for help and had wept when the answer came.

Returning Greg's ring had turned into another nasty scene. He'd told her the only way she'd find a husband now would be if she found someone who wanted her share of the ranch badly enough to put up with a repressed old maid. She knew he was hurt and striking at her vulnerabilities, but she hadn't wavered even though she wondered if he was right. The prospect of never marrying and having the family she desired brought a lasting ache to her heart.

"Stop this!" she ordered herself. Vigorously she applied polish to the old upright piano. As she polished she deliberately turned her thoughts to wondering how the original owner had managed to drag the heavy musical instrument up the mountain. Someone must have cared a great deal about music to go to all the work of hauling the thing over thirty miles of dirt roads in a wagon!

Idly she ran her fingers over the ivory keys. She didn't play well, not like her mother, but she'd had four years of lessons and had once been confident enough of her ability to accept a calling as pianist for the Primary. Her fingers stretched for a familiar chord and the melody ran through her mind. She played the first two measures, then stopped. She used to hammer out this song on the piano at home to work out her frustrations when her little brothers got to be too much. Maybe it would work now.

Anxiously she flipped open the piano bench. She halfway remembered an old orange Primary hymn book. Triumphantly she pounced on it, and it practically fell open to the page she sought. Seating herself on the bench, she took a deep breath. The music was supposed to be played boldly. Well, she would play boldly! Her fingers attacked the keys and her toe reached for the pedal that would intensify the chords.

> *Book of Mormon stories that my teacher tells to me*
> *Are about the Lamanites in ancient history.*
> *Long ago their fathers came from far across the sea,*
> *Giv'n this land if they lived righteously.*

* * *

Pain in his head and behind his eyes caused him to stagger. As he clutched his head, his feet stumbled against a half-buried log, plunging him to his knees. He drew in a couple of agonizing breaths. The pain was too much. He couldn't regain his footing; he was going to die. He felt the blackness move closer. All he had to do was reach out to it, then he would be warm and safe. Nothing would ever hurt him again. The blackness was an old friend. No matter how much they beat him, the blackness sheltered him.

No! He couldn't trust the blackness any more. If he surrendered one more time, it would never let him go. But he was so tired and the pain . . . The pounding in his head took up a rhythmic beat. He raised his head. Indian drums! They were calling him. He had to find the drums!

"Please, Father, help me," he pleaded and wondered what distant remnant from the past led him to expect God would come to his aid. "Help me reach the drums." The sound of drums faded behind the howl of blowing snow.

He rose unsteadily to his feet and wavered, wondering which way to go. "Play the drums again. Please play the drums!" he shouted into the whiteness. Then came the pounding beat again. Turning to face the sound, he stumbled on.

He had to find someone. Sam. No, he was Sam, wasn't he? The wavering shape of a man with long black hair drifted before him on the wind, mocking his assertion. He wasn't searching for just any man; he had to find an Indian. Was the Indian named Sam? Something told him that the Indian knew all the secrets.

A child's voice carried on the wings of the storm and his eyes searched for the elusive figure of a little girl. He had to find the girl. He had to find Julie. Julie and Sam and the drums. They were all mixed up and he needed them. There was a light up ahead. He had to reach it before the blackness overcame him. If he stepped into the darkness this time, there would be no more light—ever.

* * *

Courtney lifted her hands from the keyboard and laughed. The music felt good and it felt wonderful to play just as loudly as she wanted to. Again she crashed through the song. Oh yes, it felt good! Perhaps like those long ago Lamanites who were awfully good at going on the war path, a little war path music might do her good, too.

Over and over she pounded out the song until a shiver slid down her back. The pages of her music fluttered in a sudden breeze. Her hands froze above the keys and her heart pounded as she turned her face toward the door.

A snow-shrouded figure stood in the open doorway as though her music had called forth the ghost of one of those ancient Lamanites. He stared at her through hollow, sunken eyes and she stared back in frozen horror.

"Julie?" he croaked in a hoarse whisper and slowly slid to the floor.

THREE

As Courtney scrambled to her feet, her elbow caught the edge of the song book and sent it crashing against the keyboard in a jarring chord before it smacked against the floor. Instinctively she ran toward the fallen man, then stopped abruptly a few feet from his side. The man was a stranger. All the warnings and horror stories of men who preyed on women found alone in isolated places thundered through her mind. She had no idea who he was or why he'd come. He was a big man; he could hurt her.

He lay still and her tender heart would not allow her to do nothing. Slowly she sank to her knees and stretched forth a hand to wipe away the snow matting his beard and hiding his face. He didn't open his eyes, but she could feel his harsh breath against her hand. He muttered an indistinct cry and she shivered. Glancing around she realized the door still stood open. Rising quickly, she started toward it, only to see she'd have to move the man's feet in order to close the door.

By tugging and twisting, she was able to move his legs far enough so she could close the door. She slammed it shut and dropped the bar into place. Leaning her back against the wood panel, she took several deep breaths as she surveyed her unexpected visitor and asked herself what she should do. Briefly she considered calling the ranch on the cell phone, then dismissed the idea. The phone wouldn't work in the canyon, and during a snowstorm not even static would get through.

The man appeared to be about the same size as Luke and Jake, though thinner. His coloring was darker than either of her brothers, and it appeared he hadn't shaved for several days. His clothes were good quality and had the same plastered and frozen look she'd seen all her life on her father and brothers when they'd been caught in winter storms while feeding or moving cattle. As he came through the door, he'd called a woman's name. For just a moment she wondered if he might have been trying to tell her a woman was still stranded out there in the storm.

No, she didn't think so. He'd called *her* Julie. Somehow he'd confused her with someone else. For a moment she envied the woman whose name was on a man's lips during his last moments of consciousness. She must be someone terribly important to him.

Briefly she closed her eyes and muttered a quick plea to her Heavenly Father to guide her actions. Then straightening, she shook off her curiosity and came to a decision. She'd treat this man the way her mother had always treated her men. Warm and dry first, then food. There were plenty of quilts and towels in the bedrooms. She'd collect them, then see if she could wake the man enough to gain his cooperation in moving closer to the fire.

She'd done her share of babysitting as she grew up, but she didn't recall that getting a wild two-year-old undressed and into pajamas had been nearly as difficult as peeling away the layers of clothing from this inert six-foot-tall man. Once she got the frozen zipper of his jacket down, removing the jacket itself had been easy compared to stripping away the layers of shirts beneath.

Hearing the crackle of paper in his pocket as she tossed the jacket aside, she promised herself to check later for clues to the man's identity.

Once the shirts were out of the way she reached for a thick terry towel to pat his face dry before vigorously rubbing his straight blue-black hair that made her wonder if he might be Native American. She guessed the man was probably a few years older than herself. In spite of the stubble of whiskers on his face and the crooked bump on his nose that hinted of a fracture at some time, he was attractive.

He moaned softly when she turned her attention to his chest and her hands stilled as she stared in horror at the dark bruises that dotted his much-too-pale skin. It hadn't occurred to her he might be injured. She'd assumed cold and exhaustion were the only problems he faced. At the same time, she realized that his skin was so pasty he couldn't possibly be from the Uintah and Ouray Reservation just across Colorado's western border. He shifted as though flinching away from her, drawing his arms in front of his face in a protective gesture, and she noted the tell-tale marks on the back of one hand. He'd recently had an IV there.

Small marks in the crook of his elbow and higher on his arms looked like needle marks. Could he be an addict? She shrugged away her speculations. Whether he was an addict or a recent hospital patient, he'd die without care. She piled two quilts over him and drew them close to his face, then tugged an old knitted hat that belonged to one of her brothers over the top of his head.

Courtney couldn't pick the laces of his frozen shoes with her fingers and had to run to the kitchen end of the room for scissors to free his feet. While there she ladled several cups of the water she'd put on to heat earlier for cleaning into a basin and added enough cold water to cool it to lukewarm.

Returning to the body sprawled on the floor, she cut his laces and worked his feet free of his heavy running shoes, then tugged until his socks were off. She carefully examined his feet for frost spots as she'd seen her mother do with her father and brothers. She wasn't certain what exactly she was looking for, other than patches of white, but it did seem to her that his feet were much paler than they should have been. She needed to soak them in the tepid water, but first she needed to get the stranger out of his wet clothes.

Though the man was much too thin, he was still heavier and more difficult to handle than she'd imagined an unconscious person could possibly be. She'd never undressed a man before in her life and she felt uncomfortable doing so now. *Stop being prudish,* she chided herself. *This is an emergency. The man's life depends on getting him out of his wet clothes, and I'm the only person around to do it.*

She wasted several minutes glaring at the luckless man before grabbing a third quilt from the pile she'd dumped on the floor and throwing it over him. It took a few minutes, but she managed to finish undressing him without dislodging the quilt. Triumphantly she tossed the wet clothing aside. Next she carefully bathed and massaged one foot, then the other.

When she finished, she rocked back on her heels and gazed expectantly at the object of her ministrations. He should be waking up. The next step was food and she certainly couldn't stuff food down an unconscious man's throat.

"Mister?" She leaned over to pat his cheeks, but he only moaned without opening his eyes.

"Come on, wake up," she urged, clasping his shoulders and giving him a slight shake. His eyelids fluttered, then suddenly she found herself staring into eyes so dark the irises and pupils seemed almost indistinguishable. A puzzled expression flickered across his face for an instant, then vanished, to be replaced by a mask-like neutrality.

"You need to eat and drink something warm." Courtney tried to hide her nervousness behind a smile. "And I think you'd be more comfortable in a chair." She waved vaguely toward the recliner a few feet away. "I'll help you."

"No," he declined her help. She winced as she watched his painful struggle to raise his head and shoulders. As he sat up, the quilt slipped from his shoulders and she reached to secure it, but the scowl he sent her way restrained her hand.

"I'll get you something warm to drink," she muttered as she turned toward the other end of the room. Deliberately keeping her back turned to the man, she reached into a cupboard for a heavy stoneware mug. While listening for the man to fall, as she strongly suspected he would, she filled the cup with hot water, added chocolate powder, hesitated, then added a half inch of milk to cool the drink to a comfortable temperature. When she finished, she steeled herself to turn around.

He stood with one hand braced against the piano for support, while his other hand clutched one of the quilts he'd somehow wrapped around himself. Bewilderment and pain were clearly etched across his face. He raised his head as though he would challenge her in some way.

"Who are you?" he croaked in a dreadful whisper.

"I'm Courtney Grant." She tried to inveigh her voice with both warmth and confidence. "Please sit down." She nodded her head toward the chair. "I'm sure you'll feel much better once you drink this."

She could see suspicion and doubt in his eyes, then once more the smooth mask dropped into place. Warily he reached for the chair, turning his back as he half slid, half collapsed onto it. She gasped at the brief glimpse of his back. Dozens of long, thin, pink welts crisscrossed the surface and near his left shoulder blade a soggy, blood-soaked bandage dangled by a piece of tape, revealing a recently stitched wound. Rushing forward, she set the cup on a low table.

"Lean forward," she commanded, all her doubts and suspicions pushed to the back of her mind. He appeared ready to refuse, then slowly did as she ordered. What she saw made her ill. She'd never had a strong stomach and it had always been her mother, not her, who patched up the inevitable wounds of man and beast on the ranch. She closed her eyes and slowly counted to three before looking again. The welts on his back reminded her of the time Luke had been stretching fence wire and the winch slipped. The flying wire had slashed through her brother's jeans, leaving a single, long lash stroke across his thigh.

Swallowing hard, Courtney turned her attention to the jagged tear that appeared to be about four inches long. Though it had been stitched, most of the stitches had broken, leaving tiny bits of black thread dangling on either side of the broken skin. She could see where it had bled, though thank goodness, it wasn't bleeding now.

"I'll have to tape it," she grumbled, placing one hand on his shoulder as she leaned forward to see better. "I don't have anything to stitch it with. But I'd probably pass out anyway if I tried."

"It's all right," his voice rasped and she felt a shudder go through his body beneath her hand.

"No, it isn't," she objected. "It needs attention. I'll tape it as soon as you've emptied that cup." She busied herself tucking a towel behind his back and draping another quilt around his shoulders, before turning her attention to the fireplace. She added another chunk of wood then turned back to the man. He hadn't touched the cup of hot chocolate.

"You need the warmth on the inside," she spoke reasonably as she lifted the cup toward his mouth.

"I don't . . . like . . . coffee." He pursed his lips and Courtney felt a smile tug at her mouth. He sounded like a petulant toddler.

"It's not coffee. It's just plain old hot chocolate made from a mix." She smiled and offered the cup again. He took a tentative sip, then reached to hold the cup himself.

While he slowly drained the cup, she returned to the stove to stir the chili and place her forgotten loaves of bread in the oven. The man's eyes followed her as she moved about the room, and she felt self-conscious picking up his clothing and spreading the various pieces in front of the fire to dry. Even though the clothes were crumpled and wet, she could tell that all but the sweat pants were new. She returned to the spot where she'd struggled to undress him and bent forward to retrieve the rest of the blankets from the floor. Something hard rolled out of the quilt to land at her feet.

It was a gun! A black no-nonsense handgun! She stared disbelievingly at the weapon he must have carried tucked in the back of his belt, which had become tangled in the quilt as she tugged at his pants.

She knew her eyes were wide and revealed her shock as she turned to look at the man. He didn't speak and she didn't know what to say. After a few minutes she reached for the gun. It felt heavy in her hand, far heavier than the .22 caliber pistol her brothers had given her and taught her to use years ago, the gun she knew Luke had tucked into the small front compartment of her snow-mobile minutes before she left the ranch yard and which she'd promptly forgotten all about.

Carefully she checked the safety, then one by one removed the shells and slipped them into her pocket. She noted one shell was missing. Did that mean the gun had been used? Or had the shell been removed as a safety precaution? She didn't ask.

"I'll get the first-aid kit," she announced abruptly as she carried the gun to the bedroom. She looked around uncertainly, then placed the gun in one of the many drawers of an old roll-top desk. She stood in the center of the room for a moment and breathed deeply while she struggled to regain her equilibrium. Her eyes fell on the bed, and it occurred to her that she'd have to let the stranger sleep in this bed. The day bed in the smaller bedroom was too small for a man his size.

Spending the night in the remote house alone with a stranger might not be wise, a voice of caution warned. Especially one who carried a gun. She knew it wasn't uncommon for a man traveling alone across the great expanses of the West, or even a businessman visiting any of the major cities in the country, to carry a gun. Still it made her uneasy.

Her father would know what to do. If she rode the snowmobile to the bottom of the canyon, she might be able to summon help. But one look toward the snow-caked window told her only a fool would risk leaving the cabin for any reason.

She picked up the metal box that held first-aid supplies and returned to the living room. The man appeared to be dozing and she questioned whether she should wake him, but his shoulder really did need attention. Reluctantly she walked toward him. He hadn't said anything when she found the gun, but he'd been watching her. He knew she'd taken it.

Moving closer, she whispered a cautious, "Mister . . ." She wished she knew his name. She felt silly calling him "mister" or thinking of him as "the stranger."

His hand suddenly snaked forward to clasp her wrist. Startled she tried to back away, but he tightened his hold.

"Let me go," she struggled to free herself. Fear shot through her and she wondered if he'd kill her quickly and mercifully or if he'd make her suffer. The sound of her thundering heart beat louder in her ears than the fury of the storm pounding against the log walls of the cabin.

"Why are you here . . . ?" The question didn't make sense. He was the one who didn't belong here. "Where is Julie?"

"I-I don't know," Courtney stammered. The fierce grip on her wrist relaxed though he didn't release her. His head suddenly lolled to the side and he breathed heavily.

"I heard the drums," he rasped after a few minutes. "The drums called me."

"Drums?" She was alone with a crazy man. Should she play along or try to make a run for it?

His free hand slapped the arm of the chair, then tapped lightly three times. When he repeated the action several times, Courtney began to understand.

"I was playing the piano," she spoke hesitantly and he nodded his head.

"Would you like me to . . . ?"

"Yes." He nodded his head again.

This time, when she attempted to free herself, he released her wrist. Carefully she walked toward the piano where she stooped to pick up the orange hymn book before seating herself and quickly thumbing through the pages.

Her hands shook as her fingers reached for the first chord. The beat of Indian drums filled the room. She played it through twice, then paused. Slowly she turned her head toward her silent audience. The pain etched across his face stirred her compassion, wiping out fear.

"Are you all right?" she whispered.

"Yes," he mumbled, but she didn't believe him.

"Who are you?" He seemed to be asking for more than her name.

"I told you I'm Courtney Grant. I'm an English teacher at Pine Creek High School."

"Why are you here?" He made a small gesture indicating the cabin.

"This is part of the Grant ranch. It belongs to my father and brothers, but I come here sometimes . . ." Her voice trailed off. She didn't want to remind him that she was alone by telling him that she'd come to be alone.

"Where is . . . Joe Anka—?" He spoke the name hesitantly as though groping for the words.

"You mean old Mr. Ankabruch? Did you know him?"

"Yes, I . . ." He paused, as if still looking for the right words.

"Poor man. His daughter and her family were all killed in a car accident several years ago. When he knew he was dying he asked my father to buy his land so a developer wouldn't be able to buy it up in an estate sale after his death. An environmentalist group tried to block the sale, but they failed," she added, remembering her father's frustration with the amount of time he'd had to spend away from the ranch fighting the frivolous suits brought by the group.

Looking at the stranger's face, Courtney saw his reaction to her news. The man appeared shocked and seemed to withdraw without moving a muscle.

"I'm sorry." Courtney realized she meant the words. The man hadn't known the old man was dead. The sense that he was grieving in some way disturbed her and she felt a need to keep him talking though he showed every sign of drifting off to sleep.

"What should I call you?" She tried to pretend this was a normal conversation. She didn't really expect an answer. She got one, though. At least she thought he answered.

"Sam." It was little more than the release of air through his lips as he slipped into sleep.

Again she debated whether to dress his wound or just back away. This might be her only chance to get the snowmobile and leave. He'd twisted to his right side as he slumped against the arm of the chair, exposing the ugly wound on his back. She could easily reach the wound, but should she? She really didn't have a choice. She couldn't leave him like this. Biting down on her bottom lip, she crept toward the left side of the chair.

She cut tape into narrow strips and lined them along the back of the chair. The man—Sam, she remembered—flinched, but didn't open his eyes when she began pulling the sides of the wound together and applying the make-shift butterfly stitches. Between stitches she mopped at the thin trickle of blood that escaped to run down his back and took deep gulps of air to keep from being sick.

Two thirds of the way down the laceration, she encountered difficulty pulling the two sides together. After three attempts ended in failure she gave up and reached for the roll of tape. Using longer, wider pieces she clumsily covered the wound the best she could. As she smoothed the tape in place she felt a hard ridge beneath the skin. Her imagination conjured a picture of herself probing for a bullet, and her hands began to shake and her stomach roiled. A buzzing began in her ears and she hastily sat on the arm of the chair and lowered her head. She closed her eyes and reminded herself the wound had previously been stitched. Sam showed every sign of having been under a doctor's care, so if there ever had been a bullet in Sam's back, the doctor who cared for him would have removed it.

She felt regret that she didn't have the skill to reclose the wound properly. She sprayed it with an antiseptic spray she found in the first-aid kit and thought how her attempt would keep the wound clean and reduce the risk of infection, but the man would be left with a large scar.

When she finished, she taped a gauze pad in place and stepped back to survey her handiwork. She noticed Sam was awake again, his dark eyes following each movement she made. His silent appraisal made her nervous.

"Bread." The single word startled her.

"Are you hungry? I baked . . ." The unmistakable odor of scorched bread assaulted her nose. She screamed and ran to the stove. She'd forgotten the loaves she'd placed in the oven.

Grappling with hot pads she jerked the old-fashioned cast iron handle to open the oven and stared inside. The tops of the two loaves looked a little crispy, but they weren't exactly burned. The bread would be edible.

She fussed with buttering the tops of the loaves, then broke off two chunks of the hot bread and dribbled a generous amount of butter and honey on them. Placing one chunk on a plate beside a bowl of chili, she carried the food to Sam. She didn't look at him as she set the plate on the table at his side, but she knew he was awake.

She hurried back for her own plate which she carried to the chair on the opposite side of the fireplace. Pretending tremendous interest in her own food, she tasted her chili, and immediately jumped up to fetch two glasses of water.

"I'm sorry," she murmured as she set a glass of water at Sam's side. "I got it spicier than I intended."

"It's fine." She stared in astonishment as Sam emptied his bowl without pausing. He attacked the bread in the same ravenous manner.

Hesitantly she returned to her own chair. After a couple of bites, she asked politely, "Would you like some more?" When the only answer she received was a low rumble, she raised her head and stared in astonishment. Sam was asleep again. She'd meant to tell him he could sleep in the bedroom. Well, she wasn't going to wake him to tell him to go to bed!

Carefully she tiptoed across the room to gather up his dishes. When the dishes were washed and put away, she returned to her puzzling guest. Drawn by curiosity, she reached for his jacket, and just as she suspected she found a sheaf of papers stuffed deeply in one pocket. She pulled them out and found that they were soggy and indecipherable; they told her nothing of her unexpected guest.

As she separated the wet sheets of paper, a small square fell to the floor. When she picked it up she saw it was a photograph. Turning it over she could see it had fared better than the papers. Though faded, its slick finish had protected it from total destruction.

The faces of two people met her curious gaze. The man looked a little bit like Sam, though his nose and his cheeks were different. His hair was shorter and styled. The woman was vaguely familiar, and Courtney suspected that if she thought about it a while she'd remember where she'd seen the woman with long black hair and exotic eyes. Their arms were around each other and they seemed to be sharing a joke.

Sam made some small sound and she set down the papers and the photograph to go to him. She stood near the chair and watched him for several minutes. Relaxed in sleep, he was, she could see, very good looking; also, asleep he didn't look so frightening. Something about the man intrigued her and some instinct told her he'd been through a terrible ordeal. Her heart swelled with compassion.

Kneeling she adjusted the foot rest, then pulled a quilt to his chin before turning off the lamps in the room. For just a moment she stood still listening to the crackle of the fire in the fireplace and the howl of the wind. He looked so peaceful lying there with a lock of his straight, black hair obscuring his forehead. An urge to brush his hair back with her hand to feel its silky texture shocked her with its intensity.

Abruptly she added a thick log to the fire and turned toward the smaller bedroom. She wasn't letting her heart get carried away with romantic nonsense again. She'd fallen in love with one good-look-ing man who seemed romantic and exciting. She'd rather stay sin-gle the rest of her life than fall for another man who didn't share her love for the gospel, and some instinct told her this man hadn't seen much of civilization, let alone religion, for a very long time.

FOUR

Keeping his eyes closed, he savored the feeling. He'd been asleep, but he wasn't in a bed. Neither was he on a cold stone floor. He was warm, but not sweltering in heat so thick and wet, it felt like syrup. Cautiously he sniffed the air, catching only the lingering odor of bread and wood smoke; no rancid jungle rot or antiseptic hospital odors offended his senses. It wasn't even the absence of pain that held him motionless, dreading the moment when he'd have to open his eyes. It was the peace.

For the first time since he'd awakened in the hospital he felt a peace so real it was nearly tangible, and he suspected it was the first peace he'd known in almost a year. They'd told him at the hospital he'd been missing for ten months, and he could remember bits and snatches of that time, enough to know it was probably best he didn't remember it all. There had been a cement floor and stone walls, moldy bread and rotten fruit. The only light had come from a crack where the massive boulders of the wall didn't quite meet the stone slab that served as a ceiling. He remembered praying, but he didn't remember why he stopped. Neither did he remember his life before the jungle prison.

At first his captors had interrogated him every day and when he wouldn't or couldn't answer their questions, they'd beat him. Then the blackness was his friend. Later they ignored him—some days forgetting to bring him food. Then, toward the end, the beatings resumed along with taunts that no one cared about him, that he'd die in that jungle hole and no one would know or care. They'd threatened to kill someone, someone he cared about if he didn't cooperate. But who? Their threat had frightened him, frightened him so much he'd let everything he was fade until the blackness consumed him and returning became more and more difficult.

He didn't want to think about the blackness. Sometimes that was all he had to do, just think about it and he would begin to fade. Once it had been his friend, carrying him to a place where there was no pain, and no one could force him to reveal his secrets. But now he feared the blackness. It didn't want to let him go.

Slowly he opened his eyes and more recent memories flooded back. He'd followed the drum beat to the cabin where a woman undressed him and covered him with quilts. She'd said the cabin was her father's, but he knew this cabin. A long time ago he'd come here. There had been an old man and a little girl. And another boy. It felt more familiar than his condo back in Texas did.

Excitement filled his heart as he remembered the little girl sitting at the piano where the woman had sat last night making the piano throb like Indian drums. He wished he could remember more, but when he concentrated, trying to force the memories, the pain in his head became unbearable and he found himself reaching for the blackness. But it was a beginning. He'd remembered something.

The fire was almost out and faint light filled the room through uncurtained windows. Snow was still falling, but it lacked the intensity of the night before. He estimated a foot of new snow covered the tracks he'd made. No one could follow him. He was safe for the time being.

Once more he glanced at the fireplace. The fire had died down to red coals. If he'd slept as long as he suspected he had, the woman must have replenished the logs at least once during the night. He marveled that he had slept so long. Usually he slept only in brief snatches, waking at frequent intervals. Only the pain pills gave him a couple of uninterrupted hours of sleep.

A strange feeling swept over him as he thought of the woman. She was pretty; slender, but not skinny. Her brown hair was thick and sleek like mink fur, and he liked the way it turned under just about at her chin. She was afraid of him, but she didn't lack courage. She'd placed caring for him above her fears. The irony of her being afraid of him twisted his mouth in a mocking grimace. He was the one who had reason to fear. He was afraid of every-one—except her.

For a moment he wondered why he didn't fear her. He couldn't explain it. There was something deep inside him that told him she wasn't part of the madness that pursued him. Instead she imbued him with a sense of connection to his past and hope for the future. She filled him with a sense that once he'd been able to trust. He didn't know why she'd come to the cabin alone nor why her being there seemed so right, almost as though she'd come to be there for him.

His clothes drying before the fire caught his attention and he decided to put them back on before the woman awoke and returned to tend the fire. He eased himself out of the chair and stood unsteadily for a few minutes before reaching for his jeans. He pulled them on, then picked up his t-shirt. He winced as he pulled it on. His back was still tender and the tug of muscle against the tape reminded him of his last conscious memory before the hospital.

Two guards, thick heavy animals, who did as they were told without thought or emotion, dragged him up the stairs outside his cell to a room where brilliant light streamed through a wall of win-dows, painfully blinding him. A slender, militarily-erect man in some kind of khaki uniform shouted questions at him that made no sense. Another man watched. He was older, heavier, and he wore expensive shoes. If he could only see the man's face, he would know who he was. The darkness in his mind would not lift enough to reveal the man's identity.

When he didn't answer the uniformed man's questions, the guards ripped away the tattered, filthy rag that clung to his shoul-ders. He saw the uniformed arm lift a whip with a lash as fine as piano wire. He felt the stinging, burning pain only once before the blackness took him away.

A dull throb made itself known behind his eyes and he looked around for his jacket. As he reached for it, he saw the papers lying on the arm of the other chair and remembered taking them from the wrecked car. Anxiously he reached for them, only to face frustration when he saw the ink had smeared or washed away, leaving no clue to the driver's identity. His eyes settled on the photograph and he held it up to see it better. The man didn't look quite the same, but some instinct told him it was a picture of himself he held. He turned his attention to the woman in the photo and blinding pain slashed through his head.

Pain sent him stumbling the few steps to where Courtney Grant had draped his jacket over the back of a chair. His hand fumbled in the pocket until he found the bottle of pills. With trembling hands he shook one of the small white tablets into his palm. He stared at it, momentarily confused. One part of his brain told him not to swallow the pill; he didn't trust the doctor who gave it to him. Was it paranoia or was the doctor somehow connected to the man who beat him? The pain pulsed and pounded now—growing, expanding, tearing him apart. It was either the pill or the blackness.

"What's wrong?" Courtney spoke softly as she entered the room to see him standing near the fireplace with a small brown bottle in one hand and a look of torment on his face that tore at her tender heart.

"Do you need help?" She moved closer.

As he opened his hand to show her the tablet, it fell from his trembling hand to the floor. He dropped to his knees to begin a frantic search for it.

"It's all right," Courtney murmured and reached for his arm to help him to his feet. "Sit in the chair while I get your tablet and a glass of water for you." He surrendered the vial of pills without an argument and sat with his head clasped between his hands staring at the fire.

Grabbing a glass from the cupboard, Courtney filled it with bottled water she'd brought from the ranch house. She glanced at the wet and torn label on the pills and her hands stilled. The writing was smeared, but she could read the name of the same powerful drug, only many times stronger, which had been prescribed for her following a riding accident two years ago. After her arm had been surgically set, she'd been given four pills and warned that because of its strong addictive nature, the drug could only be used immediately following surgery to offset the worst of the pain. After that she'd used Tylenol.

She read the name of a Texas hospital pharmacy, but she couldn't tell how many pills should be in the bottle. Curiously she checked the name on the bottle. She couldn't quite make it out, but it didn't appear to be Sam. After peeking to make certain he wasn't watching, she set the bottle in the cupboard and reached for the Tylenol bottle she kept there. The pills were almost the same size and color.

Sam reached with shaking hands for the pill she offered him. Holding her breath, she watched him swallow it with the glass of water she handed him. He didn't seem aware of the substitution, so she urged him to remain in the chair and rest while she prepared breakfast. After only a few minutes he relaxed and seemed to fall asleep, suggesting he was psychologically addicted to the drug even if he wasn't physically addicted.

She'd just placed bran muffins in the oven when she heard the back door open. Her eyes went automatically to the chair where she'd left Sam sleeping. He wasn't there and his coat was gone, too. She ran to the door and jerked it open to stare in astonishment as he made his way unerringly to the outhouse. With mingled embarrassment and relief, she softly closed the door. She should have told him there was no indoor plumbing, but it was strange he hadn't asked. Of course if he knew Joe Ankabruch, perhaps he had been here before.

If Sam had visited the old man she wondered why she'd never met him. The only access to the homestead cabin, unless you counted the old logging trail from Isadora, went right through the Grant ranch and the only visitors she'd ever seen were Joe's daughter and her family. She'd seen them a few times when she'd been much younger, but the children weren't her age and she'd never gotten to know them during their brief visits. She'd just returned from her mission and had been away at college when Joe's family died. A touch of sadness colored her thoughts as she remembered her parents speaking of how broken and depressed the old man had become five years ago when he learned of the horrible accident which had claimed his daughter's entire family.

Shaking off gloomy memories, she slid omelets onto plates and set them at the back of the stove. She poured two mugs of hot chocolate while she waited for Sam's return. When he bumped open the back door, his arms were full of firewood. Evidently he not only knew his way to the outhouse, but he was familiar with the wood shed, too.

"Breakfast is ready," she indicated one of the kitchen chairs as she invited him to join her after he finished dumping the logs into the nearly empty box beside the fireplace.

"I'll get one more armful first," he volunteered before heading back out the door. He moved with rapid, nervous strides, then returned in minutes to fill the box beside the cookstove. When he finished he removed his jacket and hung it beside her coat behind the door, then stepped to the washstand to wash his hands. He lifted the steaming tea kettle from the back of the range to add hot water to the tin bowl on the stand as though he'd done it before.

When he joined her at the table, she hesitated before beginning. Greg found praying before meals an irritant. But Sam wasn't Greg and she was through worrying about how anyone else felt about the religious observances in her life.

"I always say a blessing before I eat," she told Sam. She'd been mistaken to let Greg's attitude make her self-conscious about asking a blessing on her food. If praying made Sam uncomfortable, that was too bad; she'd do it anyway.

"All right." He took her announcement in stride and bowed his head. As soon as she finished the brief prayer, he reached for his fork and began eating with obvious enthusiasm. He devoured food as though he expected to have it suddenly jerked away from him. By the time he buttered his fourth muffin she raised enough courage to speak.

"You seem to know your way around this house. Did you visit Mr. Ankabruch often?"

He paused and let his gaze wander around the room before he spoke. "I don't know. The house seems familiar to me, and I knew how to get here, but I don't really remember being here."

"You don't remember? How could you not remember?" Courtney asked.

He looked uncomfortable and lifted his cup to his lips to take a deep swallow. "I like this much better than coffee."

"You told me that last night," she responded in exasperation. "You said you don't like coffee."

"I did? Don't you think that's kind of strange, an adult who doesn't like coffee?"

"No, I don't drink coffee either."

"In the hospital they told me all adults drink coffee."

"Well, some of us don't. I think you're trying to change the subject. I want to know, have you been here before or not?"

"I told you the truth. I really don't remember . . . there are a lot of things I don't remember."

"Are you trying to tell me you have amnesia?" Courtney set her cup down with an audible thud.

"No, not exactly," Sam hedged. She could see he was trying to decide what to tell her. She hoped whatever he decided, it would be the truth.

"I've been out of the country for a long time," he finally admitted. "Something happened to me there, and I was sent to a hospital in Texas. I remember some things and the doctors at the hospital filled in the blanks so I know other things, but there are gray areas I'm unsure of. I don't remember ever being in Colorado, but this place seems familiar and I—I think I have been here before."

She didn't know whether to believe him or not. "What about your family and friends? If they're not in Colorado, why did you come here?"

"The shrink at the hospital told me I was an only child, raised in Vermont by my maternal grandparents who passed away a long time ago, and that I've lived in Dallas since leaving college with an MBA. I visited the condo where I used to live and spent a few hours at the business I started there with a partner four and a half years ago, but nothing there seemed as familiar as this place does. I can't explain why I felt I needed to come here."

Courtney watched him for several seconds. He seemed sincere; still his words sent a shiver down her back.

"You think I'm crazy, don't you?" he asked glumly. "To tell the truth, I sometimes wonder the same thing."

"No, Sam, I don't . . ."

"What did you call me?" Excitement suddenly lit his face.

"Sam. Last night you told me that was your name."

"Oh." His face fell. "That's another thing. They told me my name is Nicholas Mascaro, but that name doesn't feel right. I think I'm Sam, but my old neighbors and the people I worked with all called me Nick. In a box of things someone put in storage for me I found a driver's license issued by the state of Texas almost five years ago. It had my picture and the name Nicholas Mascaro."

She cocked her head to one side and studied his face. "You don't look like a Nicholas," she finally offered.

"What is a Nicholas supposed to look like?" He raised his eyebrows.

"I don't know. It just seems to me a Nicholas should have curly hair and be kind of stocky, especially with a name like Mascaro. When I first saw you I thought you were an Indian—I mean, Native American."

"An Indian?" He seemed faintly amused. "Why did you think that?"

"Your hair is the same straight, blue-black as some of Dad's cowhands who come from the reservation."

"What changed your mind?" He seemed intrigued by her early assumption.

"Your skin is much too pale."

"I've been ill," he reminded her. "But I remember an Indian. And the drums."

"The drums were only a song I like to play on the piano and I don't know who the Indian you remember might be unless you were thinking of Old Joe. I vaguely remember his coloring was dark. But not even a sick Indian could be as colorless as you looked last night." She laughed to hide her embarrassment. She hadn't meant to remind him she'd undressed him.

He seemed to understand and sought to change the subject. He rose to his feet saying, "You fixed breakfast, I'll wash the dishes."

"No, it will only take a few minutes to wash these dishes. You should rest," she argued.

"I'm fine," he disagreed and continued gathering up plates and glasses.

They did the dishes together and Courtney found working at

his side strangely comfortable. When they finished she showed him the larger bedroom and suggested he might like to rest. He wandered over to the window and stood staring out at the white landscape where only lazy flakes of snow continued to fall.

"A nap might help your headache."

"My headache is gone and I'm not sleepy," he told her in a puzzled voice. "I usually sleep for several hours after I take a pain pill and the pain never quite goes away. Instead of being sleepy, I feel jumpy and keyed up."

"Perhaps you're getting well," she told him in an encouraging voice. "You might not need the pills anymore."

"I do need them—the pain is too much without them." He turned to face her and she saw the panic in his eyes. She couldn't help wondering if his long, debilitating illness was linked to drug dependency. Nevertheless, she sought to reassure him even as her own fears gained new momentum.

"I'll keep the bottle handy and if the pain gets too bad, let me know, and I'll get a tablet for you," she assured him.

"Thank you," he whispered before turning his back to stare once more at the hillside almost obscured by the falling snow. He didn't want to be cold and wet again, but he ached to be outdoors. The uncurtained windows drew him like magnets. It had been so long since he'd seen mountains or trees or snow. He sensed he truly would go mad if he had only walls to look at day after day again.

He heard her leave the room, closing the door behind her and a twinge of fear sent his pulse racing. He didn't like the sound of a closing door and he already knew closed places led to attacks of panic. Carefully he schooled himself not to race across the room and fling the door wide. He wasn't locked in and there was a wonderful view of trees and the falling snow from the window. He concentrated on the snow and willed his pulse to slow.

Courtney's concern hadn't left him untouched. There was something about the pain pills that upset her. Her reaction lent credence to a worry of his own. Was he dependent on the pills? He didn't want to think about it, yet he knew he had to. The pills brought merciful oblivion to the pain, but they muddled his thinking and clouded his judgement. And he needed another one now. That word *need* made him uneasy. If he *needed* the drug, then he was too dependent on it.

He'd made it more than twenty-four hours between his last two pills and he'd felt better today than he had any day since he awoke in that Texas hospital. Maybe he could cut back and be fine. Besides the prescription was half gone and he had no idea when he could get it refilled; he'd have to make his supply last as long as possible. He wouldn't take another pill now. He'd lie down and try to sleep.

Stretching out on a soft bed was an unaccustomed luxury. He wouldn't think about the pain or the blackness. He'd enjoy the moment, think about the woman, examine the memory that had surfaced of an old Indian and a little girl. Narrowing his focus he concentrated on the past twenty-four hours. But the pills refused to stay out of his mind. Perhaps just one . . . No! He despised the hunger, the need. He wouldn't give in. He'd made it twenty-four hours; he'd make it another twenty-four. Activity and exhaustion had overridden his need until now. Exercise was what he needed. Sliding off the bed, he dropped to the floor, braced his arms and began the first push-up.

* * *

When Sam didn't appear for lunch Courtney peeked into the bedroom and found him lying face down on the bed sleeping soundly. Perhaps he needed rest more than food. She'd fix an especially nice dinner tonight to make up for the meal he was missing. She started to withdraw, then noticed the room was chilly so she tiptoed inside to place a quilt over him. Her hand brushed his back as she pulled the quilt up and she was surprised to feel the dampness of his shirt. Puzzled she wondered if he might have caught a cold and become feverish. Lightly she touched the back of her hand to his forehead and was relieved to find no noticeable fever. She felt a strange reluctance to withdraw her hand. When she recognized this feeling for the attraction it was, she hastily stepped back. This time when she left the room she decided to leave the door open to allow some of the fireplace's warmth to heat the room.

Returning to the kitchen, she ate her own lunch, then curled up in the rocking chair to read her well-thumbed and carefully marked

Book of Mormon. She loved to read the book, but had found little time to do so since she'd started dating Greg. Until lately he had occupied the little bit of time she had left after preparing lesson plans and grading papers. When she first returned from her mission, she had vowed to keep scripture study a daily part of her life and now regretted that she had let her relationship with Greg erode her commitment.

She read for several hours, glancing occasionally toward the bedroom where Sam slept. As the afternoon wore on and he didn't awake she grew restless. Finally she put her book down, added a new log to the fire, and walked to the bedroom door. She stood watching his rhythmic breathing for a long time. She couldn't explain what it was about the man that drew her to him. Finding out more about him was almost an obsession, and the growing feeling that he needed her in some way occupied more and more of her thoughts.

Thinking he'd be hungry when he woke up, she turned back to the kitchen and busied herself stirring up a chocolate cake and preparing pork chops and potatoes to go into the oven while the cake baked. She'd wake him when dinner was ready.

A glance through the kitchen window reminded her the snow had stopped falling. Sam would probably be anxious to be on his way soon. Thinking of his leaving, of never seeing him again, filled her with melancholy. She frowned, wondering where he would go. He seemed so lost and confused, and if his memory was as sporadic as he claimed, he really should go back to Texas where he would be around people and places that might help him remember. At dinner she'd offer to drive him to town on the snowmobile and help him find transportation to Denver where he could catch a flight back home.

The back door crashed against the wall. Startled, she spun around. When she reached the open door she saw Sam halfway down the outhouse path, kneeling in the snow. His shoulders convulsed and she realized he was ill. Grabbing both her coat and her brother's old parka from the pegs beside the door, she hurried down the path.

"You'll freeze out here," she spoke softly as she slipped the coat around his shaking shoulders. "If you can stand up, I'll help you back to the house."

"I'm okay." His voice trembled, but he managed to stand. When she would have led him back to the house, he grimaced and pointed to the outhouse. Slowly she released his arm, and he walked away with wobbling steps and one hand clinging to the rope Luke had stretched between the back door and the outhouse to prevent anyone from getting lost during the frequent snow-storms that blanketed the Rockies.

She stood in the gathering dusk, waiting for him to return. Isolation and loneliness swept over her, heightening her awareness of the silence around her. Belatedly she questioned whether she should have allowed Sam to continue down the path alone. What if he were really ill? How would she get him back to the house?

Her eyes sought the fading light at the canyon rim. Billowing darkness instead of fading rays of light warned of the approach of another storm. She should have wakened Sam earlier this after-noon and insisted on leaving. Perhaps it wasn't too late. If they left immediately they could still reach the ranch before it began to snow again.

Uneasiness crept over her as she noted Sam had been in the small structure at the head of the path much too long. She knew she'd feel stupid calling through the door to check on him, but she'd do it; she certainly couldn't leave a sick man alone in an icy cold outhouse! With determined steps she marched up the path. Just as she reached the door, it opened and Sam staggered as he stepped toward her.

"Here, lean on me," she prompted as her arm slid around his waist. He didn't resist her offer of support and together they moved slowly toward the house. For a man six feet tall, he was lighter than she'd expected. She remembered he'd appeared thin to the point of gauntness under the layers of shirts he'd worn the night before. Twice they stopped as he doubled over in pain.

Once he was settled in the chair back in the house, Courtney fetched a basin to set at his elbow and added wood to the fire. She brought him a damp cloth and a towel. When she ran to the bedroom and returned with a quilt, he protested.

"Don't fuss," he spoke through clenched teeth.

"The snowmobile has lights. I think we should head back to the ranch. We can be there by midnight."

"Storm coming." He grimaced in pain and tightened one arm across his abdomen.

"You're in pain! What if you have appendicitis?" She watched in growing alarm as he reached for the basin. Dry heaves racked his body and when they eased, she returned the basin to the end table while he slumped lower in the chair.

"Not appendicitis," he croaked and mumbled something about a scar. "Bring . . . bottle . . . pills." She rushed to do his bidding.

She returned to his side in seconds with a glass of water and the small brown bottle. She set the glass on the table and opened the bottle. Before she could shake out a tablet, he took the open container from her hand. Carefully he poured the contents into one hand. For several seconds they both stared at the handful of pills, then she raised her eyes to his face and felt a numbing horror at the longing and hunger she read in his eyes.

Slowly, deliberately, he separated one pill from the others and let it slide back into the bottle. Never taking his eyes from the pills cradled in his palm, he slowly raised his hand.

"No!" she screamed. He'd die for sure if he swallowed that many pills.

With sudden violent force, he flung the pills into the fire. Blue flames sparked upward as Sam took the bottle lid from her nerveless fingers. With deliberate calmness, he returned the lid to the bottle and slipped it into his pocket before leaning his head back against the chair. Except for the occasional grimace of his facial muscles, he appeared to be asleep.

FIVE

Courtney ate dinner alone, then settled into the rocking chair to read while Sam slept. Each time she raised her head to study his restless figure in the opposite chair, she wondered if she should leave him alone long enough to ride out of the canyon to a point where she could call the ranch. The evening wore on and she didn't go. Whether it was the fury with which the storm arrived or Sam's weak exhaustion that convinced her to stay, she didn't know.

Concern for her guest made concentration difficult, but she'd set a goal and she wanted to keep the promise she'd made to herself that she'd read the Book of Mormon all the way through while here at the homestead house. During the two months since she'd broken up with Greg, she'd questioned why she'd let herself drift into a kind of semi-activity in the Church. Though she hadn't thought of herself as inactive, she'd attended social functions and activities with Greg more and more frequently on Sundays as their relationship progressed. She'd asked to be released from teaching Sunday school and had gradually stopped a daily or even weekly scripture study, so she had no one to blame but herself for Greg's assumption that the Church meant so little to her, and she'd accept his way of life as her own. She felt a kind of chagrin that she had allowed her desire to marry Greg to cloud her commitment to the gospel and imbue his character with qualities she now knew resided only in her imagination.

This time at the cabin wasn't merely to escape the sympathy and embarrassment that would come her way as word of Greg's wedding plans circulated throughout the small community. It was to be a time to refill her reservoir of faith and make plans to redirect her life. Rereading the Book of Mormon was the first step. She knew from experience that reading the Book of Mormon would bring her more peace and comfort than anything else she could do. She'd discovered that fact while tracting in the Honduran slums where baptisms were scarce and she and her blond companion were decidedly unwelcome.

Looking up as she turned a page, she found Sam was awake and watching her. His steady gaze both unsettled and warmed her.

"Do you feel better?" she asked.

"I can handle it," he responded. "But I should warn you I will probably get worse before I get better."

"If the snow stops, I can take you to the ranch in the morning. My Dad and brothers will help you get to a hospital."

"No hospital. It will be better if I stay here."

"But—"

"Listen, Courtney . . ." He leaned forward and she could see small beads of perspiration on his face. "There's nothing a hospital can do for me that I can't do right here. Fluids, rest, and time are all I need. I'll try not to be a bother."

"You're not a bother," Courtney protested. "And though I don't know anything about illness or taking care of a sick person, I know you're in pain and that you threw away your pain medication."

"I had to."

"Sam, I think it's my fault you're sick. This morning when you wanted one of the pills, I put it back in the bottle and gave you Tylenol instead."

"Why did you do that?"

She attempted a weak smile. "I was afraid you might become addicted to the pills. Your prescription is much stronger than a normal dosage."

He was quiet for several minutes and appeared deep in thought. Finally he said, "I'm glad you did, and that explains . . . almost forty-eight hours . . . that's good, better than I thought . . ." He leaned his head against the back of the chair and she thought he'd once more fallen asleep until he asked softly, "Would you mind playing the piano? It's been a long time since I listened to someone play."

"I'm not very good," she spoke apologetically, but rose to her feet.

"That's all right. I think I used to listen a lot to someone play the piano who wasn't very good at it."

The orange hymn book was the only music in the old piano bench and she'd never learned any number beyond her first-year recital piece well enough to play without reading the music. She sat down and leafed through the pages until she found a song that looked familiar. When she finished it, she picked her way through several more, carefully avoiding those with too many sharps or flats.

After a half hour of stumbling through Primary songs and Christmas carols she hadn't played for years, she turned to face him.

"I think you should go to bed. There are two bedrooms and I've made up both beds. I'm sure you'll sleep much better in bed than in the chair tonight."

"All right." He looked uncertain and she noticed with alarm how pinched and pale his face had become and that his hands visibly trembled. "Will you play one more song first . . . the Indian drum one?" he pleaded.

She turned back to the music and flipped unerringly to "Book of Mormon Stories." She hit the first strong chord and the beat of Indian drums filled the room. When the last chord faded away, she glanced over her shoulder at Sam. His face twisted in a grimace of pain, and he clutched his midsection, doubling over as a wave of agony washed through him.

"Sam!" She ran to his side and slipped her arm around his shoulder. "You've got to go to the hospital. I don't know what to do to help you."

"Listen!" he gasped. Something in his voice made her pause and lift her head. Wind screamed down the canyon and screeched around the corners of the sturdy log cabin. Ice rattled against the window panes, and snow like a sifting of flour crept beneath the front door. It was too late. She'd hesitated too long and now they were snowbound. It could be days before the storm eased enough to allow them to leave.

Closing his eyes, Sam struggled to control his trembling limbs while clenching his jaw in an attempt to thwart the nausea. He'd seen men and women who craved narcotics so intensely they stole from children and churches, sold their bodies, or committed murder to satisfy their need. A memory surfaced of a young man writhing on the ground, screaming that spiders had gotten under his skin. The boy had plunged into a croc-infested river, either to escape the spiders or in a desperate mistaken search for the drug. Either way, he'd died.

Sam felt a jolt go through him. He'd remembered a piece of his former life, and some instinct told him those memories were of a distant place far from this cabin that felt so familiar. He didn't just know *about* exotic jungle life; he *remembered* it. He also remembered a lot about drugs. Where that knowledge came from he didn't know, but there was no question the knowledge was real. He abhorred drugs. He knew that much about himself. He also knew every symptom of cocaine addiction forward and backward. When he first suspected he was addicted to the white pills, he'd experienced a keen sense of denial. He'd spent time in South America and he might have had some connection with cocaine, but Percocet wasn't derived from cocaine and it didn't come from South America. A legitimate painkiller, it contained small amounts of morphine, but surely not enough to cause addiction.

Was he a dealer? Did he deal cocaine but use some form of morphine himself? Some instinct deep inside his confused mind told him he'd sooner die than deal that kind of misery to another human being. Then how did he know he was suffering from some form of morphine addiction? Had the doctor back in Dallas overprescribed? Sam had no idea what constituted a normal dosage of the powerful analgesic. And could he be certain the pills he'd been taking were really Percocet? A sense of despair swept over him as he concluded that he knew a lot about street drugs, but very little about prescription medication.

"Sam . . . *Sam!*" Courtney's frightened voice reached him. He'd have to explain. In his deranged condition he might hurt her. He had to give her a chance to protect herself.

"Courtney, listen to me." The words lacked the strength he wanted to convey. Shrugging away her hands, he pulled himself upright. He forced the words between clenched teeth. "I'm addict-

ed to the drug in those pills I was taking. I think you know that."
He heard her sharply indrawn breath but went on relentlessly. "I'm
crashing now without the drug. Sudden withdrawal is likely to
make me irrational, even violent. I need your help."

"I don't know what to do and the storm's too bad for us to leave
the cabin." He could hear the fear in her voice.

"If either of us leaves the cabin in this blizzard, we'll die," Sam
conceded baldly. "I don't want to hurt you, but I might during the
next forty-eight hours unless we can make certain I can't reach you.
Can you lock your bedroom door?"

When she nodded her head, he continued, "Take my gun to
your room and lock yourself in." He saw the shock and horror on
her face. She took a couple of steps away then stopped.

"What are you going to do? If you become irrational you can't
be responsible for keeping the fire going. And what's to prevent you
from running outside and getting lost or freezing to death?"

She made sense, but he couldn't bring himself to ask her to lock
him in one of the bedrooms. He broke out in a cold sweat just con-
templating being locked up again.

"I can't . . . I was . . . locked in a cell . . . ten months . . . I'll die
if . . ." Not even the look of horror on her face was enough to
induce him to agree to being locked in the bedroom. Besides, the
lock on that door wasn't sturdy enough to hold a man bent on
escaping. But she was right. They'd both freeze to death if she
couldn't tend the fire. He remembered the coil of nylon cord in his
jacket pocket. Would it be any better?

"You'll have to tie me to the bed." He heard himself say the
words as pain sliced through his stomach. Would being shackled be
any better than being locked up? But what choice did he have? He
handed the coil of nylon cord to Courtney.

* * *

Drawing her feet up under her robe hours later, Courtney
stared into the fire. Sam was quiet now and she hoped he was sleeping. She knew there wasn't much chance she'd be able to go back to
sleep, so she might as well read, but she couldn't force her eyes to

remain focused on the open book in her lap. She found it difficult to concentrate on the problems of people who lived more than two thousand years ago when the problems she faced right now inside this cabin were impossible to ignore.

She'd been reluctant to tie Sam to the bed in the larger bedroom. He'd be helpless if the cabin should catch fire—and what about eating or taking care of his body's needs? But he'd insisted and she'd finally agreed. Following his instructions, she'd wrapped the cord around each arm and leg, then secured them to the metal bed frame. She'd barely gotten to sleep when his screams awakened her. She'd dashed to his room to find him straining against the cords that held him and shouting words that made no sense to her.

She spoke to him and he quieted. Once more he'd called her Julie and said he was sorry, that he'd only done it to keep her safe and that it had all been for nothing. Courtney reached for his hand and winced at the indentations visible on his wrists where he'd jerked his arms trying to free himself. His hand felt warm and clammy. She glanced at his face and saw beads of perspiration on his forehead.

She bathed his face and talked to him until he drifted asleep. Less than an hour later his cries had her stumbling from bed once more. Again she bathed his face and spoke soothingly to him. His cries faded and he began speaking in rambling torrents of an imprisonment more horrible than she could fathom.

The fire leaped high in the fireplace and popped as the flames reached a small pocket of sap. The room was cozy and warm, but she shivered recalling Sam's almost incoherent rambling. She wondered why he'd been imprisoned and how he'd gotten free. She knew so little about him, yet she didn't believe he was a bad man in spite of his drug addiction. Had the doctors at the hospital where he'd been treated known of his addiction? Were they perhaps responsible for his drug dependency and thus for the nightmare he was now living? The fact that he'd thrown away the remaining pills, and his concern for the possibility he might hurt her in a drug-hungry craze were sufficient evidence in her mind that there was goodness in him.

A sound from the bedroom interrupted her reverie and she jumped to her feet, her heart pounding.

"Help me." Sam called. She stumbled toward his voice as her eyes slowly readjusted to the darkness.

"I'm here," she spoke softly as she knelt by his side.

"Water," he croaked and she reached for the bottle she'd placed on the bedside table earlier. She poured a small amount into a cup, then placed one arm behind his head to help him lift his head far enough to drink. He sipped slowly for a moment, then she returned the glass to the table and her patient closed his eyes.

Thinking he'd fallen asleep, Courtney prepared to leave the room. The sound of Sam gagging had her rushing back to his side. Frantically she tried to turn his head far enough to keep him from strangling. When the retching stopped and Sam lay exhausted, she began picking at the knots in the cords that secured him to the bed. No matter the potential for violence, a man who was sick to his stomach could not be secured in bed flat on his back!

"No, I might hurt you," Sam protested as she struggled with the knots her father had taught her too well how to tie.

"You won't hurt me. You're as weak as a newborn calf," she spoke with more confidence than she felt. "Besides I need to change these sheets." She finished loosening the knots and tossed aside the cord before lighting a lantern and selecting another set of sheets from the closet. She made half of the bed, then urged him to roll onto the new sheet so she could finish the job. He didn't argue when she insisted on helping him trade his soiled shirt for a dry one and wiped his face.

When she finished she pulled a chair to the side of the bed and sat down. She folded her arms and lowered her head, wishing she knew what to do.

"Are you praying?" An almost childlike voice came from the bed.

"No, but I ought to be," Courtney muttered.

"I'd like you to pray . . ."

Surprised, Courtney lifted her head until her eyes met the intense dark eyes staring back at her. Warmth flooded her as she recognized that somewhere in this man's hazy background, he'd been familiar with prayer. Slowly she slid off the chair to her knees and reached for his hand. Gripping it between her clasped palms, she began to pray, asking God to give Sam the strength to overcome his dependency and to grant her the strength and the knowledge she needed to care for him. When she finished she thought she heard Sam echo her amen. She continued to hold his hand and felt calmness settle over and around her.

"Go back to bed now," Sam whispered.

"No," Courtney responded. "You're too sick to be left alone. I'm staying right here."

"You need to get some sleep."

"I'm not sleepy," she retorted. "You're the one who needs to rest."

"I don't think I'll be sleeping either."

The cabin grew quiet and though Sam's eyes were closed, she knew he wasn't asleep. Occasionally he grimaced or drew up his legs as though experiencing abdominal pain. After almost an hour she tiptoed out of the room to fetch her book. When she returned she curled up in the chair and began to read.

A short time later Sam began to twist and moan and beg for water. She gave him one small sip, then waited to see if it would stay down. After ten minutes she gave him another tiny swallow, then settled back to her book.

"Would you read aloud?" She didn't know how to respond to his request. "Please . . . if it's not too much . . . trouble."

"It's not too much trouble," she hastened to assure him. "It's just that I'm partway through and, well . . . it's a religious book. You might not like it."

"You like it?"

"Yes, I like it. It means a great deal to me."

"Read, please . . . I need to . . . hear your voice."

"All right. Should I start at the beginning?"

"No. Anywhere is fine."

She wondered if the story of the Nephites and Lamanties would make any sense to him without an explanation of the first few chapters, but Sam had indicated he didn't really care what she read, only that he wanted to hear her voice. If hearing her voice would ease his distress, then she'd read. She meant to continue on, but some instinct had her turning back to the beginning. "I, Nephi, having been born of goodly parents . . ."

* * *

The window lightened to a lighter shade of gray as her voice began to feel strained. Laying the book down, she looked over at Sam. His eyes were closed and she was uncertain whether he was asleep or awake. As she watched, he opened his eyes and attempted to smile.

"Thank you," he croaked and in spite of his unshaven face and rumpled hair she felt her heart quicken, and she had to resist a powerful urge to reach out and smooth his thick dark hair.

For two more days while the storm raged outside the cabin, Courtney fed the fire and fixed quick snacks. Sometimes Sam swallowed a little juice or soup broth, and sometimes he rolled and twisted in a kind of delirium racked by wrenching nausea. When he began slipping into a world of depression and lethargy, her worry intensified and she slipped to her knees to ask for God's help in dealing with a situation she felt inadequately prepared for. She continued to read to Sam, and the sound of her voice at times soothed him to sleep. Sometimes as she read, he watched her avidly with a perplexed expression on his face.

Gradually he slept for longer periods of time, and when he awoke he seemed more alert. His nausea subsided and with it the depression lessened. He began questioning passages she read, and his questions led to long discussions reminiscent of her missionary days. His quick mind and probing questions challenged her to find half-forgotten answers.

The storm blew itself out at last, and Courtney began planning for a trip out of the canyon. A feeling of urgency had her moving about the cabin gathering those items she needed to take with her. She hadn't felt this strong need to leave while the storm blanketed the cabin, but now that the skies were clear and her patient seemed to be recovering, she felt the need to return to the ranch house as quickly as possible. Sam was still too weak to leave alone in the cabin, but as soon as he regained enough strength that she could comfortably leave him for a few hours, she'd ride down to where a cell phone signal could reach the ranch house.

"Courtney?" She turned to find that Sam had made his way from the bedroom to the chair in front of the fireplace. It wouldn't be long now until she could make the trip.

"Yes?" She walked across the room and sat opposite him.

"How long have I been here?"

"Eight days."

"That long?"

"Yes."

"It probably seems more like eight years to you." His mouth twisted in a self-deprecating grin.

She smiled. "It hasn't been so bad. I came here to forget my own problem, and you've certainly taken my mind off it."

He looked at her speculatively for several minutes then asked, "That problem wouldn't happen to be a man, would it? Your husband? A boyfriend?"

"Why does everyone always assume that if a woman mentions having a problem, it concerns a man?" she asked peevishly.

He raised an eyebrow and she laughed. "Oh, all right," she admitted. "You're right. The problem in question is my former fiancé who just announced his engagement to a girl I used to babysit!"

"Sounds more like wounded ego than broken heart to me," Sam observed with a twinkle in his eye, which for some reason lightened her heart.

"You might be right," she agreed loftily. Suddenly her broken engagement appeared insignificant beside the problems Sam faced, even though he seemed much better this morning.

"Do you think you'll be all right now?" she asked.

"I do," he assured her. "But if my knowledge of the filthy drug is correct, I may have flashbacks for quite a while. My digestive system will remain touchy for several more weeks, and anytime I'm under pressure or overtired, the craving may return."

"Will you be all right if I leave you for a few hours this afternoon? I'd like to take the snowmobile to the mouth of the canyon and contact my parents by cell phone."

"You have a cell phone? Why haven't you called them before now?"

"It doesn't work here in the canyon. A person has to be up on the rim or down at the mouth of the canyon to make contact."

He seemed to consider for several minutes before answering her question. "I wasn't going to say anything, but perhaps I should. Ever since I awoke this morning I've had an uneasy feeling that we should both get out of here. It might be just drug-induced paranoia, but the feeling is pretty strong. If you can give me twenty-four more hours to rest and try to eat a little bit, I'll be strong enough to leave with you."

She didn't know whether to agree with his suggestion or not. He looked as though a gust of wind might blow him over. His eyes had become sunken holes and his hands still trembled. This morning was the first time he'd walked from the bedroom to the main room. She didn't know whether he was paranoid or not, but she couldn't deny her own sense of looming disaster. If they were both experiencing this restless uneasiness, she couldn't ignore the feeling. Suddenly she knew she'd feel much better taking him with her and heading for the ranch, rather than striking out alone to request assistance. She'd wait until morning and if he wasn't well enough to go with her, she'd follow her original plan. Otherwise, they would leave together.

As the day wore on, Sam ate small spoonfuls of applesauce at careful intervals, and by evening he was able to eat a bowl of chicken noodle soup. He slept in the chair for short periods of time and spent hours gazing out the window. Just before dark he made his way alone to the outhouse and back by clutching tightly to the rope. When he returned he collapsed once more in the recliner.

Courtney considered whether it would be safer for Sam to ride in the small tow trailer or behind her on the snowmobile seat. When she put the question to him, he urged her to leave the trailer behind so they could make better time. Reluctantly she agreed and began packing the saddle bags that would fit on the snow machine. She'd return later for her clothes and the rest of the supplies she'd brought to the cabin.

"Will you play the piano tonight?" Sam asked as she joined him before the fire. He looked longingly toward the old upright and she couldn't refuse. After playing a couple of songs, she returned to her chair and picked up her Book of Mormon. She'd read a couple of chapters, then go to bed. She was only two-thirds of the way through it and she felt a twinge of regret that she wouldn't be able to finish the book before leaving the cabin as she had planned.

"Would you mind reading aloud?" Sam asked.

"No, of course not. I just thought that since you're so much better you might not want me to read aloud anymore."

"I like listening to you read . . . and there's something about that book. Sometimes I think I've heard it before, or I'm right on the edge of remembering something."

Courtney smiled inwardly. While serving a mission for the Church, she'd heard people express themselves similarly concerning the Book of Mormon. Several of her best contacts had told her that when they'd read the Book of Mormon, they'd experienced that same sense of familiarity.

Courtney began to read in Helaman about Ammon and his brothers who were cast into prison and who went for many days without food, and about the suffocating darkness that filled the prison when their enemies came to kill them.

Some small sound caused Courtney to lift her eyes from the book. To her amazement, Sam leaned forward in his chair with tears streaming down his face. "Read that part again," he asked.

"Which part?"

"Where the Nephite dissenter tells the Lamanites how to get rid of the cloud of darkness."

Courtney returned to the forty-first verse of Helaman, chapter five: "You must repent, and cry unto the voice, even until ye shall have faith in Christ, who was taught unto you by Alma, and Amulek, and Zeezrom; and when ye shall do this, the cloud of darkness shall be removed from overshadowing you."

Sam leaned back in the chair and closed his eyes. Is that what it would take to escape the cloud of darkness that hovered at the edge of his consciousness? Repentance and faith. The words alone invoked some kind of memory. For just a moment he saw two young men wearing white shirts and ties kneeling in a shabby room with a Latin couple and a large number of children. As quickly as the picture formed in his mind it was gone.

Had he once had the kind of faith in Jesus Christ that could thrust away the blackness? And could he call on that faith now?

"Are you all right?" Courtney's worried voice penetrated his thoughts.

"Yes," he paused considering whether he should elaborate. "That story reminded me of the time I spent in a crude prison."

Courtney reached across the short space between their chairs to touch his hand. "You don't have to tell me about it. You said enough while you were delirious to give me a pretty good idea of the horror you experienced."

"Did I tell you about the blackness?"

"In a way. I know you fear some kind of blackness taking you away."

"I think I must have served in the military at some time. I think it was there I learned a kind of self-hypnosis. When my captors tried to force me to tell them something they wanted to know, I used that technique to block out the unbearable pain. As I became more and more adept at letting my mind fade to black, I began to lose the ability to return to the real world."

"Is that why . . . ?" Courtney gasped.

"I think that's only part of it. My last conscious memory before waking up in a hospital is of being struck by an extremely thin whip. I immediately faded into that world of blackness. I suspect that while in that unconscious state, my captors injected me with drugs either to bring me back to consciousness or to try to force me to give them information."

Courtney sat back in her chair. "Did you tell them what they wanted to know?"

"I don't know." He pounded his fist against the arm of the chair. "I don't know what they thought I knew."

"But how did you get back to the United States?" Courtney puzzled.

"I don't know that either, but I was told my incarceration was a matter of mistaken identity. When the mistake was discovered, I was turned over to the American consulate, who arranged for a visiting dignitary to fly me back to Texas. My mind is gradually becoming more clear as I move further away from drug dependency. Today I've recalled enough to know there's a trigger, or some kind of signal, that brings me back to full awareness, but I don't know what that trigger is. When you read that story, I knew I was close."

"Perhaps it's prayer," Courtney whispered.

"I think it might be. I remembered that, too, while you read; that prayer was once an integral part of my life. Whether my faith still exists, I don't know." He rose to his feet. "There's only one way to find out."

"Yes," Courtney rose to her feet to stand beside him. "As the scripture says, pray until you get the faith to chase away the darkness."

"Thank you, Courtney." Sam brushed her cheek with his fingers, then paused. One hand cupped her chin and he leaned forward until his lips barely brushed hers. "Good-night," he whispered before turning toward the bedroom. He didn't dare look back. It had been a long time since he'd kissed a woman. Some instinct told him the feelings this woman was beginning to stir inside him were one more reason they must leave the cabin as quickly as possible.

SIX

Courtney dressed in her warmest pants and sweater without turning on a light. It was still dark out, but she felt an increased urgency to return to the ranch house. As she dressed, she reviewed the essentials she'd packed in her saddlebags last night, and made plans for a hasty breakfast. She tiptoed past Sam's room until a swift peek revealed his room was empty.

She found him wrapped in a quilt before the fireplace where the fire had dwindled to little more than ashes. It was an old patchwork quilt that had belonged to the previous owner. She'd noticed he preferred it to any of her grandmother's quilts. He held her Book of Mormon in his hands and at first appeared too engrossed in the book to notice her arrival, but in seconds he glanced up as she started to move past him.

"I heated water for hot chocolate, then let the fire go out. I didn't think you'd want to leave fires burning when we leave."

She smiled her approval as he handed her a cup. She took a swallow of the warm liquid and reached for a slice of the buttered bread he'd left on the low table by the recliner.

While she ate she noticed Sam's eyes return to the book in his lap. He read for a few minutes, then his eyes jerked toward the window. He appeared puzzled, yet thoughtful. Again his eyes returned to the book, but only for a few seconds. He closed the book and shoved it into his pocket as he rose to his feet. A kind of agitated excitement showed on his face as he paced toward the window and stood staring out. It was replaced by a troubled expression as the first rays of light turned the snow of the opposite canyon wall pink.

"Are you ready?" He suddenly turned toward her, and she shoved the last morsel of bread into her mouth before nodding.

"Are you sure you're strong enough? We could wait a few hours . . ." Her voice trailed off as he shook his head adamantly. She couldn't hide her relief. She too felt an urgency to leave.

"The snowmobile is in the lean-to attached to the house."

"I saw it when I got the wood."

"You'd better wear Luke's parka." She tossed him the heavy brown fleece-lined coat, then scrambled into her own snow pants and zipped up her sleek blue and white nylon parka. Last of all, she reached for the heavy saddle bags she'd packed the night before and gave the cabin one last cursory glance before following Sam out the back door.

She shivered as the cold air struck her face. Some uneasy premonition within questioned whether it was the cold alone that made her shiver. Sam seemed to feel it, too. Clinging to the deepest shadows, they made their way around the corner of the house. He unlatched the double doors at the front of the shed, and Courtney hurried inside. She stashed the saddle bags in the boot and climbed astride the machine.

Just as she reached for the ignition, a loud boom that sounded like dynamite rolled across the canyon. Stunned, she paused long enough to hear a deep rumble begin to grow on the slope above the cabin. She remembered the burgeoning clumps of snow like massive feather pillows clinging to the top of the steep cliff.

"Go!" shouted Sam in her ear. His body slammed against hers as he vaulted onto the seat behind her. "Head across the canyon. There's a rock wall . . ."

His words were lost in the roar of the engine as she shot from the shed. She didn't know how he knew about the stone wall, but she knew he was right. The old wall was approximately fifty feet up the opposite side of the canyon and had once led between two barns where old Joe had stored winter feed for his stock. The barns were long gone, but the stone foundations remained. Neither the foundations nor the wall would stop an avalanche if they were directly in its downward path, but on the opposite slope they might slow the upward motion of snow carried by the avalanche's momentum from the other side of the canyon.

Instinctively she turned the machine up the canyon, angling her way toward the highest point where the wall began. If they didn't make it, the closer they were to the outside edge of the flowing mass of snow, the better their chance of survival would be. She ducked her head against the sting of slapping pine bows and found herself praying that her passenger was strong enough to hang on.

She couldn't distinguish between the cracking of timber and the splintering of the cabin; she only knew the noise behind them was rapidly increasing in crescendo. A cloud of dustlike snow obscured her vision, daring her to glance behind. She wanted to look, but didn't dare. An illusion of a massive wave towering over them and an undertow sucking them backward added to her panic. She gave the machine more gas and prayed it wouldn't stall.

With one last furious roar, they swept around the end of the wall and kept climbing until the canyon slope became a cliff. They could go no higher, and the engine stuttered and died as if to emphasize that point. Too terrified to turn, she huddled over the handlebars and braced herself for the expected onslaught. A thick cloud of white swirled around them, settling on her coat and eyelashes.

"Courtney . . . Courtney . . ." Sam's voice gradually penetrated her fear. "We're safe. It's okay." She first noticed his arms were around her, then she became aware of the eerie silence. Suddenly she turned to bury her face against his coat, and deep wrenching sobs tore from her throat.

He held her for long minutes as she cried. He wished he could cry too, but his tears were spent a long time ago. Feeling her body tremble against his, he felt her tears were his, too. There was so much about this woman that seemed a part of him. He'd feared for his own life and suffered so much pain for such a long time; yet moments ago, as a wall of snow thundered toward them, it had been her life, her safety, that had been uppermost in his mind. If he lived to be a hundred, he'd never forget the glimpse he'd caught of snow sweeping down the mountain in a massive ripple and exploding in a blinding cloud as it struck the cabin.

A distant sound reached his ears, and he glanced up through the thick pine foliage to the canyon rim across from them. Where the avalanche had begun were silhouetted two snowmobiles with riders. They were too far away to pick out any identifying features other than the rifles each rider appeared to be carrying.

A sudden cry had him turning back to Courtney. She was furiously staring at the same scene he had been watching. "They shot that avalanche down!" she exploded. "Couldn't the idiots see there was a cabin down here? There was still smoke coming out of the chimney! How could they be so irresponsible?" Her face paled and he knew she'd made some connection to him in her mind.

"I guess there's no chance they were from your ranch, shooting down potential snow slides to protect cattle or men?"

She shook her head. "All our men know I'm up here. They sometimes shoot down threatening snow, but not here. None of them would trigger an avalanche near the cabin where both of my brothers spent their honeymoons. None of them would risk upsetting Amy and Lillian, even if they didn't know Jake and Luke would fire them for such negligence."

Long after the two snowmobiles disappeared, they continued to hold each other. He felt a deep wrenching sadness at the loss of the cabin. The only pleasant memories he could fully recall had transpired in that cabin. And they involved the woman he was now holding in his arms. Never again would he hear her play that Indian song on the old upright. Never again would he sit before that huge stone fireplace and listen to her read about a quarrelsome people who were given so much and who had raised up such valiant leaders, only to fall away when greed and pride entered their hearts.

Careful, he cautioned himself. He couldn't allow himself to care for Courtney Grant. His own life was too uncertain. Belatedly he suspected the warning had come too late; he already cared for Courtney more than he cared to admit.

"They did it on purpose, didn't they?" Courtney's angry voice interrupted his thoughts. "They were trying to kill us!"

"Not you, Courtney. It's me they're after."

"Why, Sam? Why do they want to kill you?" Her gloved hands framed his face. Gently she brushed at the snow turning his mustache white.

"I don't know. I wish I could remember." He couldn't bear the hurt and fear in her eyes or the guilt that swamped his own heart. He'd done this to her. If he hadn't come to Colorado, none of this would have happened. He looked away and his eyes drifted over the field of snow where the cabin had stood and saw it littered with broken trees and boulders. The top of the chimney poked through the far side of the churned snow in angry defiance of the destruction that had swept down the mountainside. Somehow it cheered him to see it still standing, like a soldier arrogantly defending its own.

"Do you think they saw us? Do they know we escaped?" Courtney's voice echoed the fear in his own mind.

"I don't think they saw us. We left from the back door, and from where they were, they couldn't see the front of the shed. The avalanche created a cloud of snow in the air above it that would have hid us until we were into the trees. We're pretty well hidden now in these big pines and behind the wall." He glanced at the wall and stiffened.

"What is it? Are they coming?" Courtney's voice penetrated his haze and her hands tightened against his arms.

"I remembered something," he whispered. "I almost remembered this morning when I was reading about that prophet in your book who stood on a wall and told everyone the Savior would be born in just five years."

"Can you tell me?" Courtney asked when his voice trailed away. Excitement filled her breast and she felt a burning sensation in her heart.

"I used to play here on this wall," Sam continued in a wondering voice. "There was another boy about my age and a little girl much younger than either of us. We took turns standing on this wall and singing a song or reciting a poem while the other two tried to knock the one on the wall off with snowballs."

"Like Samuel the Lamanite," Courtney laughed softly.

Blinding pain crashed through his head without warning, and he slumped to one side, landing in the soft snow. Over the ringing in his ears he heard Courtney's frantic voice.

"Sam, wake up. What happened?" Her arms circled his shoulders and she struggled to raise him out of the snow. A jumble of pictures, fragments of memory, ran chaotically through his head. He clapped his hands over his ears and struggled to make sense of it all. Pain and blackness waged war inside his head with a brilliant light and a flood of faces and memories. Instinctively his hand groped for the pill bottle in his coat pocket. His fingers closed around it, then slowly relaxed, letting it drop back to the bottom of the pocket.

"I-I'm all right," he mumbled as Courtney's face came into focus.

"You're not all right," she argued. "You're in a great deal of pain. I thought at first you'd been shot, but there's no blood anywhere or bullet holes in your clothes."

"The pain will go away." It would go away faster if he took that one last pill. No, he wouldn't give in. He had too much to lose. He could break the pill in half, just take part of it. That would take the edge off. No, he had to save that one pill. It had become a talisman. As long as one pill was left, he had the security of knowing he could choose a few hours of oblivion if necessary. He placed one hand over the container in his pocket and begged the God he'd once known for strength.

He bowed his head and rested it on up-drawn knees, forcing his thoughts away from the memories he longed to fully explore. He had some answers now; the rest would come in time. Right now he must focus all of his strength and energy on getting them both away from here. He couldn't risk his enemies returning and harming Courtney. And he had to warn Sam, the playmate and cousin he'd grown up with. Sam was the mysterious Indian he'd vaguely recalled, and his life was in danger.

Courtney insisted they rest until he felt better. With his back against the wall, he took deep breaths and felt the pain slowly recede. Some time later, he pulled himself to his feet, leaning heavily on Courtney and swaying only slightly as he once more straddled the snowmobile. She gave him a worried look, but said nothing as she took her own place on the seat and he wrapped his arms around her waist.

She started the engine and eased into motion slowly, fearing she might jar her passenger. Occasionally she lifted her eyes to the canyon rim and prayed the sound of the snowmobile wouldn't carry to the two men with rifles. That side of the canyon marked the beginning of a wilderness area managed by the Forest Service. If the men followed the canyon rim, traveling east, they could either make their way upward to the old logging road or they could move down the canyon parallel to their own route and end up at the ranch.

Weaving their way down the canyon called for all her powers of concentration as she struggled to avoid rocks and trees where no trail existed. Several times she caught her breath as the hands about her waist seemed to slip. But each time Sam's grip tightened, and she continued on.

As the canyon opened up into a series of rolling hills and meadows, Courtney slowed the machine. Spotting a familiar pile of rocks, she pulled up behind them and cut the engine. As the sound died away she listened intently, but no roar of snowmobiles reached her ears. She felt Sam release his grip and swing one leg over the snowmobile. He swayed, then seemed to hold himself upright by the force of his will.

"Can you call on that phone of yours from here?" he asked softly.

"No, I have to be out in the open. I just stopped here to get a better look before leaving the canyon."

"Good thinking. If I climb to the top of these rocks, I should be able to see for quite a distance." He turned toward the jumble of boulders.

"I can do it," Courtney protested. "You're not well."

"I'm not helpless." There was a new tone in his voice she hadn't heard before. Silently she stepped back and watched him scale the rock. A few minutes later he scrambled back down to stand beside her, breathing heavily.

"There's no sign of snowmobile tracks as far as I could see, but I saw where several other valleys or canyons open into this larger valley ahead of us. I remember this valley."

She nodded her head. "If you visited the Ankabruch ranch very often, you probably do remember this valley. It used to belong to Joe Ankabruch. If you recall, I told you back at the cabin that my father bought the Ankabruch ranch a few years ago. It's now the smallest of the three major valleys that comprise the Grant ranch. At one time Joe owned timber rights to the mountain at the other end of the canyon beyond the cabin, but there's no more timber cutting around here now." Her voice faltered as she thought of the cabin buried beneath the avalanche.

"We call this the upper valley now. South of here is a canyon that runs parallel to this one. It connects at one end with the middle valley of the ranch and at the other end to an old county road that leads to an abandoned sawmill near the small town of Isadora."

"Which way do you think those men were likely to go?" His returning memory, or instinct, suggested they had returned to the nearest town. His mind scrambled to piece together the bits and pieces he remembered of the mountainous terrain.

"North of here is rugged wilderness without roads. They'd have to cross to this side of the canyon and either follow the route to Isadora or go down the other canyon to the ranch."

"They have to have a truck or van to carry their snowmobiles. They could have left it at the sawmill or along the road that leads to the ranch."

"Yes," she agreed. "That's why I think we should cross this valley and approach the ranch house from the far western edge of the ranch. It'll take longer, but keep us out of range of those rifles we saw."

Sam stared thoughtfully into the distance. He appeared to be silently sectoring and appraising each rock and tree in the vast valley. Finally he nodded as though satisfied.

"Do we have enough fuel?" Courtney thought he appeared to be seeing their situation with a new awareness.

"There's a line shack tucked in the trees on the western side of middle valley. There's extra fuel stored there."

"Okay, let's go."

Courtney climbed back onto the snowmobile and felt the comforting presence of Sam's large body settle behind her. In minutes they reached a ridge where she knew she could call the ranch. Once they reached a ridge where she knew she could call the ranch. Once more she cut the engine and glanced around before reaching for the compartment where she kept the small digital wireless telephone.

Sam didn't speak, but she could see the methodical way his eyes moved across the white wilderness, taking in every detail of the snow-covered landscape. His face had become an impassive mask, and she couldn't tell whether he was impressed by the spectacular scenery or wholly focused on detecting any hint of danger.

Using her teeth she pulled free the thick glove on her right hand and pushed back the hood of her parka. Quickly she punched in the code for the ranch house and held the instrument to her ear, listening to it ring. She counted the rings and when the sixth ring brought no answer she clicked the "off" button, then quickly dialed Luke's number. Dad and her brothers were probably working outside, and Mom had most likely run over to Luke's to check on Amy.

As she listened to the rings, once more she began to worry. What was taking Amy, or Mom, so long to answer the phone?

"Hello!" A voice suddenly roared in her ear above a shrill spate of static.

"Luke!" Courtney shouted back.

"You all right?"

"Yes, but—"

"Look, Court. I can't talk. Amy's in labor and some idiot snowmobilers cut the fence down by the highway. Mom and Dad and Jake are rounding up cattle, and I've got to get Amy to the hospital. Weather's good. Come on home." Abruptly he hung up.

She stared at the phone in stunned surprise, barely remembering to click it off.

"Well?" Sam watched her face. "You didn't say much."

"I didn't get to say anything!" she wailed. "Luke's wife is having a baby, and he's rushing her to the hospital. The rest of the family is out rounding up cattle and mending fence. Someone cut the wire so they could get snowmobiles into the field near the highway and . . ." She stopped. She didn't need to see the confirmation of her thoughts on Sam's face to know who had cut the fence.

"How did they know?" she whispered. "You told me you came

along the Isadora road. I thought they had somehow followed you."

"I thought so, too," he answered grimly. "They must have a terrain map." He didn't mention the tracking device. He'd expected them to locate the Cherokee, but he hadn't expected them to zero in on the cabin so swiftly. Could they have planted the device in his clothing rather than the Jeep?

"Sheriff Boulter has a big map on his office wall that shows every road, logging trail, and cabin in the county. Do you think those men have one like that?"

"They might. They have access to some pretty sophisticated devices." He spoke with a surety that rang of conviction in her ears. She didn't like the helpless feeling that assailed her.

"Have you remembered who they are and why they want to hurt you?"

"I've remembered some. Not everything, but enough to know you're in a great deal of danger as long as you're with me. As soon as we reach the ranch, I'll leave; then you'll be all right."

"But you won't. I'm calling the sheriff." She clicked the phone back on.

"No." Sam covered her hand with his.

"But he'll help you," she argued.

"I don't know that." His mouth was set in a grim line.

"I've known Sheriff Boulter all my life. I teach his kids in school. You can trust him."

Sam shook his head. "I've been betrayed before by those I thought I could trust. I've learned not to trust easily, especially where my life is concerned."

Something bleak in his eyes made her shiver, and she wondered how much he trusted her. Sensing that he didn't fully trust her left her strangely depressed until a surge of anger rose in her heart for whoever had destroyed his faith in humanity.

"What have you remembered? Are you going to tell me?" she asked with a touch of belligerence.

"Courtney," he said with quiet determination, ending her speculation about his past, "we're kind of out in the open here. I think we should head for the timber surrounding the valley and make our way to that line shack you mentioned."

He was right. She flipped the phone closed and reached for the ignition.

His hand stilled over hers for just a second. "When we get to the shack, I'll tell you what I can."

"But not everything." The bitterness in her voice surprised her almost as much as him.

"No, I can't." There was genuine regret in his voice. "If you're thinking it's because I don't trust you, you couldn't be more wrong. I do trust you. But sometimes knowledge is dangerous, and I won't endanger you any more than I already have."

He removed his hand and Courtney, instead of reaching for the ignition key, opened a small compartment in front of the seat. Reaching inside she pulled out goggles and a ski hat. "Put this on." She thrust the cap into his hands and jerked the goggles over her own face. "We'll be moving a lot faster now and you'll need the protection."

The engine roared to life and she swept the machine in a long curve, taking advantage of the slight seclusion provided by the ridge to angle toward the trees. All the while, her heart asked the plaintive question, who would protect it from the enigmatic man who gripped her waist and whose big body sheltered her back from the wind?

SEVEN

His mind functioned on two levels as he and Courtney skimmed across the frozen mountain. While the memories flowed inside his head, he studied and surveyed the frozen expanse around him. There was no indication of any human movement other than their snowmobile on the snowy mountainside, but still he watched. His eyes swept not only the vast frozen panorama around them, but searched the sky at frequent intervals as well.

He knew now his name wasn't Sam. It wasn't Nick either. He was Mark Stewart, though it had been so long since he'd used his own name, it felt almost as uncomfortable as the other names he'd used. As he thought of his parents, his sister, a cousin who had been closer than a brother, and his crusty old grandfather, his memories came back to him, and he felt both joy to have remembered and sorrow that all but the cousin were gone now.

All the skills drilled into him by his grandfather mixed with those that had become second nature during his stint as an Army Ranger. It was in that elite unit that he'd been taught to "fade to black." He remembered his military service now and the government service that had followed. He remembered, too, why someone wanted him dead.

Rabbits and birds scurried away at the sound of their passing. Twice he spotted deer, and once a magnificent bull elk caught his eye. Snow flew outward from the two skis on the front of the machine, and a kind of joy filled his heart at the dazzling brilliance of the day. His only regret was that the roar of the small engine cut through the tranquility of the mountain, causing him to long for a return to his youth when he and his cousin had hiked mountain trails in summer and skimmed over the snow on cross-country skis in winter.

As he pondered how much to tell Courtney, he made and discarded one plan after another to protect her. He owed her as much of the truth as was safe to give her. How did he determine how much knowledge would protect her and how much would further endanger her?

* * *

Night comes early in winter and with it deadly cold in the mountains. Shadows were growing long when Courtney brought the machine to a halt in a stand of willows near a frozen stream. He looked around, but saw no sign of the line shack.

"Are we out of fuel?" he asked.

"No." She shook her head. "Perhaps I'm being melodramatic, but it occurred to me that there's an elk herd that winters in the middle valley. If we drive into their feeding ground, they'll run, then return to wipe out any trace we passed through. Jake and Luke sometimes bring a load of feed up here for them during particularly hard winters, and we all ride up here occasionally just to watch them, so they're not completely unaccustomed to people and engines."

"And if I were to drag a pine bough behind the snowmobile, our trail would disappear even more thoroughly." He spoke slowly remembering how he and his cousin had played at tracking and hiding trails when they were boys. Thinking of his cousin Sam brought a twinge of pain. They'd been so much alike when they were boys, except that he'd grown up in the city while Sam had spent his youth on the reservation. Grandpa had insisted the three children—Mark, Sam, and Julie—stay with him for at least a month each summer and for a week of the Christmas holidays, and there had been long weekends also. They'd shared so much. Now, if he didn't find his old friend before the men following him did, they would both die.

Searching out a bough large enough to drag was surprisingly easy. The recent heavy snowfall had broken several branches from the trees near the meadow's edge. Soon a large fir branch tied to the back of the machine served as a kind of broom to brush away their tracks as they left the shelter of the trees.

Confident they were hidden from prying eyes on the other side of the valley by the hills and islands of trees in the great meadow, they proceeded carefully into the open. The elk were there, as Courtney said they would be. He estimated upwards of fifty or sixty animals in the herd. Some leaped toward the willows and some faded into the trees along the mountainside, while others only warily lifted their heads and watched the snowmobile's progression with suspicion.

Once clear of the herd Courtney turned the machine toward a larger streambed and followed it for twenty minutes into a small depression between two hills. The shack was hard to see, but at last he spotted it nestled in a cluster of thick trees. It didn't look like much more than the hastily constructed clubhouses of his own boyhood. It was about the size of a suburban toolshed, built of thick planks and topped by a tin roof. A six-foot-high stack of wood rose on one side of the small structure. The roof's extended overhang provided partial protection for the firewood.

Courtney drove right past it, but before he could wonder why, she shut off the engine and pointed toward a small dark cave.

"The fuel is stored here. Let's gas up, then head back to the shack on foot," she suggested as she stood and arched her back. "We can push the snowmobile inside where it will be out of sight."

He liked the way she thought. There was no reason to believe they'd been followed, but he'd learned long ago not to trust what appeared obvious. It would be better to refuel before seeking food and shelter for themselves, and if the snowmobile remained hidden in the small cave, it wouldn't give away the occupants of the shack even if someone managed to track them this far. His eyes scanned the huge pine trees looming over the roof of the shack, and he breathed easier knowing the small structure would be impossible to see from the air.

He'd expected danger from the sky all day. With the return of his memory came a picture of the man he knew had hired others to pursue him, a man he and his partner had code-named "the Snow King" partly because of his investments in winter sports parks, and also because his fortune was derived from trafficking in cocaine, known on the streets as "snow." The Snow King carried a great deal of financial and political clout. He certainly had the resources at hand to pursue his quarry by chopper. The fact that he hadn't seemed a pretty good indication that Mark's old nemesis believed he'd perished in the avalanche.

With great care he helped Courtney erase all sign of their passing as they made their way back to the shack. Once inside, he surveyed the small space with resignation. They'd get neither much warmth nor rest in the small space. A pot-bellied stove occupied one wall. Next to it two wooden crates had been hammered to the wall to serve as a cupboard. The opposite wall sported two narrow bunks, one above the other, and the center of the room boasted a rickety table and two mismatched chairs. On either side of the door were small square, four-paned windows.

Courtney walked to a metal box at the foot of the bunk beds and withdrew a nail from the clasp holding it closed. She reached in and pulled out two coarse brown blankets.

"I think you should lie down while I fix us something to eat," she told him as she offered him the blankets.

"I'll help you." He tossed the blankets toward the lower bunk.

"No." She shook her head vehemently. "You've been ill. You need to regain your strength."

He was tired, but he knew she had to be, too. "I can at least start the fire," he argued.

"Is it safe to have a fire?" she questioned. He considered for a moment before answering.

"Yes, we should be safe with a small fire. It's dark now so the smoke won't be seen and we can cover the windows so no light escapes. Besides we're both cold and the night promises to get colder. We need the heat."

It didn't take long to set out the meager dinner she prepared; he'd watched her make sandwiches and pack them in the saddlebags the night before. Now she heated water on top of the stove and when it was barely warm they added chocolate powder and drank it. Ice crystals crunched between his teeth as he bit into the half-frozen sandwich and she looked apologetic. She'd expected to be back at her parents' home by now and had accordingly left most of her food supply at the cabin so they could travel light. He couldn't have eaten much anyway; his stomach was still touchy and a dull throb pounded in his head.

He saw Courtney's head jerk and he knew she was as close to falling asleep as he was. He'd also noticed her rubbing her arms and arching her back earlier, which told him she was stiff and aching from their arduous day. His body ached, too, but in a way he enjoyed the ache. It reminded him he was alive, and in spite of all that had happened, the day had held a kind of joy as his eyes had swept the vistas of open landscape, and memories unlocked the bars of his mind, allowing him to know the man he once had been.

"Go lie down," he told Courtney. "I'll just go out and get more wood, then I'll turn in, too."

"You don't have to go out," she mumbled sleepily.

"It's all right. I can manage that much." He hadn't meant to sound peevish or ungrateful, but he was growing increasingly frustrated with his physical weakness. He'd taken strength and quickness for granted most of his life. Courtney had taken care of him for more than a week; now he wanted to care for her, or at least do his share of the work.

"I just meant—" She stood and walked over to a space to the right of the stove, then stooping, she twisted a peg nailed to the wall and lifted a square panel of boards "—you don't have to go outside to reach the woodpile. Luke built this to save himself trips when he was about twelve." There was a gap of several feet between the opening and the chunks of wood where various visitors to the shack had reached through the trap door to deplete the stack from the inside.

Mark chuckled. "I like that brother of yours sight unseen!" He stooped and crawled forward to grasp several rough lengths of wood and pulled them into the shack.

When he turned around, Courtney was sitting primly on the edge of the bunk with a blanket wrapped around her shoulders.

Her hair was plastered against the sides of her head from the hood of the parka she'd worn all day, and there were dark shadows under her eyes. She was beautiful. And he cared more about her than he had a right to care about any woman.

Along with memories of his family and his work had come memories of the woman who had once been his wife, a woman who had convinced him unhappiness was all he had to offer a woman. Deep in his heart he acknowledged that he'd never experienced the feelings for Venita in the year they'd been married that Courtney had stirred in him in less than two weeks.

She looked up at him with huge haunted eyes and asked without any subterfuge, "Tell me what you remembered. Tell me who you are."

He couldn't deny her, though he'd hoped her fatigue would postpone this discussion until morning. He'd been glad in a way during their long trek by snowmobile that the noise of the little machine made conversation impossible. Underlying the myriad emotions that swamped his senses with the return of his memory was a sadness for the piece that was still missing.

He picked up the other blanket, wrapping it around his own shoulders. Carefully he sat beside her. He wasn't sure why, but some instinct warned him it would be easier to tell her what he had to say if he wasn't facing her. The facts of his past were simple and would be easy to relate, but how could he tell this woman whose faith had carried him through the nightmares of drug withdrawal of his own betrayal of those principles she cherished?

"My name is Mark Ankabruch Stewart," he began. He heard the sharp intake of her breath and knew she recognized the name, but he didn't stop. "My dad was a cop in Denver when I was a kid, but I spent most of my summers and holidays here with my mother's father."

"Old Joe," she murmured.

"Yeah. My mother gave me his name as a middle name."

"They said you all died, that your mother was driving too fast for the conditions. No one survived."

"I wasn't in the car."

"Not in . . . but the bodies were all identified . . ."

"My cousin was the first officer on the scene. He made some quick arrangements and I disappeared." How long had it taken the Snow King to discover his body wasn't in that car? Had he known from the beginning?

"Why did you disappear? Your grandfather needed you."

"I have to go further back to explain. My cousin and I enlisted in the Army when we were quite young. We both applied to become Rangers and were accepted. I won't go into detail about the training, other than to say it was arduous and saved my life more than once. We thrived on undercover missions and were eventually transferred to an elite intelligence unit. When our enlistments ended, my cousin joined the Denver Police force while I accepted an offer from a federal agency. From that point on a great deal of my time was devoted to tracing the conduits by which drugs enter our country. I was in South America following up on a lead when I stumbled onto an assassination attempt on a highly placed leader in an international drug cartel by a rival organization. I saved the man's life and he was appropriately grateful and trusting. It was the big opportunity of my career. Unfortunately, the rival group wasn't happy I had thwarted their assassination attempt. Among their members was a prominent local law enforcement official who set the wheels in motion to have me arrested. I suspected that if they caught me there would be no trial; I would simply be shot in a staged escape. Needless to say I was desperate to get out of the country. Finally a fellow American came to my rescue and assisted me in my escape.

"In little more than a year I uncovered a string of connections between the South American drug lord and his contact back in the United States. My investigation showed a link between the drug money and a strange conglomeration of special interest groups, both conservative and liberal. These fringe groups had only one thing in common—they all contributed large sums of money to the same political figure—and I became increasingly suspicious that he was the real head of the organization.

"The more evidence I uncovered, the more certain I became that the top man was someone I knew well, but because I knew he had inherited a comfortable fortune and had increased his financial holdings many times over, I couldn't understand why he'd take the risk. Because I lacked the final pieces of evidence concerning motive and because I hesitated to hurt those close to him, I didn't tell anyone, even my partner, the name of the man I suspected.

"I was close to proving my case when the Justice Department insisted we act on the information we had. I pleaded for more time to complete my investigation, but my superiors feared we'd lose the element of surprise if we waited any longer to arrest those we already had evidence against.

"I felt the agency was acting with undue haste, but I was assured the investigation would continue, and that by bringing charges against those we had solid cases against, we could improve our chances of gaining a witness who would testify against his boss. I had to go along with it but kept a copy of all the evidence I turned over to my superior.

"Within six months a Wall Street financial wizard, a popular actor, the head of a huge business conglomerate, and a dozen other highly placed individuals went to prison, but not one of them revealed their leader's name. He was clever and they may not have even been aware of his real identity."

"You think he knows you suspect him and that he's the one trying to kill you," Courtney spoke thoughtfully.

"More than that," Mark continued, "I think he knows about the duplicate file I kept and who has it. My superiors went to great lengths to keep my identity a secret. Only four people—my partner, my superior and his superior, and my cousin—knew who I was and the part I'd played. I didn't have to testify, so when the trial was over I believed I was free to continue building a case against the man I suspected. Instead I discovered that large sections of my investigation had disappeared and that I was being reassigned to other cases. I protested to my superior and gave him my suspect's name. That night my apartment was firebombed, and two days later my parents and sister died."

"Oh, no." Courtney grasped his arm and leaned her head against his shoulder.

"The next step was the witness protection program." The mere mention of his family made continuing difficult, but he cleared his throat and went on, "I got a new face, a new life, and became Nicholas Mascaro. I was afraid someone might discover my real identity since there was a good possibility of a leak in my office, so before I disappeared into the witness protection program I turned my copy of the investigation report over to the one person I knew I could trust."

Courtney thought of the picture she'd found in his jacket pocket. "You're the man in the photograph I found in your jacket," she voiced her thoughts aloud even as she wondered if the woman in the photograph was the one person he believed he could trust. "But why were you carrying a picture of yourself? It doesn't make sense that a man who wished to hide his identity would carry around a picture of himself."

"I found that picture, along with that useless bunch of papers and the gun I was carrying, the night before I stumbled into the cabin. They were in a car that had been following me until it slid off the road, killing the driver. I can only assume someone gave it to the man in that car to help him identify the subject he'd been hired to pursue."

"What about the woman? Who is she?" It shouldn't matter who the woman might be, but something compelled her to ask.

He could see she wouldn't allow him to sidestep explaining about Venita although he had hoped he wouldn't have to explain that part of his past just yet.

"She's my ex-wife," he said bluntly and saw her head jerk as though she'd taken some kind of blow, but she didn't say anything. "She was the American I told you about earlier. She helped me escape the clutches of a South American police chief—the one connected to the drug gang I told you about earlier," he reminded her. "My partner received word that I was on my way to Washington, and he flew on to Guatemala without me. Unfortunately he had my passport and the papers I needed to exit the country. I was stranded with no way to make contact with the agency without blowing my cover.

"A stuffy little airport official was determined to block my exit and was getting dangerously close to calling the very police chief I was trying to avoid, when an American reporter took pity on a fellow American she believed had simply lost his passport. She called her father, a prominent American politician, hoping that with his connections he could find a way to get me aboard an outgoing plane. He told her the fastest, surest way would be for us to get married so I could leave the country with her on her passport. She made the suggestion and I accepted. When we got back to the States, we decided to see if we could make our marriage a real one, but with her jetting off to one trouble spot after another to report various news stories and me disappearing for months at a time, it didn't work out."

"Does she know you're alive?" Was he imagining it or did her voice hold a hint of jealousy? The thought warmed him a small amount.

"Our marriage was over before I began building a case against the cartel." He knew the answer was an evasion. Something inside him balked at telling Courtney of his brief marriage, a marriage that had its beginning in lies and deception and that had ended equally ignobly.

"If the leader of the organization wasn't identified or charged, why does he want to kill you? And how did he find out you were behind what must have been a crippling blow to his organization?" Courtney was clearly seeing inconsistencies in his story, the same inconsistencies that had plagued him while he struggled to build a new life as Nicholas Mascaro.

"When I first entered the witness protection program, I needed time to mourn my family and adjust to the loss of my career. It was also a tremendous challenge living as Nick Mascaro although I enjoyed setting up a new business. But in time I became frustrated when it looked like the case I'd been working on had been dropped. I found myself constantly reviewing the evidence in my head. Then one day—it was almost a year ago—I picked up the paper and read an article hinting that my suspect might be a candidate for president of the United States. At the bottom of the page was an amusing little story about a drug bust in Georgia. It described how a couple of small-time thugs smuggled pot across the Mexican border so they could buy assault rifles and become generals in a good old boys militia in their neck of the woods that was, ironically, cracking down on crime and drugs. A little piece of the puzzle I'd had in my head all along fell into place. A man who coveted the power and prestige of the White House more than he honored the people and nation he wished to represent was like the militia boys who were more interested in being generals than cleaning up crime. Both chose to break the laws they supposedly stood for in order to satisfy their personal ambitions.

"Now that I had a motive, I understood that drugs were never the real name of the game; they were only the means to an end. Power was the real prize. Our boy had his eye on the White House, and the more special interest groups who were beholden to him, the better his chances of grabbing the prize. Besides, a presidential campaign requires big bucks, even more than his well-padded pockets could afford.

"Naturally, I couldn't sit by and let him go unchallenged. I sat down at a computer and punched in a few addresses I remembered and guessed at a password or two. Bingo, I had the link I needed. With me out of the way and the Justice Department no longer pursuing the case, his people had become careless, leaving a paper trail it took me only three weeks to piece together. I carefully coded a message to my former superior in Washington and a duplicate to my cousin, Sam. Then I packed my car and closed up my condo, knowing I was voluntarily leaving the witness protection program and once more placing my life in danger. I planned to drive to Colorado, find Sam, and retrieve the information I'd left with him earlier. The files from my earlier investigation, along with the new data I had retrieved, would be enough to get a conviction. But I never reached Colorado. Instead I wound up in some stinking South American jail."

"You were kidnapped?" She stared at him aghast.

"I think so, though I don't really remember. A man who claimed he represented our government came to see me while I was in that hospital in Texas. He told me that I had gone to South

America voluntarily to deal with a business emergency. All I know is that I was on my way to Colorado, not South America."

"And your name's not really Sam." There was a tinge of regret in her voice. "Should I call you Mark or Nick?"

"It might as well be Mark. Nick's cover is blown, and I never really was Sam. Sam was only a code name my cousin and I chose when we were kids."

"It seems strange to think of you as Mark instead of Sam."

Mark chuckled. "It sounds silly now, but when we were boys Grandpa read that same story of Samuel the Lamanite to my cousin and me. He painted Samuel as a real Indian hero, hoping to instill pride in our heritage in us. He had a theory that Samuel the Lamanite was one of Helaman's stripling warriors grown older. My cousin was named for him, but we figured out that both of our initials spelled SAM, his forward and mine backward, so we adopted the name as a kind of code between us."

"You're a member of the Church, aren't you?" He knew she had drawn that conclusion as soon as he'd told her of the game he and Sam used to play. The easy thing would be to tell her yes. He remembered attending Primary, passing the sacrament, and even serving a mission, but something was missing.

"I was baptized," he admitted cautiously. "And I have a feeling my membership once meant a great deal to me, but . . . I don't know if I can explain it. I find it difficult to think about the Church. There's something to do with the Church that I still don't remember. It's as though there's a blank page in my mind where once there was something terribly important."

She was quiet so long, he thought she had drifted to sleep. But she must have been mulling his words over in her mind because when she spoke, it was to refer back to something he'd said earlier. "You said your grandfather told you and your cousin about Samuel the Lamanite to instill pride in your heritage. But you're not really an Indian, are you?"

"My great-grandmother was. She and the first Joe Ankabruch were the parents of the Joe Ankabruch who was my grandfather. Grandpa was nine years old when an old Indian woman from great-grandma's tribe arrived at their door with a boy about the same age as Grandpa. She said that a terrible illness had devastated their people and all of the boy's relatives were dead, so she had brought the child to them to raise. He and Grandpa grew up as brothers. When they were adults, Grandpa married a Swedish immigrant named Inge Sorensen from one of the Mormon settlements. His adopted brother married the mixed-race daughter of a trader, but they remained close. Sam and I used to claim that made me a little bit Indian and Sam a little bit white."

"How will you find him? Is he still with the Denver police?" She stifled a yawn and he smiled at her continued questions in spite of her fatigue. He knew he should tell her that further explanations could wait until morning. They needed rest. Instead he attempted to answer her questions.

"While I was in the witness protection program, we continued to communicate through the old code we worked out when we were boys. A short time after I entered the program, he left the Denver police department, and we agreed we wouldn't tell even each other our exact locations. I don't know where he is, but in spite of not hearing from me for a year, he'll still be looking for a message from me." He'd probably told Courtney more than he should have, but there was something about her that compelled him to communicate with her as he had with no one else—except his cousin, Sam.

A soft sigh escaped Courtney's lips and he felt her body relax against him. He didn't have to be able to see her face to know she'd fallen asleep. He placed an arm around her for support and she snuggled closer. Strange how natural it felt to hold her, almost as though he'd done it hundreds of times before. He had no right to feel this pull toward a woman he'd known less than two weeks. His presence endangered her, yet he felt almost happy—an emotion he hadn't experienced since those halcyon days when two young boys had taken turns climbing a wall with each declaring himself Samuel the Lamanite in their own version of the King of Bunker Hill.

He suspected Courtney still didn't grasp the significance of the words she'd uttered this morning. Back in his military days when he'd been taught to fade to black when he ran out of all avenues of escape, even death, he'd been instructed to choose a trigger, a phrase no one would casually use, but one that held deep significance to himself. Something he would remember if he forgot all else.

And he had forgotten all else. The blackness had swallowed everything he'd once valued the most, even the faith he'd embraced since boyhood. He had forgotten the two years he'd spent in small Peruvian villages sharing that faith. He had forgotten his parents and his little sister, Julie. No, perhaps he hadn't completely forgotten Julie. Julie's song, the one she'd pounded out over and over on the old upright, had reached out to him and led him back.

* * *

He didn't know what awoke him. He lay still listening, but heard nothing. Slowly he became aware he'd fallen asleep with Courtney in his arms. He'd never moved to the top bunk as he'd intended. The fire in the stove had gone out, and with the windows still covered with the towels she'd found in the metal box, the room was dark. He could barely make out the darker outline of the stove across the room.

Perhaps it was the cold that had awakened him. He'd restart the fire then move to the other bunk. Gently he eased his way off the sagging bunk and rose to his feet. Courtney protested the cold that rushed in to take his place, and he wrapped both blankets around her. She still wore her pretty nylon snow suit. She hadn't even removed the heavy boots she'd worn all day. She wasn't the only one who had fallen asleep completely clothed. He, too, was still dressed in the clothing he'd begun the day with, but then he didn't have much choice.

He frowned, remembering an earlier suspicion. Could there be a tracking device hidden somewhere in his clothing? He couldn't see how anyone could have planted it. His clothes were all new, purchased since he'd left the hospital, some en route to Colorado, long after he'd known someone was following him.

Kneeling beside the stove, he paused in the act of reaching for kindling. Something wasn't right. Perhaps it hadn't been a sound that had wakened him, but the absence of sound. Grandfather had cautioned him from the day he'd hunted his first buck, to listen for the silence. When the creatures of the mountain huddle in stillness, it is because death stalks, he had told him.

No! he screamed silently as he dropped the wood and raced to the bunk where Courtney slept. Glass exploded into the room followed by the stench of gasoline and a whistle like that of rapidly escaping air. Flames ran like rivulets of melting snow, racing across the room and up the walls.

Scooping Courtney into his arms, blankets and all, he stood frozen. They were cut off from the door and even if they made it through it, he had no doubt a sniper would pick them off.

The sound of breaking glass brought Courtney suddenly awake. She caught a glimpse of an inferno, with flames lapping their way across the table top and nipping at the foot of her bed. Before she could scream, a blanket covered her face and she felt herself lifted into familiar arms. Too terrified to struggle, she cringed against Mark's chest. She felt him move toward the back of the shack. She heard him gasp and felt him sink to his knees. A vision of flames attacking his clothes replaced her fear for herself and she began to struggle.

Just as she wrenched the blanket from her face, a blast of cold air touched her cheeks and she felt her blanket-wrapped body being shoved through the narrow woodpile door. The blanket hampered her movements, but she rolled away from the trap door as quickly as she could. Mark would need all the space she could give him to make his own escape.

In seconds she freed herself of the confining blanket and scrabbled frantically to locate Mark. There wasn't much time. The woodpile would burn too, so it was, at best, only a momentary haven.

He lay prone, partially through the opening, and he wasn't moving when she located him. Frantically she tugged at his coat.

"Mark!" she whispered. "Mark, hurry!"

She grasped his arm and heard him mumble, "Run . . . Up the mountain."

"No! I won't leave you!" She was practically sobbing. She clasped both of his shoulders and pulled. When she felt him slide a few inches toward her, she doubled her efforts. His coat shredded beneath her fingers. Slowly, agonizingly, he wriggled forward a few more inches, and she reached forward to grab his legs and pull them through the opening. She used the blanket to beat at the flames clinging to his pants, then reached for handfuls of snow to finish the job.

"Got . . . to keep . . . moving," Mark gasped.

"Can you run?" she whispered, knowing he couldn't. He could scarcely breathe and she had no idea how badly burned he might be.

"No . . . crawl."

"They're out there, aren't they?" She shivered and instinctively lowered her head.

"Yes . . . out front . . . watch the door." He coughed and she knew the cold air burned his smoke-filled lungs. He groaned and lay still, his head resting in a pile of snow. One hand gripped a chunk of firewood as though even in his enfeebled condition he sought a weapon of defense.

Nausea suddenly gripped her stomach. Someone lurked out there in the darkness, waiting for them to die. Almost absently she noticed the flames eating through the thin wooden walls, voracious tongues licking at the wood near Mark's feet. Soon the wood pile would be engulfed and the shack would collapse. Anger woke her to the danger. They had to move.

"Mark!" She shook his shoulder. "Come on, we'll crawl together. The shack is going to collapse, then we won't have any cover. We have to move now."

His body trembled with the massive force of his will as he rose to his knees. When she would have led the way, he indicated she should follow. Stubbornly she shook her head. She knew this mountain better than he did.

On hands and knees she scrambled toward the thick trunk of one of the sheltering pines. When she reached the tree she turned back to watch Mark with her heart in her throat. He scooted slowly through the snow, stopping frequently to brush snow over their tracks with the chunk of firewood he still carried. Flickering flames danced in the air, lending a macabre air to the shadows of the great fir trees swaying above the burning inferno.

Courtney's inner clock warned that dawn was not far away. They must keep moving and be well hidden before morning illuminated their escape. Mark's harsh breathing scraped at her heart, but pity could cost him his life. She'd keep him moving, even if it cost her own.

EIGHT

Higher would be better, but she'd reached the end of her strength and Mark was nearly unconscious. She'd managed to drag him the last few feet over the frozen ground to the cleft hidden among the roots of ancient pines where she'd once played with her brothers while her parents and the ranch hands worked with the herd on the plain below. She sat now with Mark's head in her lap and stared woodenly through a small gap in the thick branches.

Pink and silver streaked the sky to the east and she sat unflinching, even when a low groan sounded from the face in her lap. Then she saw them. Two ghostly snow machines topped the ridge beyond where the shack had stood. Slowly they circled the still smoldering ruin. Near the front door they paused and the two riders appeared to be arguing. One pulled a black object from his pocket and lifted it to his masked face. Obviously cell phones were used by the criminal element as well as worried about-to-be-fathers and independent daughters.

"They're trying to decide whether or not to raise that tin roof to look for bodies underneath," a voice spoke softly in her ear. "Fortunately it's still so hot they'll melt their gloves if they try." She hadn't even been aware that Mark had revived and struggled to a sitting position beside her. She had never before felt such intense anger, or was it hatred? But then no one had ever tried to kill her before, not once, but twice in less than twenty-four hours. Don't dwell on anger, she reminded herself. She'd need all of her strength and energy to keep herself and Mark alive.

Neither spoke as the two machines with their ski-masked navigators circled the burned shack once more then swept back over the ridge. When the sound of the engines died away, Mark and Courtney continued to sit watching the meadow. Finally two dots emerged from behind the hill to scatter the elk as they had done the day before. The dots moved slowly across the valley and eventually disappeared altogether.

"Are you all right?" Mark finally spoke. Something in his voice roused her from the stupor that held her locked in its embrace. She slowly turned her head and gasped.

"Oh, Mark." Her fingers gently touched his soot-covered face where red splotches told of the sparks that had landed on his face as he'd carried her to the wood pile door. She reached for his hands and brought them to her lips. Tears squeezed from the corners of her eyes as she viewed the blisters on his palms, and she remembered the frantic way he'd patted and slapped at her blanket-draped body as he'd pushed her through the small door to safety.

She turned her eyes to his hair and found it singed and ragged. His borrowed parka was black and split from hem to yoke up his back, so that it barely clung to its wearer's shoulders. Raw scratches and blisters peeked through the many holes in his jeans, and his shoes showed signs of cracking and melting.

"Do you think our snowmobile is still in the cave?" she asked worriedly. "I thought of taking refuge in the cave last night, but didn't dare because of the gasoline stored there. If they'd followed us . . ."

"You made the best choice," Mark wheezed. "Let's go . . . get it."

"Do you think they'll come back?" Courtney hesitated.

He was quiet so long she faltered as she began to rise to her feet. "Surely they won't. They think we're dead," she argued as though he had answered affirmatively.

"Courtney." He struggled to stand beside her. "They couldn't have followed us. Even with binoculars and daylight they couldn't have watched us because of the trees and hills in the valley between us and them. No one is good enough to have tracked us at night. Somehow they knew where we were without following."

"But that's impossible," she objected.

"No, listen to me." He grabbed her wrist when she would have turned away.

"You're scaring me."

"I know, and I'm sorry, but you need to know what we're up against. These people have access to sophisticated tracking equipment. I assumed the tracking device they were following was attached to my vehicle, but after I destroyed my Jeep, they found us at Grandpa's cabin, then they followed us here. The transmitter has to be hidden somewhere on my person. As soon as I leave this area, they'll know and follow."

Her eyes looked like sunken hollows in her white face as she stared at him speechlessly. She swallowed several deep gasps of air before she found her voice.

"Then we'll just have to get rid of your clothes. They're not going to get away with this." Her fierce declaration sent a shaft of warmth through his heart.

"Even forgetting propriety, I really can't forego clothes on a snow-covered Colorado mountainside." He shook his head and winced as he disturbed a previously unnoticed blister at the back of his neck. "Therefore," he touched her cheek in gentle understanding. "I want you to climb on that machine of yours and get out of here as fast as you can go. When you're safely at the ranch, call your sheriff and tell him to bring a posse after me."

"I can call him now!" She brightened. "The phone is in the snowmobile. I didn't take it inside. I meant to. I'd planned to try to call Dad again, but I wanted to know what you had remembered and as you talked I forgot all about the phone."

"How far can you call on that little phone of yours? Can you make long distance calls?" A glimmer of hope pushed through his despair.

"I can call anywhere, just like on a regular phone. The only place I can't call is to or from a place like the homestead canyon where satellite signals can't reach."

"All right. Let's get your phone, make some calls, then you're leaving." Her chin rose at a stubborn angle, and he suspected she wasn't through arguing the point. Eventually she'd have to see reason. There was no hope for either of them if she stayed without food or shelter. And he couldn't go with her, knowing that his movements would invite an attack on her and her family.

Working their way back down to the cave took longer than she expected. Though the sun shone brilliantly, their breaths left little cloudlike puffs each time they breathed out. Their bodies ached and their hands throbbed with cold as their gloves had been left behind in the cabin. Mark's hands suffered, too, from the effects of the fire, but finally the two survivors slid the last few feet into the tight maze of trees and shrubs concealing the small cave.

Her numb fingers fumbled with the catch to the compartment where the phone was concealed, then fumbled again as she punched in the ranch house code. She held her breath waiting, but she didn't have to wait long.

Her mother answered on the second ring.

"Mom, is Dad there?" She found herself struggling with a sudden surge of emotion at the sound of her mother's voice.

"Yes, I'll call him, but are you all right? Luke said you called yesterday and he thought you were on your way home. He didn't tell us until nearly eleven o'clock. What with the baby and everything, your call slipped his mind. Oh, the baby is a darling, just beautiful. He weighed nine pounds and—"

"Mom, I can hardly wait to see him, but I've got to talk to Dad. Please get him."

"Yes, of course." She knew she'd hurt her mother's feelings, but she knew, too, that Mom would forgive her when she knew the whole story.

"Court! What's the matter? Do you need me to come get you?" Her father's gruff bark was balm to her soul.

"Yes, Daddy." She gulped back the sob in her throat. "But I'm not at the cabin, and I'm not alone." There was silence at the other end of the line and she rushed on.

"A very sick man stumbled into the cabin that first night. Yesterday he was well enough to travel and we started for the ranch, but there was an avalanche. Two men deliberately shot it down."

"What?" her father roared. "Did you see them? Were they driving snowmobiles?"

"Yes, Dad. They were after the man with me. We headed across the valley and made it as far as the line shack along Goose creek. We holed up for the night, but they found us before morning and burned us out. We escaped and hid in the trees until dawn. We're at the cave behind the line shack now where we left the snowmobile last night."

"Are you hurt?" She could hear the shock and fear, coupled with growing anger in his voice.

"No, I'm fine, but the man with me is hurt and needs clothes. He's Luke's size."

"Jake, warm up the Cat!" Her father bellowed in a none-too-subtle aside, then his voice lowered as he turned back to his daughter. "You sit tight. We'll be there by noon."

"Thanks, Daddy."

"Love you, baby." It had been years since he'd tucked her in bed at night with that gruff reminder and she found herself fighting tears. Suddenly Mark took the phone out of her hand.

"Mr. Grant," he spoke into the tiny instrument. "These guys play rough. Bring rifles, and call the sheriff." He took a deep breath and plunged on. "Sir, please call this number and ask for Lieutenant Draper." He repeated a number he'd apparently memorized years ago. "Tell him everything your daughter told you and tell him Mark Stewart asked you to call." He listened briefly then handed the phone back to her. She held it to her ear then pressed the "Off" button.

Once more Mark took the phone from her hand. He pushed a quick succession of numbers, then paused as though listening. When he spoke again it was to rattle off from memory what she assumed was a credit card number. When he finished he spoke slowly and distinctly into the mouth piece. "HEL 7-1, 8-27, NE 3-4, night of the sign. SAM." He listened intently for several seconds as his message was read back, thanked the person on the other end of the conversation, then turned off the phone and handed it back to Courtney.

"Isn't it risky to use a credit card number if you don't want to be found?" Books and television had taught her that credit card use could be traced.

"It wasn't my card, but don't worry. My old partner has buckets of money, and he's the one who insisted I memorize the number, just in case I should find myself stranded without any funds."

They stood, each deep in thought, until Courtney broke the silence. "We need to start checking each piece of your clothing for that bug. You can keep Luke's coat; there's no way the bug could be in it."

"That's part of the problem." Mark sank against the snowmobile seat. "I don't see how anyone could have gotten to any of my clothes. They're all new, though I'm sure they don't look it now. From the time I purchased them until right now, the only time they've been off my body was at the cabin when you washed them while I slept or bathed."

"How about your wallet?"

"I thought of that. Again it's new, purchased on my way out of Dallas. Just in case, I kept the cash and left the rest behind back in the canyon."

"There must be something else." She paced to the edge of the trees. Slowly she reviewed in her mind every item she'd stripped from Mark the night he'd stumbled into the cabin. Her steps halted and she whirled around to face him again.

"The gun! Do you still have the gun?"

Slowly he shook his head. "The gun is gone. I wish I still had it; I'd certainly feel more confident while we wait for your father if I did, but it was in your saddlebags on the table inside the cabin."

"If having a gun will make you feel safer, I suppose my gun is still under the snowmobile seat. That's where Luke usually puts it."

"You have a gun?" Mark stood staring disbelieving at the spot where he'd been sitting, then at Courtney.

"It was Luke's idea. He convinced me several years ago that he'd feel better if I kept it with me whenever I went out alone. Jake insisted on teaching me how to use it."

Mark lifted the seat and reached for the small revolver. As he cradled it in one raw, bleeding hand, he whispered, "Now I know for sure I like your brothers." She didn't doubt he would like them if they ever had the opportunity to meet. When it came right down to it, Mark was a little too much like her brothers.

Once again she turned her thoughts to the problem at hand. Something niggled at the edge of her mind. There was something else, something she should remember.

"How big is this bug we're looking for?" A horrible thought occurred to her. "Can they hear us talking?"

"No, I don't believe it's a listening device," he answered her second question first. "I got a good look at the monitor that was in the car of the man following me. It was simply for tracking. I've seen that kind of tracking system before. The signal device is quite small, about the size of a dime. It can take a lot of abuse and still send out a signal for several months."

"Well, if it's that big, that rules out it being hidden in your clothes. There's no washing machine at the cabin, so I scrubbed every inch of your clothes by hand."

He looked pained at her admission and she felt an urge to grin. It never hurt to remind macho types like her brothers that it was the women in their lives who did the really nasty chores. Her smile died before it began as she remembered he'd saved her life. Without his quick thinking, she would have never made it out of the shack. She looked at his face and remembered that he'd suffered a number of burns in rescuing her. They had to be extremely painful.

"A gun isn't all I carry under that seat." She started toward the snowmobile. "There's a first-aid kit in there, too." She reached for the small square box blazoned with a red cross. Hastily she removed the cap from a tube of ointment and began gently smearing it on the blisters on his face and hands. Next she wound gauze over his hands and around his fingers. When he protested, she insisted that even if he didn't need the burns and abrasions covered, the loose wrap would take the place of the gloves he'd lost in the fire.

"There!" She put the cap back on the tube and stood back to survey her handiwork. "That should help until we can get you to a doctor. If you'd like some, there's some Tylenol in . . ." She stopped. Silence crashed around them as she slowly lifted her eyes to meet his.

"The pill bottle." He breathed the words and his hand moved in seeming slow motion toward his torn and blackened pocket. Slowly he withdrew his gauze-wrapped hand. In it lay a flattened, melted chunk of brown plastic. As Mark stared at the twisted pill bottle in his hand, his face revealed the agony of his thoughts. The dime-sized bug would have fit easily beneath the liner inside the lid that made the bottle child-resistant. Now both the bug and his last pill were forever fused with the plastic. Slowly he stepped to the edge of the trees and with one mighty thrust, he flung the bottle toward the smoldering ashes below.

He stood there gazing down, his shoulders trembling, and she obeyed the urge to go to him. She slipped her arm around his waist and leaned her head against his shoulder, choosing to wait with him in silence. Finally he squared his shoulders and turned to face her. He took her face between his two large battered hands and seemed to touch her soul as he stared deeply into her eyes. For just a moment she thought he meant to kiss her, but then he dropped his hands and turned away.

"Let's go meet your father," he spoke gruffly as he moved toward the snowmobile.

She stared after him, her thoughts in a turmoil. She'd wanted him to kiss her! But she'd sworn she wouldn't get involved with another man who didn't share her commitment to the Church. From what he'd told her she assumed he was an inactive member. She remembered his head bent over her Book of Mormon. At least he wasn't indifferent to the gospel as Greg had been. Her spirits rose, then plummeted just as sharply. She was building rosy dreams, seeing what she wanted to see just as she'd done with Greg. It was too soon and she was too smart to succumb to a rebound romance or confuse the quickly formed attachment of shared adventure with the enduring bonds of real love.

"Courtney?" She turned to follow Mark back to the cave, expecting to see him beside the snowmobile, waiting for her to climb aboard. Instead he stood staring at the mountains that bordered the northern boundary of the ranch.

"Who owns all that land?" He gestured vaguely in the direction he faced.

"It's government land. In case you've forgotten, the federal government controls greater portions of all of the western states than the states themselves do."

"But isn't there a mine and a timber company that operate in that area?"

"The mine hasn't been profitable for a long time. When the owners couldn't raise the money to meet new environmental guidelines, they closed. The timber company applied for a renewal of their timber cutting permit, but Roy Perry, our state senator wouldn't back it. Then a couple of loggers were injured when some save-the-forests group spiked the trees, so its owners dissolved the company and left the state. With both the mine and the mill closed, Isadora is well on its way to becoming a ghost town."

"Not for long," Mark muttered under his breath, but Courtney heard him.

"That's what Greg says."

"Greg?"

"My former fiancé." She hadn't meant to bring up his name, though surprisingly his name didn't evoke the hurt it usually did. "He works for the real estate arm of a large land and property management company. He's handled the sale of quite a bit of property in and around Isadora."

"Has he mentioned who is buying up the property and, no doubt, getting a real bargain?" She saw a hint of bitterness in his eyes and wondered if he resented her family for buying his grandfather's land.

"No, but he hinted once that a major developer was interested in turning Isadora into the next Vail or Aspen. When I asked Greg for more details, he got upset and said I shouldn't talk about it because it would raise hopes and inflate land prices." Anger stirred inside her. She'd argued with Greg that night trying to make him see that the people in the small town had a right to know their area was being considered for development so they could get the best prices for their property or choose to stay and become part of the new community. Or even fight the development if they chose. Greg had warned her that if some of the more militant environmentalist groups heard of the planned development, they'd create so many delays no one would benefit.

"Let's go!" Mark's curt command broke her reverie, and she hurried to take her place on the machine.

"Here!" Mark thrust her goggles and what looked like an old pair of gloves into her hands. "They were under the first-aid kit." He read the question in her eyes, and she remembered leaving them there several weeks ago when she'd helped Jake throw feed to the herd down on Willow Flats. When they'd finished, she'd placed the work gloves under the seat and pulled on the heavy insulated gloves she used for snowmobiling or skiing, the gloves that now were nothing but ashes.

Impulsively she turned to her companion. "Mark, why are they trying to kill you now? It seems it would have been much simpler while you were being held in that prison or even during your hospital stay."

He too questioned why the chase had turned deadly. He could only surmise that simply by coming to Colorado, he had revealed what they'd tried to torture from him for so many months—the identity of the person to whom he'd given his copy of the case report. He'd agonized for months wondering how the Snow King had learned there was a copy and that someone was holding it for him. He'd told no one in the department, not even his partner and friend, Desden Draper, about the duplicate file he'd asked Sam to keep safe for him.

He looked at Courtney, feeling uncertain how he should respond to her question. Her head was bowed and her eyes closed. Why hadn't he thought of that? Once he would have been on his knees thanking God for their escape as soon as they reached the trees where they'd hidden. And Courtney wouldn't be quietly praying by herself before leaving this hidden cave. A hunger to share her faith had him quietly placing his hand over hers.

A few moments later she reached for the ignition and felt a surge of satisfaction when the engine roared to life. Carefully she picked a trail through the trees, then when she reached the meadow, opened the throttle.

Making no attempt to hide their trail, she chose the most direct route to the ranch. Snow flew on either side as they skimmed across the meadow. Squinting against the dazzle of sun on snow, she raced toward the foothills separating this middle valley from the lower valley where the herd wintered and the ranch buildings waited.

It became necessary to reduce their speed once they reached the hills. Courtney was more accustomed to moving through a notch in the hills further to the east where a road had been cut to accommodate ranch vehicles and provide access to the Ankabruch ranch. As she searched out an old trail she hadn't ridden for years, she found she had to concentrate to avoid disaster.

She began watching for the big snow Cat as they emerged from the hills, though she didn't expect to meet up with her father for an hour or more. He would follow the road until he reached the middle valley, and the Cat was much slower than the sleeker, smaller snowmobiles. She wanted to cut him off before he followed the road into the hills. She glanced toward the east where the two snowmobiles had disappeared earlier, then turned that direction also and gunned the engine.

At last she topped a ridge and far in the distance caught a glimpse of the big yellow tractor laboring up a slope nearly two miles away. The big machine was slow, but it was as sturdy as a tank and the cab was enclosed and heated. It cut through massive drifts to carry feed to stranded cattle no matter how much opposition a Colorado winter threw its way.

She raised her hand to wave and heard the unmistakable whine of a bullet slice the air beside her ear. Suddenly she found herself tumbling in the snow with Mark on top of her. A second shot hit the snowmobile and its roar ceased instantly. Panic struck as she floundered in the snow while rifle shots kicked up little puffs of snow all around her. She had to get off this hill; she had to reach her father.

"Courtney! Hold still!" Mark's voice brought her back to reality, and she stopped her struggle. They were pinned down with only the body of a snowmobile between them and two men with rifles. And what kind of protection was it? One well-placed bullet to the machine's gas tank, and they'd be right back where they'd been last night.

NINE

Courtney stared in amazement as a pine shuddered, dropping a load of snow on the ground halfway up the hill from where the shots had erupted. An explosion near her ear had her turning to face the man who sprawled at her side, his body half concealing hers. Her gun was in his hand and he was returning fire. She understood the hopelessness of their situation. His gesture was heroic, but futile. There was no way a .22 pistol could hold off two high-powered rifles.

Without glancing her way, he seemed to read her mind. "They're out of range, but they can't see us well either. I can't hit them, but I can keep them from coming closer, perhaps buy us some time." Her hopes lifted.

Anxiously she peered over her shoulder to see how far away her father was. Evidently he'd noticed their predicament. He'd left the road and was now moving slowly, but inexorably up the slope toward them. She held her breath fearing the snipers would turn their fire on him.

The crack of a rifle rang through the still, cold air and Courtney cringed. It was followed by the swift tatoo of two shots fired almost together.

"What the–?!" Mark exploded. "Those shots came from behind the others. Is there a whole army out there?" They both tensed listening to the crack and whine of rifle fire. Gradually Courtney realized the fire was no longer directed at them. Mark came to the same conclusion.

"They're shooting at each other! Whoever is out there, they're on our side." He reached for her arm and gave her a squeeze even as his eyes were already measuring distances, looking for an escape route.

"Jake and Luke! They must have gone ahead on their snowmobiles, and when they heard shots, circled back." She was glad she and Mark were no longer targets, but her heart hammered in her throat as she envisioned her brothers facing the killers she knew those men to be.

"If we scoot backward and stay low, I think we can drop beneath the rim of the ridge and get out of sight while your brothers keep them entertained," Mark suggested.

Accordingly she moved. Wriggling like a snake, she felt snow work its way beneath her coat and fill her boots. She swallowed a mouthful of snow and moved faster. The ground dropped away and she began to slide, faster and faster, until she careened into a clump of brush, and Mark slid to a halt beside her.

The gun fire suddenly ceased and the only sound reverberating across the valley was the steady drone of the Cat coming ever closer. In minutes it churned its way over the crest and shuddered to a stop beside them. Her father flung open the door. She didn't need his gruff order, nor Mark's hasty shove, to scramble inside as quickly as she could.

Her father allowed only a brief hug before he slipped the tractor back into gear and began turning the machine toward home. Warmth wafted across her face, and she collapsed onto the bench seat gasping for breath. They were safe. It took several seconds for her brothers' plight to register.

"What about Luke and Jake?" she cried when she realized her father was making a straight run for the shelter of the ranch buildings nearly fifteen miles away.

"They'll be along," Ted Grant shouted over the drone of the diesel engine. "I saw those two skunks heading east as fast as they could go with your brothers and a couple of our hands about a half mile behind just before you two started down the hill. They'll probably head for the pass into Isadora. Sheriff Boulter's deputies will try to cut them off there. Don't worry, Jake and Luke won't follow them up the narrow pass. Too many places for an ambush."

He was right and both brothers, along with a couple of the younger ranch hands, returned to ride a kind of outrider escort before they reached the edge of the herd. As they approached the first barn, she spotted two more of the ranch hands with rifles keeping watch. When her father pulled to a stop in front of the shed where he stored the big Cat and the smaller snowmobiles, both brothers were off their machines and pulling at the doors of the Cat. She stumbled first into Jake's arms, then Luke's.

"Whooeee, sis!" Luke shouted. "You smell like the *piece de resistance* at one of Jake's cookouts." His graphic description of the burnt aroma clinging to her clothes and hair brought a smile to her lips.

"Wait a minute, little brother," Jake protested. "I'm not the one who burns the hot dogs."

Her mother and Lillian sprinted across the yard with a deputy at their heels, and Courtney staggered to meet them. Her mother's arms came around her, and hot tears burned the back of her eyes. For just a moment, she felt nine instead of twenty-nine years old and it felt good.

Remembering Mark, she freed herself from her mother's arms and turned back in time to see him watching her with a quizzical look on his face. He started toward her, then suddenly pitched forward, face first into the snow.

She screamed and ran toward him, expecting to see blood forming a puddle in the snow and to feel rifle bullets slam into her own body.

"He's all right." Her father grabbed her. "He hasn't been shot. He just passed out. The boys will get him to the house where your mother can give him a good once-over." With her mother, she hurried ahead of the men to prepare Luke's old room for Mark. She knew her mother had questions, but she didn't give her a chance to ask them. She wasn't ready to face any questions about Mark just yet.

* * *

Hours later, she was no more ready to face those questions, but they would no longer stay away. It wasn't her mother doing the questioning; the questions were her own. What lay between the stranger she'd rescued and herself? What did he really mean to her?

Why had she felt as though she were dying when Mark suddenly collapsed? What was the invisible link that drew her to him? Was it imagination or did her soul know him better than he knew himself?

She sat in the low rocker in her room, snug in a thick velour robe with her toes tucked beneath the trailing edge of the quilt her grandmother had made for her. Slowly she dragged a thick-toothed comb through her still-damp hair and savored the feel of being warm and clean. She'd stood beneath the spray of her shower enjoying its pelting warmth for half an hour, refusing to think, as black grime, fatigue, and fear washed down the drain.

But her thoughts wouldn't stay away for long from the man who lay just beyond the wall in Luke's old room. He'd regained consciousness before he'd reached the house and had insisted on remaining in the kitchen while her mother checked the numerous burns and scrapes on his face, hands, and legs. Luke had found him a change of clothes, and Jake had leaned against the bathroom door waiting while Mark had taken a quick shower. Courtney was uncertain whether her brother had assumed a defensive stance or if he expected Mark to collapse again. She had personally carried Mark's clothes outside and burned them. If there was any chance of a transmitter being hidden in his clothing, it was definitely gone now.

Her family had shown remarkable restraint in withholding their questions until Mark was clean, his wounds attended to, and they were both warm, dry, and fed. Dad wouldn't even allow Deputy Franklyn to ask questions, insisting questions could wait until Sheriff Boulter arrived. Franklyn didn't like having his authority usurped and tried repeatedly to gain a few answers to questions Mark neatly sidestepped.

She grimaced thinking of the soup Mom had ladled into two bowls for them. She'd greedily inhaled hers while Mark had to force himself to swallow half a dozen spoonfuls. His stomach was still bothering him. What if all the trauma they'd faced in the past two days set his recovery back? Just as she knew he needed to be under medical supervision, she knew he wouldn't trust a doctor to help him. He'd refused both her family's and the deputy's offer to send for a doctor.

Mark hadn't told her family about the drugs, only that he'd been a government agent and had been kidnapped. He'd told them about the witness protection program and warned them they were all in danger because his cover had been blown. He hadn't told them about Sam, and a silent admonition in his eyes warned her not to speak of Mark's cousin.

When the sheriff arrived, he sent the deputy back to Isadora to continue the search there, then he sat down with Mark and the Grants as though he had all the time in the world to visit before getting down to business. Dad and the sheriff told Mark about old Joe's last days and reminisced about when Mark's mother, who had been a few years older than Dad, had been a girl growing up on the mountain. Boulter blushed when he admitted he'd dated Anna Ruth, Mark's mother, a couple of times back in high school. She'd gone over the mountain to Isadora to high school while he'd stayed on this side and gone to school at Pine Creek. That was before the county closed Isadora High School and built a larger school at Pine Creek, he'd added.

At last, the sheriff insisted on closeting himself alone with Mark, and when he emerged from the bedroom a half hour later, he looked grim. He sent for a helicopter to take him to the cabin and the burned-out shed. He barked orders into the phone to his dispatcher and demanded that Courtney's father walk outside with him when he returned to his truck.

So much had happened, yet now, warm and cozy with her family around her, she thought it all seemed unreal. Only the feelings in her heart were not unreal. Something had happened on that windswept ridge when Mark threw her to the ground and covered her body with his own to protect her from sniper fire. She'd always known her family loved her and would willingly make tremendous sacrifices for her well-being if necessary, but at that moment she'd known Greg would never have taken the risks for her that Mark had. Mark had risked his life twice to spare hers. And he didn't even profess to love her. Not once during their time together had he done or said anything to indicate he was interested in furthering their relationship. He'd offered her comfort and risked his life for her, but he'd for her, though his actions told her he wasn't indifferent to her. Her feelings for him could not be denied. She loved him. She'd thought she loved Greg, but those feelings were remote and shallow beside what she'd discovered she felt for Mark. She wasn't ready to articulate those feelings yet, even in response to her mother's gently worded questions when they were finally alone. They were too new, too precious, to speak aloud so soon.

Her thoughts returned painfully to the beautiful woman Mark had been married to, and she wondered if he still cared for her. When Mark had spoken of the American reporter who saved his life by marrying him and helping him escape a dangerous situation, Courtney had realized who the woman was in the photograph she'd found in Mark's pocket. She was the glamorous international news reporter, Venita Perry, a woman who frequently appeared on television, reporting fast-breaking, sometimes dangerous stories, from disaster and war zones all over the world. Her name was on every "most admired" list published by both the top news magazines and women's glamour magazines.

It didn't matter. Mark would probably never love Courtney as she'd come to love him. With a surge of self-pity, she acknowledged she wasn't the kind of woman who inspired undying love from wild adventurers like Mark. He didn't live the kind of life where marriage and children and the Church fit in, but that was the kind of life she wanted. Her painful experience with Greg had taught her, those were the things that mattered most to her. Unlike her, she suspected Mark was as much at ease in the drawing rooms of powerful Washington hostesses as in jungles or forests, and that she'd never fit into his lifestyle any more than she could accept the life Greg offered her.

An inner core of steel refused to give in to self-pity and she vowed that she'd marry some day and she'd have the life she wanted. She'd even learn to love the man she'd someday wed. But in her heart, she knew there would always be a hole, an empty space, that no one except Mark could ever fill.

* * *

Mark opened his eyes and blinked at the bright light streaming through the window. He glanced at his wrist then realized he had never replaced the watch he'd been wearing when he'd been kidnapped a year ago. Time hadn't mattered in that hole in the jungle, and he'd been too busy—and too confused—to concern himself with a matter as trivial as a watch since his return.

He looked around the room, recognizing it as a boy's room. There were rodeo and sports posters on the walls and a Junior Bull Riders trophy on the dresser. Old-fashioned Spanish spurs dangled from a piece of braided rawhide draped over the hinge of an antique cheval glass, and above the headboard of the bed, a rack of antlers held a dozen baseball caps. Two faded spots on the wall hinted of two framed pictures no longer there. The room had obviously belonged to one of Courtney's brothers before he'd married and moved into one of the new houses on the outskirts of the sprawling cluster of buildings he'd seen the day before.

The house was silent, but Mark knew it must be close to midday. He felt rested and wondered how Courtney was faring her first day back with her family. He felt a moment's regret that their time alone was at an end. It was for the best though. She belonged in this world, while he wasn't certain he belonged anywhere.

He wondered what she'd told her family. There was really nothing he needed to hide from the Grants, but he wished he'd thought to ask her not to mention Sam or that he and his cousin had once both called themselves Sam. Mark had recognized Courtney's father and remembered times when Ted Grant had stopped by Grandpa's cabin to discuss ranching business, and that sometimes one or two small boys had ridden with him. It was strange he hadn't remembered that Grandpa's neighbor had a little girl, too. Those small boys were now very large men who had let him know in their own none-too-subtle way that they wouldn't tolerate anyone hurting their sister.

Gingerly pushing back the covers, he stood on a rag rug and looked for his jeans. Then he remembered Courtney had burned all of his clothes. He was glad she had, but he hoped she'd remembered to remove the roll of bills from his pants pocket first. He found her charred Book of Mormon and the money on the dresser.

Hoping he wouldn't have to face the family wrapped in a sheet, he studied the room further, then breathed a sigh of relief when he spotted a neatly folded stack of clean clothing at the foot of the bed. He dressed as quickly as his stiff limbs would allow in jeans and a soft flannel shirt. The boots were a little snug, but not uncomfortably so. He picked up the money and stuffed it in a pocket, then gently touched the Book of Mormon. The leather cover was scorched and the edges of the pages curled and crumbled beneath his fingers. Snow had blurred the inked notation at the beginning of the book and left messy smears of color where passages had once been carefully highlighted.

He was sorry the little book had taken so much abuse, but he was glad he hadn't left it behind at the cabin. He'd buy Courtney a new book as soon as he had an opportunity, but he'd like to keep this one if she'd let him. He'd had leather-bound scriptures like this once, he remembered, and noticed with a pleasant sense of familiarity that Courtney had marked many of the same passages he'd once highlighted in his own book. His scriptures had been in his apartment when it had been destroyed, and again he felt the hurt and loss of personal possessions he had once loved taken from him. He'd replaced those scriptures shortly after beginning his new life under the witness protection program. He supposed those books had disappeared along with his luggage when he'd been kidnapped.

He opened the book unerringly to Helaman. This section and the one that followed it had always appealed to the sense of justice which had propelled him into law enforcement work. Knowing Christ had come to this world, too—his world—somehow strengthened his faith. Something deep inside had always rallied to the heroic stories of Alma and Helaman, and especially to the Lamanite prophet, Samuel.

What had happened to his faith in that jungle prison? Why had he ceased to call on God? He'd condemned those ancient ancestors in his mind so many times for their failure to remain true. And he'd pictured himself as one of Helaman's two thousand stripling warriors with a faith so strong he could ride into battle and return unscathed. Now he felt more like the humiliated Peter who had denied his Lord when the going got tough and seemingly never forgave himself his one-time lapse in faith.

Suddenly Mark found himself on his knees, crying out to the God he'd forgotten. He pleaded for forgiveness for his weakness even as in his heart he questioned whether he could forgive himself for his failure to remain true to his faith. He did not know why all traces of his religion had disappeared so thoroughly from his mind. Anguish twisted his soul as he prayed for forgiveness, and he found himself pleading for another chance. The sweet peace he'd once found on his knees seeped into his soul, and at last, he arose shakily to his feet, marveling that God still loved him. He wasn't certain he'd been forgiven, but he experienced a quiet assurance that though he had forgotten God, God hadn't forgotten him. Knowing he'd turned from depending on God to depending on drugs sickened him, and he vowed to reclaim the faith he'd once known.

A vague recollection of a bathroom across the hall led him to seek it out. Moments later he stared at himself in the glass above the sink and quirked his mouth in a wry acknowledgment of the stranger who faced him. It was a wonder the Grants hadn't taken one look and told the sheriff to take him away!

Ted Grant and both of his sons wore mustaches, so he'd bet he could find a pair of scissors. A little snooping produced both scissors and a razor. Fifteen minutes later with his singed hair trimmed and his face free of stubble, he felt more like the old Mark Stewart. Now he only had to arrange for transportation. He'd get a motel room and wait until it was time to meet his cousin.

He stepped out of the bathroom to the sound of the front door opening and women's voices raised in laughter. He moved effortlessly in the old way, making no sound until he reached the end of the hall. He leaned his weight against the door frame and stood with folded arms watching the scene before him. In a large room filled with Christmas decorations and comfortable-looking chairs and sofas, four women shed coats and boots as their happy chatter warmed the room. Courtney sat in a chair and held out her arms. For the first time he noticed the wrapped bundle her mother held.

Liz Grant walked to her daughter's side and gently placed the baby in Courtney's outstretched arms.

He watched Liz reach for her daughter-in-law's arm as the other daughter-in-law hurried to the new mother's other side to help her up the stairs, and Courtney was left alone with the baby. An ache made itself known in his heart as Courtney settled back in the chair and carefully peeled away the blankets covering the infant's face. She brushed her cheek against the tiny face, and an expression of both pleasure and pain spoke volumes to him.

Courtney was a beautiful young woman with a heart full of love to give some lucky man. Once he'd dreamed of meeting a woman like her and of taking her to the House of the Lord to be joined with him for all eternity. It was easy to picture Courtney as the wife he'd once visualized. She touched his heart as no other woman ever had. But that dream belonged to a time before he had learned so much evil existed in the world. Before he'd denied his faith.

Courtney should be sitting in her own home. That should be her fir tree besider her, decked out with lights and Christmas angels. And it should be her own baby in her arms. Beside her there should be standing a man like one of the sons of Mosiah, a man who would never turn to drugs no matter how great his pain, a man who would face prison, starvation, and betrayal without turning from God.

"We'll just get you settled in bed." Liz's voice carried from the stairway. "Then we'll bring up the baby."

"Mom, I'll be fine at our house. The baby's things are all there."

"Luke's bringing them. We want you right here until after Christmas. The master suite has its own bathroom and sitting room. We used the sitting room for a nursery when our babies were born; we can do it again."

Courtney lifted her eyes and caught him watching her.

"Come in," she invited. "I'd like you to meet my favorite nephew. Of course, he's my first and only nephew, too." She smiled at the baby. "This is Lawrence James Grant—Little Luke." She held up the baby for his inspection.

He reached a finger toward the baby's soft head with its covering of pale fuzz and remembered his first glimpse of Julie. She hadn't looked much like this baby. She'd been no bigger than a half-grown kitten and long black spikes of hair had stood every which way from her head. He'd watched in awe as she'd twisted her tiny red face and launched the most satisfying war cry he'd ever heard. Neither he nor his equally enraptured cousin had ever ceased being amazed by the energy and vitality that had been Julie.

"May I use a phone?" He spoke softly, afraid he might disturb the sleeping infant. "I need to arrange for a car, and I should contact my former partner in Washington. I'll pay for any long-distance charges." So formal, so polite. His heart ached, but this was the way it had to be.

"Sure, go ahead. The phone's on the wall in the kitchen right behind you."

"Thanks."

She nodded her head and he turned away, ignoring the hurt in her eyes. He didn't mean to hurt her or sound indifferent. He was anything but indifferent to Courtney. She wasn't indifferent to him either, which made keeping his distance more difficult. He'd recognized that she cared something for him. It wasn't unusual for two people who had faced a life-threatening situation together to imagine a relationship that didn't really exist. He needed to be careful not to read too much into her warmth and kindness. She'd forget him soon enough when this was over. He didn't dare question whether he would forget her as quickly.

She didn't try to eavesdrop, but an occasional angry word reached her ears. Mark was arguing with someone over the phone. It was obvious he didn't agree with whatever he was being told. When he returned to the room where she sat holding Luke and Amy's newborn son, there was a thunderous scowl on his face.

"Mark, what is happening? Do you have to leave?"

"No, that's the problem. I've been ordered to stay right here until Desden Draper arrives. I tried to explain that my presence here endangers an innocent family, but Draper won't budge."

"Who's Draper?" She struggled to remain calm. She mustn't reveal how much his desire to leave disturbed her.

"Draper was my partner. We started out working together putting the drug cartel out of business until I got an opening that necessitated my working alone. He was assigned a new partner, a move I thought was only temporary. I expected we would resume working the case together after the trial, but instead he was given a long-term assignment with a foreign embassy while I had to suddenly enter the witness protection program."

"Is he the one . . . ?"

"No, Draper's a good man," he cut her off. "He didn't know I kept a copy of the evidence until after my family was killed. I talked to him by phone shortly before I went into the witness protection program, and he told me he'd heard a rumor from someone in the department that I'd kept a copy of the evidence and had given it to someone for safekeeping. I told him I was going into the program, so he knew I was still alive, but he didn't know who I'd become or where I'd gone."

"You trust him?"

"Yeah, I guess I do."

"What about your supervisor?"

"The man's dead. He suffered a heart attack a year ago. Draper has his job now."

"Then who is behind this?" Her agitation communicated itself to the baby, and he began to whimper. While she hushed and soothed him, her eyes never left Mark. "You said there were only four people who knew you were alive. You've eliminated two of them and I assume your cousin is the third. Who is the fourth?"

"The fourth isn't the man responsible for shooting at us and burning the line shack. I suspect he is a leak, but Gary Llewelyn isn't the brains of the organization. He's the man my supervisor reported to and now Draper does. I think that when my old supervisor had his heart attack, the message I sent him concerning my report and the new evidence I'd discovered—which included a phone number where I could be reached—fell into Llewelyn's hands. Llewelyn is a brown noser. He, no doubt, went right to his old pal, who happened to be responsible for his appointment. Within a week of my former supervisor's heart attack, Nick Mascaro was pressured with the help of a bump on his head into a South American business trip, and his business partner suddenly had the necessary funds to make the company a real success."

From the stairs, Lillian's voice reached them. "Mom, I understand why you want Amy and the baby close after what happened to Courtney, but there's no reason for Jake and me to move in."

"There's every reason," Liz Grant spoke in her best no-nonsense voice. "The boys found tracks this morning where someone rode snowmobiles up the slope behind the barns during the night."

Courtney's eyes flew to Mark's face. "They followed us here," she spoke in a hushed whisper through the sick horror rising in her throat. They were still after them. Unconsciously her arms tightened in a protective gesture around the baby.

TEN

By late afternoon the ranch was overrun by officers from every law enforcement agency Courtney had ever heard of. Sheriff Boulter turned Luke's house into his own temporary headquarters while four federal agents moved into Jake's place. The four were to alternate surveillance around the ranch buildings. Two deputies were assigned as bodyguards for Courtney, and were to take turns staying in the Grant home with the family. Two arson squads, one from the state and one from ATF, were dispatched to investigate the line shack fire and another team of investigators made its way to the avalanche site.

Desden Draper arrived driving a new sports utility, and Mark introduced him to the family. He was easy-going, friendly, and looked as though he'd be right at home on the cover of *GQ* magazine. Mark had told her his old friend was rich, but now she learned he was the son of Washington's famous Senator Lou Draper and that his mother was an equally well-known federal judge.

Mark—sometimes she still had to catch herself to keep from calling him Sam—spent long hours behind the closed door of her dad's office with Desden Draper. Outside of the office they continued to argue over Mark's enforced presence on the ranch. Draper insisted he could protect the former agent and the Grant family best if Mark remained with the family on the ranch until arrangements could be made to move him to a safe house, a plan Mark vehemently disputed. There had been a leak once; there could and would be again with Draper reporting to Llewelyn. Draper seemed skeptical that Llewelyn was the leak.

Courtney prowled the house feeling restless and useless. Mom and Lillian were providing more assistance with the new baby than Amy knew what to do with; Courtney's help wasn't needed. When Liz retreated to the kitchen to prepare dinner, Courtney volunteered to help, but her mother insisted she go to her room and rest.

Lying flat on her back on her bed, she stared at the ceiling, willing herself to sleep, but sleep wouldn't come. She wanted to be with Mark. This need to be with a particular person was a new experience for her. She enjoyed being with people, but she'd never needed anyone the way she needed Mark. Even her infatuation with Greg hadn't left her feeling this way.

They'd had no time alone since they'd been shot at on the ridge. Her mind persisted in reviewing every conversation, every minute they'd been together, both before their rescue and since. She knew Mark hadn't told her family about his drug addiction or the case he'd been working on before going into the witness protection program. She wondered if he had told his former partner of his planned meeting with his cousin. If he told Desden of the proposed meeting, wouldn't that information make its way to Llewelyn? And did Desden know the name of the man Mark suspected of masterminding his kidnapping, and who was now behind the attempts on his life? She knew his failure to give her the name of his suspect was deliberate, probably an attempt to protect her, but sharing information with Desden could be dangerous. Surely he understood that.

A knock sounded on her door and she found herself hoping Mark was seeking her out. She expected he would if for no other reason than to caution her against revealing anything she'd learned while they'd been at the cabin.

"Dinner!" Her mother's voice called through the panel and her hopes plummeted, forcing her to admit she missed Mark on a personal level that went far beyond friendship. She wasn't hungry, but she'd obey the summons. Though Mom fussed over Amy and the baby and bustled around the house in her usual efficient manner, Courtney knew her mother was worried about her. The whole situation couldn't help but concern her parents, and she wasn't about to add to their worry by refusing to eat or by playing some kind of tragic heroine.

She was surprised to find Mark and Desden already at the table when she arrived. She smiled at Mark before taking her seat across from him. He barely returned her smile and his gray pallor and grim expression heightened her concern. He wasn't well. He'd warned her it would take weeks to flush the drug's lingering effects from his system and that he could experience flashbacks for a long time to come. Months of malnutrition and physical abuse had also taken their toll and weakened his stamina.

None of the others seemed to have any awareness of his ordeal before the past two days, and she wondered if she should find an excuse to speak to Mr. Draper and alert him to the physical and emotional trauma Mark had been subjected to. Tentatively she broadened her smile to include him.

"Hello, Mr. Draper," she murmured.

"Desden," he smiled. "Please call me Desden." He widened the invitation to include the whole table before turning his attention back to her.

"School teachers didn't look like you when I was in high school," he spoke approvingly as his eyes met hers. There was a twinkle there and frank masculine appreciation that went far in healing the damage to her ego Greg had left behind.

It soon became obvious Desden didn't share his former partner's gloom. He smiled easily at her as she passed him the gravy, and launched into an amusing tale about Washington. Not until she caught the speculative gleam in her mother's eyes as she glanced from Mark to Desden then back to her, did she recognize that the handsome agent, who couldn't be more than five years older than her, was flirting with her.

Instead of feeling flattered by the man's attention, she felt a surge of annoyance, then wondered at her reaction. Tall and thin with the tiniest streak of gray touching each temple, Desden Draper was handsome and in noticeably excellent physical condition; she suspected that his smile had melted many hearts. She wondered just how sure Mark was that Draper hadn't played a part in his betrayal. Just to be safe, she'd avoid rather than seek a private chat with the agent. Mark might trust him, but she wasn't at all certain he was deserving of that trust.

Before retiring that night, her father invited Mark, Desden, and Deputy Franklyn to join the family for prayer. None of the men exhibited any awkwardness or reluctance as they took places in the circle, and she couldn't help comparing their easy acceptance of her family's Mormon lifestyle to Greg's bare tolerance. With a jolt of surprise she realized she was over Greg. Her feelings for Greg had been nowhere near as intense as what she now felt for Mark. Greg's memory no longer hurt or even raised her pulse a point, while Mark consumed nearly all of her thoughts and longings.

Unerringly her gaze sought Mark as they knelt in a circle. He looked tired and the pain etched across his face was unmistakable. His eyes were closed and several times he winced as though something hurt deeply. She was glad he'd been able to eat a little more for dinner than he had at any previous meal since the withdrawal symptoms had started, but he was far from well.

She waited until the old house had settled for the night before seeking him out. She knew he wasn't asleep. She'd heard him restlessly moving about his room ever since he'd wished everyone good night and retired to his room right after family prayer. She had to try to make him be reasonable about seeing a doctor. He'd hid it well all day, but she knew he was suffering. If he wouldn't see a doctor, perhaps she could convince him to take an over-the-counter pain killer so he could at least get some sleep. She had a bottle of Tylenol PM.

She got her purse and fished out the bottle of pills before leaving her room to tap softly on his door. Not waiting for him to answer, she twisted the knob and walked in. Mark was sitting up in bed with a quilt across his lap. He didn't seem surprised by her intrusion.

"I don't think your mother would approve of your being in my room." His mouth quirked in a small grin, and the light in his eyes told her he was only half teasing.

"I brought some Tylenol." She held up the bottle. "You don't seem to be able to sleep." Moving closer, she noticed the dull gray of metal in his lap and recognized the outline of a gun against one of her grandmother's patchwork quilts. Seeing it sent a shiver down her spine. She really didn't like guns. Idly she wondered if Desden had replaced the gun Mark lost in the fire. Surely if he'd given Mark a gun, he must be on Mark's side.

Before she could comment, he spoke softly, "It's better to be prepared."

"I know. And though it's not politically correct to admit I see a need for such weapons, I do. Dad and my brothers have kept rifles as long as I can remember, and I own a handgun, which I know how to use, but I can't really feel comfortable with guns."

Mark nodded his head in approval. "I've long maintained that those who are too comfortable and complacent around guns are as scary as the fanatics who create a false aura of secrecy and power around them by forbidding their use to all but a chosen few."

Deep grooves of white outlined his mouth, and the stiff way he sat on the bed revealed his discomfort. She held out the bottle.

"Take the Tylenol." With seeming reluctance, he took it from her hand.

"You need to see a doctor," she whispered.

"I will, I promise, once this is over." He shook two pills into his hand. She handed him a glass of juice her mother had left beside his bed. Her mother firmly believed Vitamin C was the panacea for most ills that afflict the human body.

When he set the glass down he looked at her as though he expected she would leave now. Something electric pulsed in the air between them. She should leave. Not only would her mother disapprove of her presence in a man's room in the middle of the night, but she knew in her heart she shouldn't be there.

Somehow she'd always thought that if she chose to wait for marriage, she had only to make it clear to the men she dated that no amount of persuasion would change her mind. She'd never realized that one day she might have to battle her own desires. But something deep in her soul warned that she'd be unable to live with herself if she indulged in the longing she felt for this man. She had already determined that she could not settle for less than temple marriage, and from what she knew of Mark's life, preparation for temple marriage didn't play a large part in his lifestyle. His casual marriage and divorce were indications he didn't view marriage the same way she did.

Feeling as though her heart was tearing in two and her soul was caught in the grip of an intense battle, she struggled to stay outwardly calm, but betraying tears trickled down her cheeks. Why did she feel this intense connection with a man she'd known for so short a time and who was so unsuitable for the life she'd chosen?

"Don't cry." Mark reached for her hands and she dropped to her knees beside his bed. She hadn't been aware of the tears coursing down her cheeks.

"You're safe now and this will all be over in just a few days now." He attempted to comfort her and she took consolation from knowing he didn't understand the real cause of her grief.

"Have you heard from your cousin?" She attempted to divert her attention from their closeness and the gentle way Mark was stroking her arms. He couldn't possibly know his tender action was adding fuel to the inferno raging inside her.

"Not yet. Desden and I will go into town tomorrow and get a copy of the *Denver Post.*" She remembered the call he'd made from the cave. As she'd suspected, the cousins communicated through the paper's classified section using a series of letters, numbers, and cryptic phrases from the Book of Mormon. Dread filled her heart as she thought of the risk he would be taking by leaving the house and wished she knew more about the meeting he'd arranged.

"After you meet with your cousin, are you coming back?" She'd promised herself she wouldn't ask, but she did.

"I won't go away without saying good-bye." His eyes met hers and the words that neither could speak seemed to hover in the air. She recognized the same longing that tore at her heart in his eyes and knew her feelings were not one-sided. And with that message came a quiet confirmation that Mark was aware of her feelings and that he would not only give his life for her, but he would protect her spiritually, no matter the personal cost, as well.

"You're stronger than you think," Mark stated quietly as though she'd spoken her thoughts aloud.

Slowly she rose to her feet. "Try to sleep," she told him. Her throat ached and her tongue felt thick. She marshaled all the willpower she could gather and turned toward the door. As she passed the dresser, her eyes lit on the charred and battered Book of Mormon, a reminder of the faith she cherished. A feeling of great humbleness swept over her. That book had been a refuge of strength and hope so many times in her life. Through it she had learned that God's children are tried to the limit of their endurance, but no further, and that God does not leave the faithful to fight their battles alone. A moment of recognition told her he was watching over her. Whatever happened between Mark and herself, her Savior would lend her strength. She only needed to ask in unwavering faith.

She hesitated, then left the book on the dresser. Somehow it comforted her to feel it symbolized a higher being watching over Mark. The trials he faced were greater than hers, and if the only way she could help him was to share this one small book, then she wanted him to have it.

* * *

She tossed and turned for what seemed hours after she returned to her room and climbed into bed. When she did sleep, it was only for a few hours. The clock beside her bed indicated a little past five when she awoke. Unable to return to sleep, she decided to dress and go to the kitchen where she could keep herself busy by starting biscuits for breakfast.

When she entered the kitchen she was surprised to see Luke slumped in a chair beside the table with the sleeping baby draped over one shoulder. He was unshaved and his hair stood in tousled spikes.

"You're up early." She tried to keep her voice bright and cheery.

"Who's been to bed?" He growled, and she couldn't help noticing the bags under her brother's eyes. "This little guy has night and day mixed up. He sleeps and is good as gold all day, but when Daddy is ready to hit the hay, he thinks its time to party. He just fell asleep, and it's time for me to be getting up."

Courtney laughed.

"It's not funny, dear sister," Luke continued to complain. "Amy had a rough time and the doctor told me to see that she gets as much rest as possible. I brought Little Luke down here so she could get some sleep, but it snowed again during the night and I've got to be ready to haul feed to the herd on Willow Creek as soon as it's light. Dad and Jake are loading the hay now."

"I'll do it." She needed the hard work and a few hours away from the house. "You go back to bed."

"Mom will skin me if I let you go," Luke grimaced.

Courtney dismissed her mother's concern. "She's being overly protective. I need to work as badly as you need to sleep."

She could tell Luke was tempted. "Look," she argued. "Amy's nervous because of what happened to Mark and me. Between the sheriff's men and the agents, there's plenty of protection around here, but I'm sure Amy will rest better and feel more protected if you're here while Dad and Jake and all our hands are out with the cattle. Even Mark and Desden are going into town this morning, so if you don't stay, there won't be any of our own men around the house this morning."

"Okay, you win." Luke yawned and shook his head. "If I were more awake I'd probably see all kinds of holes in your argument, but since I'm half asleep anyway, I'll let you drive the Cat and I'll get some shut-eye."

True to her expectations, her mother was appalled at the idea of Courtney leaving the house. She argued through the early breakfast the four of them shared.

"She'll be as safe feeding the stock as she'd be here." Her father took her side. "Besides she can't stay cooped up in the house forever."

"Amy and Luke need some time together," Courtney added to the argument. "Luke had to come after me while Amy was in the hospital instead of being with her and the baby, and he's been so busy since then, they've hardly had any time together."

Reluctantly Courtney's mother nodded her head, acknowledging that Courtney would make her own decision and that if her husband thought she'd be safe, then she wouldn't protest anymore.

*   *   *

Cattle wintered in three major herds in the lower valley during the winter, though small groups clustered together in gullies and patches of willows in between the larger herds. When the sound of the Cat pulling its heavy load of hay reached the cattle, they came running as fast as the deep snow permitted. While Jake and her father broke bales and scattered the hay, Courtney inched the snow caterpillar along the path she knew well in spite of six inches of new snow.

Several times her father pounded on the window to get her attention and pointed toward a spot along the creek where cattle had become stranded by the deep snow and were unable to make their way to the usual feeding areas. Each time, she turned the Cat toward the bawling cattle, broke a trail, and took them feed.

The Cat was used for the cattle farthest from the ranch buildings. While she, Dad, and Jake hauled hay to those cattle, the four ranch hands who worked year-round on the Grant ranch trucked hay to the closer herds.

As they approached the northern edge of the valley, Courtney marveled at how serene the great meadow appeared. It was hard to reconcile the peace and silence with the terror she and Mark had faced here just two days ago. She found herself nervously peering at rocks and ridges where hidden assailants might lie in wait. She was glad she'd traded places with Luke, but it would be a long time before she would look at a snowy mountain landscape and see only the beauty.

The pounding on the door caught her attention, and she brought the machine to a halt. Rolling down the window, she looked around.

"I don't see any cattle," she shouted over the roar of the engine. Her father pointed to a dip between two hills, and she peered in the direction he pointed. At first she didn't see anything except snow-covered boulders, then she spotted a patch of red beside one of the white mounds. It was too early for calving to begin, but one of the cows might have delivered early. If the cow had trouble, both the cow and calf were probably dead. They'd have to check.

"Drive closer," her dad instructed. She turned the Cat, and as she drew near the patch of red, a creeping premonition nearly choked her. When her father yelled for her to stop, she didn't hesitate. Leaving the engine running, she jumped from the cab to join her father and brother who were now both holding their rifles.

Together they waded through the deep snow to the lump clearly defined now as a cow.

Jake brushed away the snow covering the red hide and Courtney gasped. The cow hadn't died giving birth—she'd been shot!

She raised her eyes from the sight to see her father and Jake already striding as fast as the snow allowed to the other mounds she'd assumed were boulders. She watched as they uncovered seven more cows. Slowly a scream rose in her throat, and she clapped her gloved hands over her mouth to prevent its escape. Eight cows were dead—shot! She didn't need it spelled out to know the cattle's deaths were some kind of warning.

* * *

Mark ducked below the dashboard as Desden backed his Explorer out of the garage. They were taking no chances that anyone with high-powered field glasses might see him leave the ranch house. It was essential he look for a message from Sam, but equally important that no one discover his interest in the *Denver Post*. He could tell when Desden left the ranch road, crossed the cattle guard, and turned onto the highway. He waited another ten minutes before straightening onto the seat beside his former partner.

Desden glanced his way and grinned. "Just like old times."

"Not quite," Mark grimaced. "Back then I was in a lot better shape."

Desden sobered. "You told me about your stint in some South American jail, but I get the feeling there's more than old injuries bothering you . . . I know, I know. You're worried about nailing some biggie with a lot of clout, but there's more than that. I have a feeling you're a lot sicker than you've been letting on. Don't you think it's time you leveled with me?"

Mark considered not answering, but he supposed Desden had a right to know. Dropping everything in Washington to rush across the country to Colorado, besides tying up a lot of manpower on the word of a man who wasn't even an agent anymore, could jeopardize his old partner's career.

"Drugs . . . morphine, methadone . . . . or oxycodone . . . . maybe cocaine. I've been taking some pretty powerful stuff."

"You're putting me on! What's the matter with you? You never used to kid about drugs. Not ever!" Desden exploded, his own abhorrence of drugs evident in his reaction.

"I'm not kidding. I don't even know when they started giving it to me or if I took it willingly. To begin with, I think I was given street drugs. I have no idea what I may have been given while in the hospital in Dallas, but a doctor there prescribed heavy doses of Percocet, and I kept right on popping the stuff after I left the hospital."

"You're not . . . ?"

"No, I'm not on anything right now."

"How long . . . ?" Desden gave him a worried look.

"I'm past the worst of it. Courtney guessed right off while we were at the cabin, and when she did, I had to face it. I got rid of the stuff and put us both through a nightmare. I'm making it, but I'm still shaky."

Desden pounded a fist against the steering wheel. He started to swear, then stopped. "I can't believe it. I never thought something like that could happen to you. You were Mr. Straight Arrow Mormon. Undercover you always found a way to avoid so much as a sip of beer. That religion of yours was like some kind of armor. I'd follow you anywhere because I thought you were invincible."

"Yeah, it bothers me, too," Mark said quietly.

They rode in silence until they topped a rise and saw Pine Creek before them.

"Skirt the town," Mark instructed. "They might be watching for me here. If we go on to the next town, there's less chance of being seen." He gave directions for going around the small town, then returning to the state road.

Both men were silent as they passed through a small canyon and a heavily forested area. Mark pointed out a couple of alternative routes back to the freeway and Desden chose one at random.

"Look, I'm sorry," Desden spoke when they were back on the paved road. "I didn't mean to sound like I was criticizing you. They must have knocked you cold, then shot the stuff into you while you were unconscious. *Why* is what I'd like to know. The stuff is worth a lot of money. Why did they waste it on a prisoner?"

"They didn't give it to me the whole time, just toward the end.

I've thought about it a lot and I think they had a reason," he spoke slowly, considering each word carefully. "I wouldn't give them the name of my contact so they came up with a plan to scramble my brain so badly I'd either tell them what they wanted to know or lead them right to the evidence I hid."

"They're not just following you now—they're trying to kill you—so you figure they've somehow guessed who your contact is?" Desden's jaw clenched and his hand tightened on the steering wheel.

"Yeah, I think I led them right to him."

"Not necessarily," Desden glanced nervously at his rearview mirror. "Just before you disappeared into the witness protection program, word got out that you were the one responsible for that big bust. Supposedly you knew the name of the top guy and had given a copy of your report to some mysterious contact, and there was a lot of speculation about who your contact might be. Most people figured he knew as much as you did and that his life was in just as much danger as yours. Rumor settled on me as the most likely candidate."

"If this guy believed you were my contact, you'd be dead now," Mark spoke bluntly.

"Someone tried," Desden spoke softly. "Only I got the feeling they were more warnings than serious attempts. I think your guy thought I might be the man, but he wasn't sure. And not being sure, he didn't want to risk the kind of investigation that would follow the sudden death of the only son and heir of the Senate's top-ranked Armed Forces chair, if I wasn't really involved. Sometimes having a famous daddy comes in handy."

Mark remembered that Desden's mother was a federal district judge and his father a powerful U.S. senator. They both moved in top social and political circles. The death of any agent would be fully investigated, but an agent with Desden's connections would draw more publicity than someone with secret ambitions would want to risk on a hunch alone.

"You're in the clear now. I headed straight for Colorado, not Washington."

"I don't think that proves anything. As soon as you got to a phone, you called me, and I came barreling out here."

"They turned deadly before I contacted you."

"What about the girl? Is she your contact?"

"Courtney?" Sweat broke out on his upper lip. He hadn't considered the Snow King might consider her anything but an unfortunate complication.

"Of course, Courtney. As far as I can tell, Courtney Grant is the only person you've had any real contact with since you left Texas. Even the brief investigation I've had time to conduct reveals she was in South America at the same time you and I were chasing a few notable drug lords across that continent."

Mark shook his head vehemently. "No, I never met Courtney until almost two weeks ago when I stumbled into my grandfather's cabin where she was staying."

"Just in case that's the way your man is thinking, I've assigned our agents to watch her particularly closely," Desden reassured Mark.

There was something about his old partner's statement that disturbed Mark. He hesitated to call it jealousy, but he hadn't like the attention Desden had shown Courtney the night before either. Even if Desden were interested in Court, it was none of his business since he wasn't in a position to stake a claim himself. It shouldn't matter one way or the other to him, but it did.

"How much does Courtney know?" Desden continued his questions.

"I'm not sure," Mark answered. "She's extremely bright and while struggling with withdrawal, I suspect I revealed a lot more than I should have. She knows I've been trying to make contact with Sam Manytrees."

"Personally I always figured your contact was probably that Indian cop cousin of yours," Desden went on. "Didn't you tell me once about an uncle who stole your cousin's share of a big ranch up by Aspen?"

"Yeah, his father's stepbrother got everything. Only it's not a ranch anymore. Now it's covered with hotels, condos, and cabins for the rich and famous."

"And, I suppose, the uncle is now counted among the rich and famous?" Desden laughed, then glanced once more at his mirror.

"Someone following us?" Mark's eyes followed Desden's to the mirror, but the angle was wrong for him to see anything.

"I'm not sure, but I'm keeping an eye on a black Buick that's been with us since we returned to the freeway."

Mark turned his head. "It's coming up fast," he warned as his hand automatically went for the gun Desden had given him earlier.

"Get down!" Desden roared just before gunfire shattered the window beside him.

ELEVEN

Mark grabbed the wheel as Desden fell toward him. Blood and shattered glass were only a faint impression as he fought to keep the vehicle on the road. Climbing over his friend's inert body he searched with his feet for the brake and clutch. Desden's legs were in the way, but he couldn't take his hands off the steering wheel to move them aside. The blast of an air horn warned him he'd strayed across the center line. He overcorrected and felt the brush of trees scraping the passenger side. With adrenaline surging, he swerved back onto the road and found the brake. Searching visually for patches of ice that could lead to a deadly skid, he slowly began to pump.

A quick glance ahead showed the Buick had continued on, but the eighteen-wheeler he'd passed was pulling to the opposite side of the road nearly a quarter of a mile back. Mark brought the Explorer to a stop and shut off the engine. With shaking hands, he turned to Desden.

"Keep going. They'll be back," the wounded man muttered and Mark groaned in relief. Desden was alive.

"They've gone. Let me take a look at you," he tried to still the other man's concern.

"There isn't time," Desden groaned and struggled to raise his head. Mark felt sick at the sight of Desden's face, torn and bleeding from the shards of broken glass.

The Buick was lower than the Explorer, so when the gunman shot, he'd aimed up. Between the angle of the shot and the speed both vehicles were traveling, accuracy had been sacrificed. The left side of Desden's face had taken the brunt of the shattered glass, and a purple knot was growing on his temple from the center of a long jagged cut that was bleeding profusely.

Looking around frantically for something he could use as a pressure bandage, Mark spotted a travel size box of tissues. Just as he pressed a wad of the paper tissues against the cut, he heard shouting and raised his head. One hand automatically reached for the gun wedged between Desden and the back of the seat.

"You guys all right?" The truckers had almost reached the Bronco. They were dressed in jeans and boots, western shirts with pearl buttons, and beneath their cowboy hats their eyes were shaded by shiny metallic glasses. Their belt buckles looked as big as dinner plates. The truck drivers looked more like cowboys than Ted Grant and his men did.

Cautiously Mark spoke through the broken window, keeping his gun out of sight. "My friend is hurt pretty badly," he acknowledged.

"Saw the whole thing," the bigger trucker exploded with a few epitaphs that made Mark wince. "Got their plate number, too. Put it on the air, so I 'spect there'll be smokies here any minute."

"Thanks." He started to turn back to Desden when another sound caught his attention. Two more diesel rigs were slowing to a stop right behind him. The first one had barely stopped when a pint-sized lady hopped out, lugging what looked like a suitcase.

"Anybody hurt?" she called as she hustled along the side of the road. In minutes she'd introduced herself and crawled inside the Explorer.

"Dorrie—that's my wife—is a nurse," a burly trucker explained. "She comes along when she can, so when we heard Rodeo Man put out a call on the CB for the smokies, Dorrie said since we were close maybe we could help."

Mark backed out of the vehicle, leaving Desden in the hands of someone who appeared to be a lot more capable than he felt. Sirens wailed in the distance, and two more eighteen-wheelers pulled off the road, followed closely by a highway patrol car.

When the troopers stepped from their car, Mark walked to meet them. He showed them Desden's ID and stretched the truth a little when he told them he was working undercover to explain why he wasn't carrying ID.

"This man needs to see a doctor!" For a little woman, the trucker's nurse-wife didn't lack volume. Her voice cut through the excited male voices around the Explorer. In minutes someone produced a mattress that filled the back of the SUV and a couple of drivers moved Desden onto it. Someone else found a blanket. One of the cowboy truckers produced a sheet of plastic and had it taped in place over the shattered window by the time Dorrie had Desden ready to travel.

"Mark," Desden's hoarse voice reached his ear as he shifted into gear, prepared to follow the highway patrol's flashing lights. "They're out there."

"Yeah, I know," Mark acknowledged. "But we're safe for now. A couple of troopers are leading the way, and we've got the darndest assortment of truckers you ever saw riding shotgun."

"Don't try to talk," Dorrie ordered from her position perched beside Desden.

* * *

Courtney paced the floor. She'd changed into dry jeans and traded her boots for running shoes, but she refused to let her mother swaddle her in a blanket and ply her with hot chocolate. She ignored the two men in the room. Sheriff Boulter had ordered two of his deputies to stick to her like glue at all times.

Dad and Jake had returned with the sheriff to the dead cattle, but they'd refused to let her go along, though Luke had gone with them. They acted like she'd been shot at again. Her mouth tightened to a grim line. The loss of the cattle would cost her Dad and brothers thousands of dollars, but their loss was also clearly going to cost her the little bit of freedom she'd enjoyed since her return to the ranch. Between her mother and the two bodyguards assigned to her, she couldn't even go to the bathroom without someone following her down the hall and knocking on the door if she were in there more than five minutes.

What really bothered her was Mark. It was late afternoon, and he and Desden hadn't returned. She felt certain they had only been planning to be gone for the morning. She pictured the slaughtered cattle and squeezed her eyes shut trying to blot out the picture that came to mind of Mark cut down the same way.

The heavy throb of a helicopter passing over the house brought the two lawmen to their feet. One deputy, Kyle Johnson, a former student of hers, grabbed her about the waist and unceremoniously thrust her beneath a table.

"What do you think you're doing?" she spluttered.

"Just following orders, Miss Grant." He sprawled beside her as though at the first threat he meant to shield her with his own body. Across the room she saw Deputy Franklyn duck behind the drapes with a drawn weapon.

"Reporters! That's a Channel Three News chopper!" Deputy Franklyn snorted. He started to say more, but her former student warned him to watch his language around Miss Grant.

"They're headed the same direction the sheriff and the others took," Franklyn continued to share information with the young deputy.

"Kyle, let me up!" Courtney pushed at the deputy's chest. He blushed as he slowly rose to his feet, then extended a hand to help her up. She brushed his help aside and scrambled to her feet and over to the window.

"How did they find out?" She glared at the older deputy before turning her attention to the chopper disappearing from sight.

"Better questions might be how did they get here so quickly from Denver and how do they know where to go? This is a mighty big ranch," Kyle spoke thoughtfully. "I think maybe I'll make a call to Boulter, warn him they're coming, then I'll just do a little checking to see if I can find out who's in that bird."

Courtney turned worried eyes toward the young deputy. Four years ago he'd sat in her senior English class. He'd been one of the best students in the class and she'd been disappointed when he'd decided not to go to college. She'd suspected a lack of money was the reason he'd chosen the military instead. Evidently his time in the Air Force hadn't been wasted. He was still asking the right questions, and she suspected that more often than not, he was finding the right answers.

The other deputy politely suggested she move back from the window and she didn't argue. Folding her arms, she hugged herself as though she were cold while listening to Kyle's side of the conversation with the sheriff. When he ended the call, he immediately called the Denver television station. As he listened, his eyes narrowed and his mouth assumed a straight white line.

He politely thanked whoever was at the other end of the line and redialed the sheriff. Courtney knew the moment the sheriff answered because Kyle immediately jerked the phone a couple of inches away from his ear. Courtney could hear Sheriff Boulter shouting to be heard over the noise made by the helicopter.

"It's a network reporter," Kyle shouted to be heard over the background noise. "The station manager said Senator Perry's daughter is home for the holidays. She got a tip from somewhere and demanded the station's chopper and pilot."

Courtney stiffened. The local weekly newspaper would certainly be interested in a story about eight dead cows, but a national television affiliate? Why would Venita Perry care? She usually covered stories of national or international interest, so what was she doing here? Or maybe she didn't care about the Grants' dead cattle. What if she'd come because of Mark? Had he let her know he was here?

"Someone's pulling into the yard," Deputy Franklyn suddenly announced, and Kyle immediately stepped between her and the door. "Colorado Highway Patrol followed by a Ford Explorer. Looks like Draper and Stewart are back and they brought a friend."

When Desden stumbled into the house supported by Mark and a state patrolman, Courtney's knees went weak.

"Mom!" she yelled over her shoulder as she hurried toward the three men. Though Desden's bandaged face and stained clothing were hard to miss, it was Mark who drew her attention. She could see no obvious wounds, but still she had to ask.

"Are you hurt?" she whispered when she reached his side.

"No, I'm fine." She wasn't sure whether he smiled or grimaced as he answered her question. "Des needs to lie down though."

"Perhaps we should move him into Courtney's room. Is that okay, honey?" Her mother entered the living room with Lillian right behind her and took charge of the injured man. "Lillian, help Court change the sheets on her bed and move what she'll need to the family room. As soon as we get your friend settled," she turned pointedly to Mark, "you should rest, too."

"I'm fine," Mark protested.

"Nothing's fine around here," Liz grumbled as she shooed the men down the hall to Courtney's bedroom. "Tomorrow is Christmas Eve and nothing is the way it should be. With bombs and avalanches and people and cows getting shot, there's precious little peace and good will going on around here."

"What did she mean, cows being shot?" Mark gripped Courtney's arm and hissed in her ear.

"I'll explain later," she said as she hurried to prepare the bed for Desden.

When Desden was settled, he asked Deputy Franklyn to find one of his agents for him, then appeared to fall asleep. The others filed out of the room.

Courtney was the last to leave. She fluffed the pillow behind Desden and made certain that a glass of water and the pain pills and antibiotics prescribed by the doctor were within easy reach. She looked at him, then glanced away as she realized the direction of her thoughts. Desden seemed to be a nice man, but she couldn't deny she was glad it had been him rather than Mark who had been injured. The thought filled her with guilt, and she compensated by fussing for a few more minutes.

Mark watched her from the doorway and despised himself for begrudging Desden her attention. It would almost be worth getting shot to have her fussing over him, he thought, then denied the thought. He couldn't allow his growing attraction to Courtney to distract him from seeing justice done. With one last glance over her shoulder at the man in her bed, Courtney followed the others out the door. Mark was so busy envying the other man because he was lying in Courtney's bed, he almost let her walk right by him.

"Court." He reached for her arm. "What's been going on?"

"I might ask you the same thing. How did Desden get hurt? You told Mom you were in an accident, but what caused the accident?"

"You first."

"Okay." Briefly she explained about the dead cattle.

He agreed with the conclusion she had drawn. "It's a warning, all right. He's letting me know we can't patrol every foot of this ranch night and day."

"Tell me about the accident."

"I'd rather not, but Desden said something that makes me think they might not be after just me. He has a theory that the guy I'm after is getting desperate and that he'll attempt to kill anyone he suspects might have been my contact five years ago. Desden put himself and you in that category."

"Me? I didn't even know you five years ago," Courtney protested.

"We know that, but there are those who may assume we've known each other a long time because I spent summers and an occasional winter vacation on the ranch next to yours. Also you were in South America serving a mission at the same time I was gathering evidence there."

Courtney didn't speak as she slowly paced the hall. The very idea that someone might consider her Mark's contact was just too ridiculous. After a few minutes she stopped her pacing to remind him, "You didn't explain about the accident."

"Someone pulled up alongside of us and fired a shot through the side window. The shot didn't hit Desden, but the flying glass tore up his face."

"Will he be all right?" Courtney interrupted, her voice anxious, and Mark once more felt a niggling jealousy at her obvious concern for Desden. She was a caring woman, he reminded himself; her concern for Desden didn't necessarily mean anything personal.

"There wasn't a hospital, just a small clinic in the town where we took him. The doctor who saw him said the big cut on the side of his head may leave a scar, but the other cuts aren't deep and will fade in time. Desden refused to go on to Denver to be treated by a plastic surgeon."

She had more questions, and he told her about the truckers and the nurse. When he finished she took a couple more steps toward the sun room, where she stood in the doorway lost in thought.

Mark watched her, enjoying the sight of a beam of light touching her hair, making it appear almost red.

"Miss Grant."

Mark turned to see a young deputy standing a few feet behind him.

"Sheriff Boulter said I should keep you away from windows and out of the sun room." Though the deputy spoke respectfully, Mark suspected there was a streak of iron behind the young man's gentle voice. Evidently Courtney thought so, too.

"I'm sorry, Kyle," she apologized and took a step back into the hallway. "We'll just be a moment more, then we'll join the rest of you in the living room."

When the deputy was out of earshot, Courtney turned her attention back to Mark. He was surprised by the fierce anger in her eyes.

"How did they know where you were?" she demanded. "I'm sure you took precautions. There's no way anyone could have followed you the first ten miles on that detour without your knowing about it. I know that road. Even if you were seen exiting onto it, how did they know which fork you took at Five Mile Creek? If someone was planning to ambush you, why didn't they take advantage of the lonely, hidden stretches, instead of waiting until you were on the interstate?"

"I don't know. I just don't know," he repeated. "I've been asking myself the same question ever since Desden spotted that black Buick coming up behind us."

"Another thing . . ." She bit her bottom lip and seemed reluctant to speak. "Your ex-wife is here."

"What?" He wasn't certain he'd heard Courtney right. What was Venita doing here? "She's here?"

"Well, not right here, but nearby." She proceeded to tell him about the helicopter.

"What is she doing here?" he puzzled aloud.

"Then you didn't call her?" Courtney's voice sounded hesitant as though she dreaded his answer.

"No, I certainly didn't contact her," he lost no time clarifying. "But someone did."

* * *

After dinner Liz Grant insisted the whole family meet in the living room. She invited the two deputies to join them, and even Desden crawled out of bed to join the group. Liz reminded them that the next day was Christmas Eve and insisted they sing carols.

"I know you probably don't feel much like it," she conceded as she spread her music on the piano. "But I, for one, don't intend to let those ruffians spoil Christmas."

While they sang, Courtney found herself watching Mark. He seemed to be enjoying the music, even if some of the others seemed less enthusiastic. As she remembered the times she'd played the old upright at the cabin, he glanced up and met her eyes, and she knew he was thinking of that time, too.

Liz paused to find another piece of music, and Luke spoke into the sudden silence. "I'm taking Amy and the baby to her mother's house tomorrow." She could tell by his belligerent stance and Amy's quick denial that they'd argued about this before.

"I don't think that would be a good idea," Desden spoke quietly.

"I want them safe." Luke's tone of voice said his decision wasn't up for discussion.

Jake, too, had concerns about his wife's safety. "I've been thinking of sending Lillian to her brother in Denver," he added.

"Believe me, they're safer here than they'd be anywhere else," Desden spoke firmly to the brothers. "The people after Mark aren't after him alone. There's plenty of reason to suspect they consider your sister and me to be threats also. They play real rough, and if they get a chance to grab your wives or the baby to hold as hostages, they won't hesitate."

Amy started to sob, and Luke sank down on a footstool beside her and took her in his arms. His face looked bleak and worried, making Courtney wish she and Mark had never returned to the ranch. She could only excuse the danger they'd placed everyone in with the feeble excuse that she'd had no idea anyone would continue to pursue them once they were no longer isolated.

"This is my fault," Mark apologized. "I shouldn't have come here. I'll leave as quickly as I can make arrangements."

"You can't," Desden spoke bluntly. "I know you. You won't leave me or Courtney as long as there's a chance we're in danger."

Ted slapped his hand against the polished surface of the grand piano. "Nobody's going anywhere!" he exploded. "We're all getting mighty fed up with this business. I've got a ranch to run, and I can't do it for stumbling over deputies and investigators. No one's getting enough sleep for worrying about everyone else; we're losing cattle and shelters, and getting shot at. We can't even properly welcome a new Grant to the family or celebrate Christmas the way we'd like to.

"But Grants aren't quitters. We don't send away guests or family. We circle the wagons and that means we're all in this until it's over. Right now everyone better get to bed and get what sleep they can. Tomorrow after we feed the stock, we'll put our heads together and start coming up with some answers."

As the group began moving toward various bedrooms and one of the deputies went off duty, Courtney remembered she hadn't removed the clothing she'd need the next day from her bedroom so she accompanied Desden to her room.

"Do you have a pair of tweezers?"

She looked up from the drawer from which she'd been removing her sweats. Desden was sitting on the side of her bed looking at a trickle of blood seeping through the shoulder of his shirt.

"You're bleeding! I'll get Mom." Dropping the stack of clothing she'd pulled from the drawer, she started toward the door.

"No, I'm fine," he objected. "It's just a little sliver of glass the doctor missed. I can get it out with tweezers if you have some."

"I think there's some in the bathroom across the hall. I'll be right back," she called as she hurried through the door.

"Oops!" Mark's hands settled on her shoulders, preventing a collision. "What's the hurry?" He glanced at her face, then back at the open bedroom door, and frowned.

She felt breathless and strangely off balance with Mark's hands resting on her shoulders. It took an effort to remember her errand. "Desden is bleeding from a sliver of glass the doctor missed. He says he needs tweezers to get it out." She freed herself and dashed into the bathroom to return seconds later with a needle, alcohol, cotton balls, and a box of bandages.

Mark was already helping Desden remove his shirt when she returned. Desden pointed to a spot just above his left collarbone. She wrinkled her nose and bravely probed the area with the needle. When the spot became obscured by a smear of red, she dabbed it clean with an alcohol-soaked cotton ball. As she lightly pressed the cotton against his skin, she felt a small lump with her fingers. Seconds later she triumphantly lifted a tiny chunk of glass from its hiding place.

"Thanks," Desden grinned. "You can be my nurse any day."

"Not me." She took in the bandages on his face and the blood on his shirt. There was some on her fingers, too. Suddenly her stomach shifted and she knew she was going to be sick. She barely made it to the bathroom before becoming ill. Minutes later, feeling embarrassed, she washed her face and brushed her teeth as she steeled herself to return to the two men.

When she re-entered the room, she saw Mark had bandaged the small wound and cleaned up all traces of her impromptu first-aid job.

"Sorry," she mumbled, feeling mortified.

"Hey, you did fine." Desden gave her an understanding smile.

"At least she waited to get sick until after the job was done," Mark teased. "When she patched up my shoulder, I practically had to scrape her off the floor."

"Ingrate!" she laughed while remembering the night she'd put improvised butterfly stitches on a nearly frozen stranger's shoulder. He'd never know her dizziness that night had been more from touching his skin than from the sight of blood. Her fingers tingled now as she recalled the sensation of running her finger along the edge of the jagged tear. There had been a bump . . . A buzzing began in her ears. She must have swayed because Mark suddenly gripped her arm, steadying her.

"Sit down. Put your head between your knees," he ordered.

"No, I'm not going to faint." Her voice sounded weak to her own ears. "It's you," she gasped. "That's how they always know where you are. The transmitter is in your back."

TWELVE

"My back? What makes you think . . . ?" But already he was beginning to see she was right. If the transmitter had been planted inside the wound in his back, his pursuers would have no trouble tracking him. Planting the device beneath his skin sounded like some television espionage show, not real life; but ditching his truck, his wallet, even the pill bottle had made no difference. He'd known drug couriers who hid drug packets in their own body cavities or surgically planted them inside, so why not a tracking device? That he still carried the device on—or in—his person was the only explanation for the ease with which he was always located. It might also explain the length of time the wound on his back was taking to heal.

"What are you talking about?" Desden demanded to know. "How could you have a transmitter in your back?"

Mark grabbed the bottom of the sweatshirt he wore and jerked it over his head. Desden blanched when he saw Mark's back.

"What did they do to you?" His voice was hoarse, and Courtney noticed a momentary sheen of moisture in his eyes. She made a silent apology for the suspicions she'd entertained earlier. Desden's concern for Mark was genuine. Besides, surely the people pursuing Mark wouldn't have shot one of their own.

"Let me show you." She reached for Desden's hand. Carefully she skimmed his fingertips over the partially healed wound on Mark's shoulder until they came to the small obstruction barely felt beneath his skin. "There!" Slowly his fingers explored the spot she indicated.

"It is the right size and shape," he muttered.

She sank down on the side of the bed while Desden continued to run his fingers over the small lump. Placing her hands over her face, she began to cry.

"Hey, what is this?" Mark was suddenly crouched beside her, tugging her hands away from her face. "I think you've hit on the key. You should be cheering instead of crying. I can get rid of the thing now."

"Oh, Mark!" She flung her arms around his neck. "I should have guessed. I felt that lump the first night I bandaged your shoulder. I thought it might be a bullet, and I was too scared to examine it closer, then I forgot all about it until I felt that shard of glass in Desden's shoulder. I'm so sorry."

"Nothing to be sorry about." He kissed her cheek and while she was struggling to control her runaway pulse he gave her a wry smile and asked, "How do you feel about a second bit of surgery tonight?"

"Me?" She straightened, alarm tingling in every inch of her body. "That's a lot bigger than Desden's sliver of glass. I can't get it out. You need a doctor."

"You can do it," he coaxed. "You're much braver than you give yourself credit for."

"No, Mark. I can't. Let me drive you to Dr. Gates' house. He's retired, but I know he'd do it."

"You know I can't leave here. They'd know the minute I leave the ranch."

"I'll get Mom."

"I don't think we should involve your mother," Desden cautioned. "She's sleeping at the other end of the house, and if we disturb her, your whole family and the deputy will be in here. The fewer people who know about this the better."

"Then you do it," Courtney turned pleading eyes toward Desden. He held up his left arm with its bandage extending from the tips of his fingers to his wrist. He hadn't been wearing gloves so the flying pieces of glass had left their marks on his hand as well as his face. His heavy coat had protected his arm, although a few shards of glass had found their way inside his collar to leave scratches and small cuts on his neck and upper shoulders.

"Sorry, I'm a southpaw. I'm barely managing to feed myself." He smiled apologetically.

"I can't do it," she wailed. "I'm a school teacher, not a nurse." The men didn't say anything, but they watched her expectantly. Bile rose in her throat as she pictured herself cutting into Mark's back. He tightened his grip on her hands, and she read the sympathy in his eyes. He was trying to comfort her, but who would comfort him? With that awful bug in his back, his enemies knew every move he made. Eventually they'd kill him, and her cowardice would be to blame.

"A needle and tweezers won't work," she mumbled the words, but both men accepted her timid acquiescence.

"Thank you," Mark leaned forward and gently brushed his lips against her forehead.

"You're one in a million." Desden grinned. "I don't think you'll have to sneak into the kitchen to nab a steak knife." He nodded toward the closed door to the adjoining bathroom. Her father had added it for her so she wouldn't have to share the one her brothers used across the hall. "When I visited your bathroom I saw a straight-edge razor like my hair stylist back home uses. It will work."

"I had a missionary companion who was a hair stylist. She used to trim my hair for me when we were in Honduras. When I came home she gave the razor to me. Mom occasionally trims my hair with it now when I get too busy to go to my beautician as often as I should." She knew she was babbling, postponing the inevitable.

"Get it." Mark pulled her to her feet and smiled encouragingly.

In the bathroom she picked up the slender tool and shuddered. How could she do this?

"Courtney." Mark's hand rested on her shoulder. She hadn't been aware he had followed her into the small space. "I wish I didn't have to ask this of you, but I have faith that you can do it."

"I don't know . . ." Her voice trailed off. Turning her to look squarely into his eyes, he gripped both of her shoulders and spoke with quiet conviction.

"Remember when we were at the cabin? You read to me from your Book of Mormon, and I knew then you weren't just reading words.

Your faith in God runs deep. It was the conviction in your voice behind the words that resurrected memories buried deep inside my subconscious that told me I once knew those truths myself. I remember serving a mission for the Church in Peru, and though I still have some gaps in my memory, and I don't know why I forgot God while I was in prison, I trust him to respond to your faith. I trust you."

"Would you give me a blessing? I'm so scared."

"I don't think I have that right anymore."

"Nothing that happened to you while you were imprisoned was your fault. You're a good man and your priesthood is still there if you have the faith to draw on it," Courtney argued.

"There's a lot I need to relearn, and much I don't understand about my past, which I have to resolve before I can feel worthy and have the right spirit with me to call on the priesthood powers I once held."

She saw evidence of deep sorrow and uncertainty in his eyes. Gently she pressed her hand to his cheek and whispered, "Then will you pray with me?"

"Yes, I can do that."

"What's taking you two so long?" Desden called anxiously.

"We're coming," Mark answered.

"What about Desden? Will he pray with us?"

"I used to call Desden 'the heathen' because he claims he's an agnostic, who neither knows nor cares whether or not there's a god. But whenever we were in a tight spot, he was the one who insisted I pray. Later he'd always claim there was no harm in covering all of our bases. I suspect he'll be more than willing to pray with us."

Courtney hid a smile as the three of them knelt beside her bed. Desden was not only willing, but eager, to join them in prayer before attempting to remove the transmitter. She put her entire heart into asking for strength and calmness for all three of them, then rose on shaking limbs to reach for the bottle of alcohol to sterilize the razor and tweezers.

Desden spread clean towels on the bed before Mark lay facedown on it.

"I've got those pain pills the doctor gave me," she heard Desden whisper to Mark. "One of those might help."

"No, they're just a weaker version of the drugs I've been fighting. I don't want one."

"I've got a flask of good Kentucky bourbon, but I don't suppose you want it either."

"That's all I need to make this a real B-grade western," Mark chuckled. "No, I don't want it either, but I saw something in the other bathroom that might help. There's a green metal box of bag balm there. Go get it."

"Bag balm? What on earth is that?"

"It's a salve farmers and ranchers use on cattle," Courtney answered for Mark. "If a cow slices open a teat on barbed wire, she still has to be milked. If it eases the pain enough to keep a cow from kicking a farmer into the next county while he milks her, it just might ease the pain for Mark."

Desden returned quickly with the ointment. He took off the lid and sniffed, then wrinkled his nose. "If this is for cattle, how come you keep it in the house?" he asked curiously.

"Every farmer and rancher knows it's the best remedy for the inevitable nicks and chapped hands that go along with tending stock in all kinds of weather." She knelt beside Mark.

"I'll never understand you country people in a million years." Desden shook his head as he placed the can beside the first-aid items Courtney had gathered.

Carefully she swabbed the area with alcohol, then spread a thin film of the ointment along the area she would have to cut, before reaching for the razor.

"Don't try to be slow and gentle," Desden warned. "Samurai warriors lop off heads and arms painlessly without even bloodying their swords by being swift and decisive."

She was no samurai warrior, but what he said made sense. Cutting slowly would be a lot like trying to ease adhesive tape from skin rather than jerking it off in one quick swoop. She closed her eyes and took a deep gulp of air.

"Better keep your eyes open," Desden cautioned and she heard the worry in his voice.

"Yeah," Mark mumbled. "I'll shut mine; you keep yours open."

Quickly, before she could think further or acknowledge the queasiness in her stomach, she pressed the razor into the old wound and drew it rapidly toward her, leaving a two-inch gash. Mark flinched and sharply drew in his breath. She struggled to close her ears to the soft moan that escaped his lips. Desden swiftly pressed cotton over the fresh wound.

Turning her head away, she fought the urge to gag.

"Are you okay?" Mark whispered. She wasn't sure if he was keeping his voice down to avoid waking the rest of the household or if pain was the reason.

"Don't worry," she tried to sound lighthearted. "I've already made my offering at the porcelain altar. There's nothing left to lose."

Turning back to the task at hand, she reached for the tweezers and wondered if they were sturdy enough to use as forceps. Steeling herself, she motioned Desden to move back enough to give her access to the cut she'd made. She knew exactly where to probe. She'd felt the razor graze the foreign object in Mark's back. She expected the sight of blood would make her sick again, but what she saw stirred her anger. A yellowish fluid seeped from the spot where she'd brushed the object. The area around the tiny transmitter was infected.

The dime-sized object came out easily, probably due to the infected fluid around it. She dropped it into the plastic lid of a can of hair spray that Desden held out to her, then turned her attention back to Mark. With great care she cleaned out the wound and debated out loud whether to use alcohol or the bag balm for an antiseptic. Desden handed her a bottle of hydrogen peroxide. He'd evidently made a thorough survey of the supplies she kept in her bathroom.

"It needs to be stitched, but I don't think I can do it." Courtney realized her hands had started to shake and the nausea was making itself felt again.

"Use tape." Mark's whisper sounded more like a groan.

"I can't hold the edges together and cut the tape, too, and with only one hand, Desden can't do it either. If I were meant to be a doctor, I would have known to cut the tape before beginning the surgery."

"I'll cut the tape. Hand me the scissors." Mark moved as though reaching for the scissors lying near his right hand on the toweled surface of the bed.

"No! When you move, the cut bleeds more."

"I'll have to risk that . . ."

"What's going on here?" All three heads swivelled to face the door. Kyle stood there with his gun drawn, a look of horror on his young face. "Are you hurt, Miss Grant? You and that guy on the bed are both covered with blood." He turned just enough that his gun was pointing directly at Desden.

"Come in and shut the door," Courtney spoke impatiently. "Everything is fine, but I could use a little help cutting some tape."

The deputy continued to stand and his gun didn't waver.

"Kyle, put that gun away and get over here."

"I think you better do as she says. Courtney is a very unwilling doctor," Desden spoke calmly as though a gun pointed his way meant nothing at all. "Blood makes her nauseated, and if she has to make another dive for what she euphemistically refers to as 'the porcelain altar,' poor Mark just might bleed to death."

She could see the hesitation in the deputy's face as he slowly returned his gun to its holster.

"That's all his blood?" The deputy looked at Courtney's blood-smeared hands and splotched shirt, then looked toward Mark. She nodded her head in acknowledgment.

"What happened to him?"

"She stuck a knife in my back, officer," Mark attempted a feeble joke.

"Come help me and I'll explain as we work." Courtney glared at Mark, then tried to smile at the deputy, but it didn't work out well. Instantly he was beside her.

"Wash your hands in there." She indicated the adjoining bathroom. "Then cut narrow strips of adhesive tape I can use for stitches."

When he returned he cut strips faster than she could apply them. After watching her work for a few minutes, he took the strip she held in her hands from her.

"I'll do it. You go wash up."

"But . . ."

"You're shaking so badly, it'll take you until next week to finish. I can do it; first aid is the first thing we deputies are taught in those police academies the taxpayers send us to." He smiled and she knew he was aware of how close she was to losing it. On trembling legs she retreated to the bathroom and left him to it.

When she returned she saw that a thick pad had been neatly taped to Mark's shoulder and the blood-spattered towels had been removed.

"I wish you'd gotten here sooner. You'd make a much better doctor than I proved to be." She spoke to Kyle, but her attention was riveted on Mark. He was sitting up, leaning against the headboard and Desden was sprawled in the only chair in the room. They were both being so casual about the situation, she tried to play it cool, too.

"You did a good job, Miss Grant," Kyle voiced his approval. "That took a lot of courage to do what you did. Draper explained what happened."

"Don't you think it's time you called me Courtney like everyone else? It's been a long time since you sat in one of my classes."

"Yes, ma'am, er— Courtney." Kyle blushed to the tops of his ears and turned away.

Mark felt a slow grin spread across his face. The deputy was still nursing a school boy crush on his teacher. Of course, he couldn't blame him. He'd felt the same way ever since he'd opened his eyes and saw her face that first time back at his grandfather's cabin.

That fiancé of hers must have been some kind of fool to have let her get away, he found himself thinking. Suddenly he wondered if he, too, would be some kind of fool if he walked away, leaving her behind when this was over. But what choice did he have? Courtney deserved someone a lot better than a beat-up undercover cop with Swiss cheese for a brain.

Sure, he knew she was attracted to him, but that happened when two people faced life and death situations together. Hadn't he once fancied himself in love with Venita after she rescued him? Courtney would get over it, and so would he.

"How do you feel?" Courtney sat down beside him, and her worried expression did strange things to his heart.

"I'm doing fine." There was no way he'd tell her his back burned like it was on fire and he was almost as woozy as she'd been earlier. He understood how hard removing that tracer bug had been for her, and it touched him that she had conquered her fear for him.

"You really should be taking an antibiotic," she told him. "It makes me so angry to think that someone put a foreign object inside you without any concern for the infection it could and did cause."

"Hey," he tried to make light of the incident. "It's not any worse than some of the other things they've tried to do to me."

"I know someone has tried several times to kill you, but there's just something so sneaky about planting that thing inside you. Whoever did it knew perfectly well that if they failed to shoot you or blow you up, you'd probably die from infection." He felt a sudden urge to kiss her as her indignation traded two spots of color on her cheeks for her earlier pallor.

"The doctor who saw Desden gave him antibiotic tablets as well as pain pills. I took a couple of those, so don't worry." He attempted to reassure her. "I'll take a couple more in the morning, and I'll be fine."

"What are you going to do with this thing?" Kyle stood in the middle of the room with the plastic lid that held the small round disc Courtney had removed from Mark's shoulder.

"Flush it!" Courtney shuddered.

"I don't think so." Kyle shook the object a couple of times. "It would just end up in your septic tank, which isn't all that far from the house, and those guys would think Mr. Stewart is still holed up here."

A sudden mental picture of the septic tank being blown up struck Mark as extremely funny, and he wondered if he might be bordering on hysteria. The sooner they were rid of the thing the better. Its removal from his back hadn't precipitated an immediate attack, but the longer it was in the ranch house, the greater the risk of an attack that might harm or kill Courtney and her family.

"You're right." Desden wandered over to stand by the deputy. "How are we going to get rid of it without endangering the guy who hauls it away? It's a simple device that can be picked up by a tracer for several months, and it's practically indestructible. Even if we smashed it, that would be sending a message that it had been found."

"Well, I've been thinking," Kyle spoke in a slow deliberate voice. I used to work part time out here for Mr. Grant during branding and roundup, so I know the place pretty well. About two hundred yards back, on the other side of the barn, there's a fast-moving creek that never freezes over. If we were to put this thing in one of those little plastic pill bottles and drop it in the creek, I'm not sure it would make it all the way to the Colorado, but it would travel into some pretty inaccessible places."

"What's a kid as bright as you are doing working for a county sheriff?" Desden was already dumping the contents of one pill bottle onto the nightstand. When he finished, he reached for the coat he'd left hanging over the back of the chair.

"No offense, Mr. Draper." Kyle reached for the bottle Desden held. "Neither of you fellows is in any shape to be traipsing down to the creek. I have a bullet-proof vest and a white snowmobile suit. Besides, I know the way and you don't. Shouldn't take me more than half an hour. I'll lay odds even your agents won't see me coming or going," he added, either to taunt or reassure Desden. He was out the door before anyone could stop him.

The kid had courage, but Mark wasn't sure he appreciated his heroic act. It might be an attempt to impress Courtney. He immediately felt ashamed for considering that possibility. The deputy was young, but he was a born lawman through and through. What rankled was that he hadn't been able to do the job himself. It didn't sit well to have a fresh-faced kid-deputy calling the shots, especially one that had a thing for Courtney. He might do well to remember the deputy wasn't really a kid either, he thought glumly.

Mark watched Courtney pace the floor while they waited for Kyle to return. Once she disappeared into the bathroom and came out wearing a clean shirt. She jumped at every small night sound, and he found himself becoming increasingly irritated. He didn't know if her obvious concern for the young man was the source of his irritation or if his own worry was the problem.

A whisper of sound reached his ears just as the door opened. Either he was slipping or the deputy had a knack for moving awfully quietly. Kyle stepped into the room and closed the door behind him. There was a sparkle in his eyes and his cheeks were rosy. To Mark's eyes, he appeared on the verge of laughter. He'd enjoyed the little trick he'd pulled, and he wasn't even breathing hard!

Courtney rushed to hug the deputy, and while she thanked him and called him brave, Mark felt his gloom deepen. Tomorrow, today really, was Christmas Eve. He'd meet Sam tonight, warn him to disappear for a while, and arrange to collect the evidence he'd left with him five years ago. Before the week was over, the case would be wrapped up, and the Snow King would be under arrest. Then he'd leave Colorado for good. With that decision made, he knew he should feel better, but if anything, his gloom deepened.

"Mark, if you want to stay in here, Desden said he doesn't mind moving to your room." Courtney approached the side of the bed.

"I'm fine. Stop fussing." He heaved himself to his feet and suddenly had to grasp the bed post to stay upright.

"I'll help him, Miss—uh—Courtney." The deputy was at Mark's side in a flash. It was humiliating to need his help, but he'd seen more than one man let pride make a fool of him, so he stoically accepted the proffered support.

When he reached his own bed, he sank slowly onto it, being careful to shield his injured shoulder. He was glad he was only wearing sweat pants and didn't need to change. He wouldn't relish having the deputy help him out of his clothes.

"Will you be all right?" Courtney chewed on her bottom lip as she looked down at him.

"Yeah, sure. A few hours of sleep and I'll be good as new." He smiled, trying to reassure her. To his surprise she bent forward and lightly brushed her lips across his. "I'll check on you about five," she whispered, her voice husky, then she rushed from the room. Kyle practically had to run to keep up with her.

Mark stared at the faint outline of the door Kyle closed behind them, and it hit him that he wouldn't be getting over Courtney soon. Maybe not ever.

THIRTEEN

Courtney fiddled with her fork. It certainly didn't seem like the day before Christmas. Fortunately she'd done her shopping weeks ago in Denver, but that was before Little Luke had been born. Not knowing whether the baby would be a niece or a nephew, she'd bought generic gifts for him. She wished she could run into Pine Creek this morning and pick out something really boyish for him. Pine Creek didn't offer a lot of choices, but the one small department store and the craft shop both carried a nice selection of baby items.

She didn't have a gift for Mark either, and she wanted to give him something. It looked like both Mark and Desden would be with them for Christmas so there ought to be packages under the tree for them. She supposed she could change the tag on one of the gifts she'd picked for each of her brothers. The quilted flannel shirt she'd bought for Luke would look good on Mark, and the box of fishing flies she'd picked out for Jake would have to do for Desden. She hoped he liked to fish.

"Have you finished your breakfast?" She looked up to see her mother watching her with a worried expression on her face.

"Oh! Yes." She scrambled to her feet and gathered up her dishes. Her mother would be wanting every bit of counter and table top space in her kitchen for preparing Christmas Eve dinner. She apologized for dawdling over her breakfast.

"You didn't eat much. Are you sure you're not coming down with a cold?"

"I'm fine, Mom," she insisted, striving to add a cheerful note to her voice. "What would you like me to start on?"

"If you don't feel well . . ."

"Mom, I don't need any more rest, and I'm not sick."

"You seem a little distracted," her mother observed. "You've been through a difficult time, but I think it's more than that. It seems to me you're more than a little bit attracted to Mark. Are you afraid he doesn't share your interest?"

Her first instinct was to brush aside her mother's question and pretend she felt nothing more than friendship for Mark, but suddenly she felt a need to talk. "I do care for Mark," she admitted. "And I feel certain he feels something for me."

"Then what is the problem? He seems to be an honorable young man."

"He's been married before . . . to a beautiful, famous woman, and I'm not certain he's over her."

"If the looks he gives you when you're not watching are any indication, I suspect he's well over her," her mother almost drawled. "But I can understand you might have reservations about his true commitment to a relationship."

"It's not just that. When I broke up with Greg, I made a promise that I'd never settle for a man who didn't share my commitment to the gospel."

"But you said yourself Mark is a member of the Church. His parents and grandparents belonged to the Church as well. Are you saying something has happened to weaken his testimony?"

"No . . . I don't know. That's just the trouble. We haven't talked about it. While we were at the cabin Mark didn't remember anything about the Church, but we read the Book of Mormon together and we had some wonderful discussions. Since his memory returned, he doesn't seem to want to talk about it. He doesn't feel worthy to use his priesthood and feels guilty about something. I don't know if it's something to do with his marriage and divorce, or if it's something that happened after he was kidnapped."

"My dear." Her mother moved around the side of the counter and placed her arms around her. "You've learned the hard way that your faith must come first, but I suspect that in the process you learned to doubt your heart. Don't turn from those inner stirrings of love. Exercise your faith to ask your Heavenly Father if your heart speaks the truth."

Courtney sniffed and wiped away the traitorous tears that dampened her cheeks. A short time ago she'd thought nothing could be harder than being single while all those around her shared their lives with someone each held dear. Now she wondered if it might be equally hard to take a chance on love when she had first-hand knowledge that being wrong could bring so much pain.

"Don't worry, Mom," she tried to reassure her mother. "I have no intention of making a decision this time that doesn't include a lot of prayer." She paused, then straightened her shoulders. "Now, put me to work. I don't think I can take any more coddling."

"Well, if you're sure. There are a couple of loaves of bread you could start breaking up for the dressing."

Courtney found the large bowl her mother had used for mixing bread before Dad had bought her a bread-making machine. She carried it to the table along with the bread.

Her mother hummed Christmas carols as she rolled out pie crust on the opposite side of the room, and Courtney found her thoughts returning to Mark. She'd tiptoed into his room before daylight and found him sleeping soundly, so she'd closed the door and returned to the family room, which was now serving as her bedroom. If Mark would see a doctor she'd feel much better, but she didn't suppose he'd go today, even though moving around was much safer for him now that the signaling device had been removed from his shoulder.

She hadn't expected to go back to sleep after checking on Mark, but she had. It had been almost eleven when she'd reawakened. She'd hurried into her jeans and gone to check on him again, only to find his room empty and his bed neatly made. Her mother informed her that he and Desden had eaten breakfast several hours ago, then had asked permission to use her washer to wash out a few of their things. When they'd finished, they'd put on their coats and gone out to the shop to work on something.

She suspected the laundry Mark and Desden had done were the towels they'd used the night before. She should have taken them with her last night and thrown them into the washer with her own stained shirt.

Not even Kyle was around this morning. She learned the sheriff had sent him home to rest and that Hal Franklyn had arrived to take his place until evening. Lillian had expressed a desire to go shopping and Courtney had seconded her suggestion, but the deputy who had taken over Dad's chair in the front room had vetoed their plans, informing them he had orders to keep all of the women inside the house. Lillian had muttered a few uncomplimentary words about chauvinistic men before returning to Amy's side to help her bathe the baby. Lillian would have been even more upset if Desden and the sheriff hadn't decided there was sufficient security for their families to visit that evening.

"Mom, you won't believe this!" Lillian stormed into the kitchen a short time later as Courtney started on the second loaf of bread. Courtney felt a flash of sympathy for her sister-in-law. Lillian liked to ride her horse no matter what the weather, and she usually accompanied Jake when he fed the stock. She insisted she only did enough housework to keep the Board of Health from condemning her house, but she actually took a great deal of pride in the home she and Jake had built. Being so close, but not being allowed to spend part of Christmas in her own home, must be hard.

"What's the matter, dear?" Liz expertly ran a knife around the rim of the pie she'd just completed.

"Amy and I turned on the TV and there they were!"

"Who?" Liz started pinching the crust of the next pie.

"There's a big crowd of people picketing the ranch!"

"Our ranch?" Courtney gasped. She glanced out the window, but saw nothing other than the snow-covered hills and a forest of pine trees that hid the house from the county road more than a mile away.

"Who are they?" Liz paused, her pastry knife suspended in air.

"I don't know who they are!" Amy's indignant voice came from the doorway. "But they're down at the end of the lane near the arched gate. They have shaved heads and holes in their ears, and they're carrying signs accusing us of being cruel to animals."

Wordlessly all four women trooped into the family room to stare at the television; the deputy followed them. There was no mistaking the log gate at the entrance to the ranch lane. Nearly thirty people milled around it, carrying signs and shouting at Sheriff Boulter who was clearly trying to persuade them to move along.

"Maybe you should go help him." Courtney turned to the deputy, who seemed to be actually enjoying the spectacle on TV.

"Uh, uh, orders are to look after you ladies." He leaned back in the comfortable chair.

"Look at that!" Lillian pointed to the screen and Courtney caught a glimpse of a van with the insignia of a Denver television station emblazoned on its side, the same station that had sent a helicopter the day before. Before she could comment, the camera zoomed to a woman in a heavy parka who thrust a microphone in front of an angry young man.

"First, let me assure you the lining of my parka is synthetic fur, not the real thing," a woman's voice spoke and Courtney knew with a sinking heart that the woman was Venita Perry. "Can you tell me who you are and what is happening here?" the newswoman went on.

"I'm Calvin Jones and I represent the Animal Rights Alliance," he spoke the words with impressive fervor. "We saw your newscast last night and knew we couldn't let this blatant disregard for animals pass without a protest. As you know, the Grants are ranchers who have stolen the natural habitat of wildlife to raise cattle for the express purpose of slaughtering them for profit."

"Surely, you're not suggesting the Grants will profit in any way from the deaths of those cattle?" The woman seemed taken aback by the accusation.

"They'll be compensated if they haven't been already," the man sneered. "It's a known fact that both of the younger Grant men belong to the Pine Creek Rifle Club, and we all know that's a right-wing militia group masquerading as a sports club."

"What is he talking about?" Lillian protested. "Neither Luke nor Jake belong to any rifle club, and though I can't speak for Luke, Jake certainly has no leanings toward any militia group."

"Luke thinks militias are stupid. Besides he doesn't have time for anything but the ranch and church." Amy's voice was as indignant as Lillian's.

"The Pine Creek Rifle Club is a shooting range where anyone can go practice shooting or to sight their rifles. It's not really a club, but the two old guys who run it charge a small fee to cover expenses," Courtney explained without taking her eyes off the screen.

"Both of the boys took their hunters safety classes there when they were scouts," Liz added.

"There's an elk herd that winters on the Grant ranch," the earnest young man continued. "The Grants have been negligent in allowing the militia to hold their maneuvers near that herd. It's bad enough allowing cows to be used for target practice, but irrational gun men could attack the elk herd at anytime, which is why we have asked Senator Perry to sponsor a bill that would return millions of acres of so-called 'ranch land' to federal control, where it should be."

"That land has been privately owned by the Grants and other ranching families for over a century. Do you think they'll give it up without a fight?" Venita asked.

"It goes back to the old homesteading laws. Those laws weren't meant for a few greedy individuals to grab thousands of acres for their private use." A snort of disgust emanated from the deputy as the activist attempted to give his views substance.

"Tell me, Mr. Jones," Venita continued. "Haven't you clashed with the Grant family before and lost?"

Anger flared for a moment, before the man continued his carefully contrived monologue. "Five years ago an old Native American owned a ranch north of the Grant ranch. When he died without heirs, Ted Grant produced a document purporting ownership of the land. He claimed he had purchased the land from the man, who died without a will or any legal heirs, but when the state claimed the untestated estate, there was nothing more than a few hundred dollars in a local bank. The judge blocked our efforts to obtain a copy of both the old man's and the Grants' financial disbursements. That left no evidence, other than Ted Grant's canceled check, of the large sum the Grants supposedly paid for the land. Our group took the

Grants to court in an attempt to force them to reveal details of the purported sale, but the same local cowboy judge threw the case out."

"Was that the end of it, Mr. Jones?"

"There's an ordinance that requires the maintenance of a buffer zone around national parks that extends to other federal property in some cases," Calvin Jones explained. "We tried to claim the Native American's ranch for the federal government as a buffer zone since it's between the original Grant boundaries and a legally designated wilderness area. But a biased judge ruled that ranching doesn't interfere with the wilderness designation as long as cattle are not allowed to roam at will in the protected area."

At that moment a new group of protesters appeared as a couple of extended cab pickup trucks pulled up behind the speaker and half a dozen men in khaki fatigues piled out of each one, carrying rifles. Pandemonium broke out as angry shouts filled the air and a scuffle erupted between a couple of men from the different factions.

The camera zoomed from one side of the milling group to the other, picking up shouted orders being issued by the sheriff. As a group of protesters clasped hands and stretched a human barrier across the road in front of the ranch gate, Venita Perry scrambled to get out of the way. At the edge of the crowd she paused.

"What is your stake in this?" she shouted as she shoved her microphone toward a bearded newcomer.

"These tree huggers and Bambi crusaders are in cahoots with the Grants. We're fed up with the Grants keeping us off some of the best hunting territory in the state. They killed their own cattle so they could blame us and get more legislation banning guns passed." He stormed off in the direction of the sheriff.

Venita swept her hood back from her head as she turned to face the camera, which had faithfully followed her through the milieu. Long dark hair spilled across her bright red coat and her eyes sparkled with excitement. "We'll stay with this story and bring you further details at six. This is Venita Perry, reporting live from Pine Creek, Colorado."

Courtney stared at the face on the screen in dismay. There was no mistaking the petite form, the exotic doll-like face, or the long dark hair. Venita Perry's face was familiar to millions of people around the world, including Courtney. She was Mark's ex-wife and the most beautiful woman Courtney had ever seen.

She wondered if Venita knew Mark was at the ranch and if that was the reason she was here. He said he hadn't contacted her, but why else would she be here? An internationally famous reporter didn't cover minor local clashes between gun-rights groups and extremist environmentalists. Desolation invaded her heart. There was no way an ordinary woman with simple country tastes could compete with Venita Perry.

* * *

Mark peered through the trees. From their position he and Desden had a front row seat to the "media event" being staged below them. And it was a media event. He didn't doubt that. He knew very well who had tipped off Venita to the story and who had leaked conveniently slanted tips to both the animal rights group and the gun-totin' rednecks.

A couple of small-time special interest groups clashing over a few dead cows wasn't Venita's usual kind of story. She usually appeared in hot spots around the world, reporting on the devastation left behind by wars and natural disasters unless she was promoting major environmental issues. She'd been in South America doing a story on some miracle drug derived from a rainforest tree when they'd hastily married. So what was she doing here? She was too smart to believe the wanton destruction of a few ranch animals constituted a major environmental story.

The mere fact that Venita was in Colorado was a pretty strong indication her father was here, too, and had demanded she come home for Christmas. Her father had never been sentimental about Christmas, so there must be more to it than that.

Mark hadn't seen his ex-wife since their mutually agreed upon divorce. There had been no animosity between them, and he didn't feel anything but sympathy for her now. She was still beautiful—a glimpse through Desden's field glasses had confirmed that—but she didn't, and never had, stirred the longings and dreams that Courtney did.

He'd known who Venita was, had even seen her a few times around Washington before their South American encounter. She moved in the same social circles as Desden, and Desden had liked her. Otherwise Mark wouldn't have trusted her offer of help as genuine.

"Beautiful as ever," Desden breathed his appreciation of the dark-haired reporter as they stood shoulder to shoulder watching. "Do you ever regret not coming home to her at night anymore?"

"I never did come home to her at night," Mark scoffed at his friend's question. Desden was one of the few people who knew about his brief marriage. "She was never home. Our marriage consisted of sharing the rent on an apartment that we never occupied at the same time. The only reason we didn't annul our marriage as soon as we returned to Washington a week after we were married was because her father wanted us to try to make it work."

"Why did he care?" It was an idle question, but Mark took so long answering it, Desden's curiosity was aroused.

"I don't think he had any personal fondness for me as a son-in-law." Mark chose his words carefully. "But my career made me privy to information he thought might aid his political ambitions. Besides, my grandfather owned a large tract of land he has wanted for a long time. I was the logical heir, and with me married to his daughter, he hoped the land would eventually fall into his hands."

"Is that what you quarreled over?"

"No, Venita and I didn't really quarrel. We just didn't share any common ground. Her career is her first love, just as mine was then. She cared passionately about the rain forests, endangered species, land destruction, and clean air. Though I don't consider the environment unimportant, I was more caught up in making the world a safer place by putting criminals out of business."

He remembered only too well one of the few real quarrels that had erupted between the two of them. Venita had actively supported a clean air bill that would prohibit use of air space by commercial or military planes over national parks and wilderness areas. She believed her father supported it, too.

"Your father has too large of a stake in major ski areas like Aspen, Park City, Sun Valley, and Jackson to want to see tourists to those areas inconvenienced," Mark had argued. He'd shown her a list of those making huge financial contributions to oppose the bill. Venita's father's name had been on it. Furious, Venita had insisted that her father knew nothing of the huge contributions his company executives had made to lobby against the bill.

"Did Venita know her old man played both sides?" Desden pointed to where the sheriff and two deputies were shepherding the gun rights people back into their trucks.

"I don't know how much she knew. She's a smart woman and I think she must have figured it out, but we never talked about it. I suspect she took a look at his voting record. She and her father were close, even though he didn't like her career and his disapproval hurt her a lot."

Venita and her crew climbed back in their van. They weren't more than a quarter mile down the road before the protesters began moving toward their vans. The show was over.

Desden's last question lingered in Mark's mind. Had Venita known how her father had used her? She hadn't talked about it, but he'd suspected some kind of rift between father and daughter about the time she'd insisted on a divorce. He hadn't needed her to point out how futile their attempts to make their marriage work had been.

Their expectations were too different for the marriage to ever work. He'd wanted her to take the missionary lessons, be baptized, then go to the temple. He'd wanted a home and family, though he would have preferred a few more years of undercover work before assuming a life much like his parents had enjoyed.

Venita wanted to travel, to reach the top in her career, and was adamantly opposed to having children or returning to Colorado for anything but skiing with some of her jet-setting friends. She'd ridiculed the one ward party he'd taken her to, and he'd been bored and embarrassed by a cocktail party to which she'd dragged him. He hadn't attempted to change her mind about the divorce, but he'd been surprised by her secrecy and haste.

Her career was the first area in her life where Venita had defied her father, the divorce was the second. He wondered if he should draw some conclusions from that, but it was probably a moot point. She and her father were obviously on speaking terms again if she was visiting him for the holidays and she'd let him sucker her into doing a story on a contrived environmental incident.

The sheriff leaned against the bumper of his truck watching the last of the protesters disappear from sight. His bored, relaxed pose said the show was over. Then he turned and nodded to one of his deputies, who began to move quickly toward the trees where Mark and Desden were hiding.

As Kyle stepped into the shelter of the thick pine grove, Mark was peeling off his jeans and Desden was holding Mark's coat. Tossing his coat to Desden as well, Kyle reached for his belt buckle and began to undress. In moments, with their outerwear exchanged, the two men looked at each other and grinned conspiratorially. Kyle's uniform fit Mark surprisingly well, but Mark's clothes hung loosely on Kyle.

"You're the only guy I know skinny enough to wear my pants," Kyle joked as he tightened the belt on the much looser pants he'd acquired from Mark.

"Hey, I didn't know he'd turned into a scarecrow, or I would have bought him a smaller size," Desden defended the pants he'd brought for Mark when he'd learned his old partner was stranded without a wardrobe.

"Wouldn't hurt you to skip a few meals," Mark playfully poked Desden's stomach, then turned to examining the items Desden slipped into his coat pocket, including a small digital telephone. "You know what happens to guys who get kicked upstairs to sit behind a desk."

"Not me," Desden grinned. "There's a couple of ladies back in Washington who wouldn't be at all happy if I turned to flab." Turning serious, he clasped Mark's shoulder and whispered, "Be careful and keep that phone handy. I won't risk calling you, but you better report in on schedule or I'll come after you."

"Good luck," Kyle spoke earnestly as he fastened the parka he wore and slipped on Mark's cap.

"Thanks," Mark acknowledged before stepping onto the road and making his way to the sheriff's truck. He didn't have to look over his shoulder to know Desden and Kyle were already making their way back to the house.

FOURTEEN

Mark could see where several vehicles had been up the old county road from Isadora to what had once been a thriving lumber mill since he'd last traveled this way. He knew the sheriff's department had checked the area several times, and it was the most likely route his attackers had followed. He hoped they weren't still hanging around. But even if they'd gone, he suspected they hadn't gone far.

It was easy to spot where he'd missed the turnoff along the unplowed road and ended up on the logging road that stormy night almost three weeks ago when he'd followed a faint memory to his grandfather's cabin. This time he deliberately passed the mill, but before he reached where he'd abandoned his Jeep Cherokee, he nosed the borrowed Dodge Durango through a screen of shrubs to a level spot where he and his cousin used to park their bikes before scrambling down the bank to fish at a stream below.

It had been several days since the last snowstorm. That made it more difficult to obscure the tracks where he left the road than it would have been right after a fresh storm. The snow was packed, with a frozen crust on top, but he brushed at the snow with a pine bough until he was satisfied that only someone on foot or possibly on a snowmobile, and who was deliberately searching, would notice the slight variation.

He returned to the Durango and removed a pair of skis from the back. They belonged to Kyle as did the vehicle. Two more reasons to be grateful to the young man—only it was difficult to feel grateful to a man who would be spending Christmas Eve with Courtney while he retraced a trail that had nearly cost him his life less than three weeks ago. He hoped he'd be back at the ranch before she retired for the night.

Once the skis were in place, he clasped the poles and used them to push off into the trees. He decided to avoid the logging road itself. In case someone managed to circumvent the precautions he'd worked out, he didn't want to lead them directly to his rendezvous point. He'd parallel it instead.

A surge of excitement filled his heart. It would be good to see Sam again. The step-glide motion of the skis brought its own exhilaration. Surrounded by trees and sky with the snow beneath his feet, he experienced a soaring freedom that healed a portion of his soul. Never again would he take space and freedom for granted.

He wouldn't take the gospel for granted again either. He remembered a long ago summer day when he and Sam had loafed beside a fishing hole and planned the missions they would someday be called to serve. He'd wondered aloud whether he would have accepted the gospel and had the courage to be baptized if he hadn't been born into an LDS family.

In a way he had his answer now, thanks to Courtney. As she'd read to him and discussed gospel principles while he recuperated at the cabin, he'd felt the conversion process taking place inside him. Someone once said no one is born with a testimony; at some point all true members become converts. But his conversion as he grew up was slow and easy, and somehow he'd always just known the gospel was true. Not until he had knelt to ask God to remove the darkness, as Aminadab, the Nephite dissident, had advised in the book of Helaman, had Mark felt such a brilliant burning of truth consume him, shattering the darkness that held him hostage.

He thought back to the morning they'd left the cabin. He hadn't slept much the night before and so had turned again and again to prayer and had pondered the passages Courtney had read and explained earlier. A burning had swept through him, centered in his chest, and he'd known it was true, and that he no longer needed to fear the darkness. The burning was followed by a sensation of peace.

That, too, had faded to be replaced by an urgency to leave the cabin. The only blank left in his memory now was a question. Why had he ceased to pray and call on God while experiencing the greatest trial of his life? Everything within him told him that in a time of trouble his best refuge would be his faith in God, so why hadn't he turned to him during that terrible time?

He paused to catch his breath and look over the terrain before him. He once could cross-country ski all day and not be winded. Now a few miles left him gasping for breath.

It would soon be dark. He'd purposely come early to check for signs that either he or the area was being watched. Using the binoculars Desden had given him, Mark surveyed the field of snow that led down into the canyon. He saw no discernible marks in the snow.

Carefully making his way to a pile of boulders, he concealed himself to watch his back trail. The silence seemed complete, then slowly he began to recognize sounds. A night bird screeched as it spotted its prey, and the wind rattled the branches of a nearby clump of birch.

At last he pulled the phone from his pocket and dialed the speed code Desden had given him. Desden answered immediately. After verifying that he had reached the meeting point and all appeared quiet, he hung up. Mark waited half an hour more before starting down into the canyon itself. He wanted to make certain he hadn't been followed.

He'd once enjoyed night skiing and experienced a familiar thrill as he swooped down the narrow entry into the canyon. The moon wasn't up yet and only a sprinkling of stars could be seen through the thin streams of clouds, but they provided enough light that he didn't fear running into obstacles. He stopped short of the wall, and behind a section of the old barn's foundation, he found a place to wait that was sheltered from the breeze which had picked up.

He didn't know how long he'd have to wait. He hadn't specified a specific time and his cousin's response in Tuesday's paper had said only, *Be there. Sam.*

Time moved slowly in spite of the jumble of thoughts crowding his mind. He didn't mind the cold. The open space and the cold air were a welcome contrast to his months in a steaming jungle prison. He doubted he'd ever be comfortable working or living within a confined space again. Once he had the file Sam was holding for him, he'd set proceedings in motion to send the Snow King to prison, then do some serious thinking about his own future. He wondered if Courtney might be a part of that future, then abruptly cut off the thought. Letting his mind wander could get him killed.

He glanced at the watch Desden had insisted he borrow and saw it was almost time to report in again. He reached for the phone and tapped in the code, but when he pressed it to his ear heard only static. Too late he remembered that Courtney had told him phones were useless in the canyon. If his cousin didn't come soon, he'd have to move back up the hill to where he could call in.

He didn't see or even hear anyone approaching, but an awareness filled him, warning him he wasn't alone in the canyon anymore. He strained to see a shape materialize out of the darkness and tensed to protect himself.

The soft trill of a meadowlark wafted on the breeze, and Mark felt himself relax. A meadowlark in December could only be Sam. Easing himself from behind the old barn foundation, he moved toward the stone wall.

When his eyes made out the shapes of two figures standing beside the wall, he hesitated. His hand went to the gun nestled in a side pocket.

"Mark?" It was his cousin's voice. "It's all right."

Hesitantly he moved forward. He recognized the stance of the closer figure as that of his cousin. He was heavier than he'd been five years ago, but still gave off an impression of coiled energy.

Nervously Mark glanced at the second person. This figure was smaller and seemed nervous. Suddenly the figure leaped across the space separating them. His first impulse was to reach for his gun, but some prompting caused him to hesitate. A woman's voice called his name as she threw her arms around him. Her hood fell back and long, dark hair spilled across his arms.

"Julie?" He reeled with shock, unable to believe his own eyes. Julie was dead; how could she be here beside Grandpa's wall? He opened his arms and carefully folded her against him, wondering if this were some horrible aftermath of the drugs he'd taken. Had a flashback conjured his sister's ghost into his mind? Was he holding a ghost in his arms? *Do ghosts cry?* The woman in his arms was sobbing so hard, the words she tried to speak were an incoherent jumble.

"She's real, old friend." Sam stood beside him, correctly reading his confusion.

"But how?" Softly he kissed Julie's temple and pulled her more securely into his embrace as he felt tears on his own cheeks. How could his little sister be alive?

"Come over here." Sam led them both to the wall. He brushed away snow and indicated they should sit. When they were seated, with Julie's hand firmly clasped in his, his cousin cleared his throat, then spoke words that were clearly difficult for him to say.

"I lied to both of you," he admitted. "Now I seek your forgiveness."

"I understand." Julie lifted her eyes to Sam' face. "It was necessary."

"I don't understand." Mark felt a sudden surge of anger. He had communicated with Sam half a dozen times through their code since he'd been informed of Julie's death and before he'd been captured. "You could have told me five years ago."

"I could have," Sam conceded. "I decided not to."

"But why?"

"Five years ago you told me your life was in danger, and that you were going into the witness protection program, and that not even I would know where you were. You left without telling your family good-bye, but you asked me to watch them for you. The accident happened that night."

"Mom and Dad were both killed," Julie picked up the story. "I would have died with them if I'd been in the car."

"But you were in the car, Julie," Mark insisted. "I held the door for you myself when you climbed inside." He didn't understand.

"Mom stopped for gas a few miles out of Denver, and I discovered Sam was following us, so I asked to ride with him."

Mark turned to his cousin. "Why were you following them? They were only coming here to spend a week with Grandpa. That's why Mom was upset. She had counted on me going with them. She'd even told several of her friends that we were all going, then I pulled out at the last minute, using work as an excuse, when I knew I was going to fake my own death and disappear. I thought my presence might endanger them, but that they'd be safe if they believed I was dead."

"That's why I was following," Sam explained. "I knew they'd be upset when they got the news. Your family had always been my family, and I wanted to be there for them when they felt the pain of your death." Sam paused. "Their deaths were not an accident. They were forced from the road and I had to make a quick decision. If I reported what I had witnessed, there would be no way to keep it secret that you and Julie were still alive. The same people would come after both of you again. My mother has many brothers." He shrugged. "I called one who arranged for four bodies to arrive at his mortuary in Denver. Then I called you. You wanted to stay in Denver, to say a final good-bye to your family, but I convinced you to go. Arrangements for your new identify were already made, and you no longer needed to fake an accident. I was the only one who knew you weren't in that car."

"But you could have told me—"

"No, he couldn't," Julie interrupted her brother. "I fainted when the car exploded. When I came to, I didn't remember what had happened. I didn't remember you'd backed out of going with us. I believed you were dead, too."

"Memory problems seem to run in the family," Mark muttered wryly under his breath. Aloud he asked, "Do you remember it now?"

"No, but before we came to meet you, Sam explained what happened."

"I made the decision not to tell her." Sam accepted responsibility for his silence. "You were going to disappear anyway, and why should she face your death twice when neither one was true?"

"You're right," he conceded. "But you could have told me about Julie."

Julie shook her head. "No, he knew you too well. If you'd known I was alive and alone, you would have felt responsible for me. You would have jeopardized your life to come back to care for me."

Julie was right, too. He would have come.

"What did you do?" He reached out to touch his little sister's face with his gloved hand. "You weren't quite seventeen. How did you manage?"

Sam answered for her. "I took her to my mother on the reservation, and she took Julie to Fort Hall in Idaho to stay with some relatives there."

"I stayed there for two years," Julie explained. "I finished high school and began college in Pocatello. Sam came often to visit me." She ducked her head shyly. "We were married just before my nineteenth birthday, and he accepted a job with the tribal police on the reservation."

"You're married?" He glanced from one to the other, feeling hopelessly confused.

"We have a son," Sam announced proudly. "We named him Mark Stewart Manytrees for you and your father."

"And in the spring he will have a little brother," Julie added.

"Or perhaps a sister." Sam placed his arm around Julie's shoulders.

He couldn't take it in. Julie was alive and married to Sam. And he was an uncle.

"Please be happy for us," Julie requested, a worried frown on her face.

"I have loved her since the day she was born." Sam's voice carried a quiet dignity, and Mark knew he spoke the truth. In his old friend's eyes was a question, asking for approval and forgiveness.

"You're cousins. Can you legally marry?" Mark asked.

"If our grandfathers had been biological brothers," Julie laughed, "that would make us second cousins, but Sam's grandfather was informally adopted by our great-grandparents. The bond our grandfathers passed on to us was not because of shared blood, but rather deep love for each other. We had no trouble getting a marriage license."

Mark felt a little embarrassed. "I've known that all my life, but I've thought of us as cousins so long, I guess I forgot there's no real biological tie. I'm glad there is now." He hugged his sister to express his pleasure, then smiled as he reached for Sam to clasp him in a fierce hug. "I'm pleased for both of you."

"Grandpa's house is gone?" Julie glanced sadly over her shoulder to where a chimney poked through the snow. It was more statement than question.

Briefly he told them of the ordeal he and Courtney had gone through and concluded with, "Soon this will be over and I can meet my nephew and we can be together again. Did you bring the file with you?"

"Not the file—only a key." Sam handed a ring with a solitary key on it to Mark. "It fits a box at Zion's Bank in Salt Lake City. I feared it might not be safe to travel with the file."

"As usual, you're a step ahead of me. Thanks, and I do appreciate the precaution." Mark tucked the key into a zippered pocket of his borrowed coat before bending to kiss his sister's cheek.

"What way did you come? The Snow King's men are everywhere, and you're both in danger. If you'd prefer to return to the ranch with me, I can ask the Marshal's office to provide security."

"We'll be all right returning the way we came, across the government land."

He didn't doubt Sam's assertion. He would protect Julie far better than any agent possibly could. He glanced down at their skis and remembered Julie was expecting a child.

"I'm strong and healthy, big brother," she gently mocked him with the impish grin he remembered. She'd always called him 'big brother' when she'd found his protective instincts toward his much younger sister a little overbearing. "We have snowmobiles and winter camping gear hidden a few miles beyond Grandpa's old timber tract."

"You'd better be on your way." Once more he hugged his sister, then watched as the couple faded silently into the shadows. They would circle the upper end of the canyon on the same side as the avalanche had been started until they reached the logging road, then follow it a mile before striking off to the north. He would retrace the same path he'd followed coming in.

He glanced once at the sky before beginning. A brilliant star shone in the western sky, and he wondered if it was the same star that the other Samuel had prophesied would herald the Savior's birth. He felt an urge to return to the ranch as quickly as possible. He wanted to spend what was left of Christmas Eve with Courtney.

* * *

Courtney let her eyes travel around the living room where the family and their guests had gathered after dinner, and though the room was crowded with people and laughter, it felt empty without Mark. She'd been disappointed when Desden had returned to the house alone. He'd said there was something Mark had to do, and that it might be late before he arrived back at the ranch. She suspected he'd gone to meet his cousin and knew she'd worry until he returned.

Both Amy's and Lillian's families had arrived at the ranch in time for dinner. Lillian's parents had wanted to whisk their daughter safely back to Denver, while Amy's younger brothers thought she was living a grand adventure. Her parents were so enthralled with their new grandchild they scarcely listened to the edited version Ted and Liz gave them of the recent activities on the ranch.

A loud knock sounded on the front door causing Courtney to start. Perhaps Mark had returned. No, Mark wouldn't knock, but would slip quietly in the back door. Had something happened to him? She watched anxiously as Kyle moved swiftly toward the door while Desden, with one hand too casually fingering the lapel of his jacket, moved to the arch separating the living room from the front foyer.

Kyle stood to one side of the door, his hand resting on the butt of his pistol, to peer through the glass. She saw his somber wariness turn to puzzlement. He reached for the doorknob, but as he opened the door, he blocked Courtney's view. Unable to see, she tried to identify the two voices other than Kyle's.

"Mr. Grant." Kyle turned to call her father, and Courtney's eyes widened before she found herself smothering a giggle. Agent Brent Glendowski stood on the step behind two men, one very old and one quite young. The agent was clearly rattled and the boy squirmed with embarrassment, but the elderly man thrust out his hand to Ted.

"What are you doing out here, Brother Clagston?" Kyle asked in exasperation. "It's Christmas Eve, and you should be home with Emma and the boys."

"Do you think I could enjoy the festivities without first doing my duty?" Parley Clagston appeared affronted for just a few seconds, then ushered his teenage grandson through the door without waiting for an invitation. He followed behind, his cane thumping against the stone floor of the entryway.

"It's all right," her father assured Kyle and the agent, who, like Desden, had their hands hovering near their holsters.

"Parley's a neighbor," Ted attempted to explain the arrival of home teachers. "They're here on a church assignment."

Parley thumped his way to the chair Ted had just vacated. He settled himself with a resounding plop, braced his cane between his knees, and rested both hands atop it, one over the other.

The boy peered through thick glasses and shuffled his weight from one foot to the other as he searched futilely for a place to sit. One of Amy's brothers snickered and his mother thumped the top of his head with a plastic cow someone had given the baby, which brought a paroxysm of giggles from his brothers.

"Here." Liz patted the piano bench where she sat and moved over to give the boy some space. With his ears glowing a fiery red, he stumbled across the room to take the offered seat.

"Well?" Parley looked expectantly at Ted who had returned to the room to lean against the wall.

"We're doing fine." Ted didn't elaborate.

Parley's shaggy eyebrows drew together in a frown, and her father looked like a guilty school boy sent to the principal. She suspected more than duty had prompted Parley to come home teaching tonight. He was an insatiable gossip who usually showed up on the last night of the month with a string of tales concerning all their neighbor's woes. He must be dying to learn the details of the "goings on" at the Grant ranch to turn up this early, she mused.

"Saw them protesters carrying signs on the TV," he announced. "Charley Bates and his boys tried to shoo 'em off, but the sheriff didn't like 'em stickin' their nose in his business." He paused expectantly, but when no one offered more details he went on, " That snippety girl of the senator's was there, too. She oughta be home with a passel of babies by now. Never did figure why ol' Roy lets her run around like that, stickin' her nose in other people's business. Don't look good, 'specially when he's gettin' ready to announce he's runnin' for president. Never thought he done much for us ranchin' folks, but I don't suppose he'll be no worse'n the one we got now. 'Spect we oughta impeach that fella, what with all his carryin's on with that . . ."

Courtney's mind began to wander. She had a pretty good idea Mark was meeting with his cousin tonight. His message to Sam made reference to the night of the sign, which surely meant Christmas Eve. Their code had been devised by two young boys with a fascination for Samuel the Lamanite; it couldn't be too complicated.

A movement across the room caught her attention, and she watched Desden slip from the room. He'd been quiet since dinner and she'd noticed him looking at the clock several times. Mark must be late. Her own worry level escalated.

As Parley droned on, she watched for Desden's return and had made up her mind to go after him when the telephone rang. She excused herself and hurried to the kitchen extension. She didn't miss the purposeful way Kyle followed her. He frowned when she picked up the phone, and she paused before saying hello. She'd forgotten she'd been instructed not to answer the phones. Desden's voice came over the line. Evidently he'd picked up the hall extension before she reached the kitchen phone.

"This isn't a secure line. I don't believe we should be discussing this," he said.

"He doesn't work for the department anymore. You're endangering his life and the whole case by turning him loose on this," an angry voice thundered in her ear.

"He has access to information the Justice Department lost." Desden's voice was stiff and controlled.

"He's carrying out a personal vendetta!" The other man's voice turned icy. "More reliable agents than you have turned up evidence he blames the senator for the failure of his marriage and that he's spent the past year working out a frame with San Bunisto."

"San Bunisto nearly killed him!"

"So he claims. He'll have his day in court, but you're off this case. I want you back in Washington by morning. I've already sent someone to pick him up." He slammed down the phone, and

Courtney stood paralyzed with shock. Bits and pieces whirled through her mind. Mark was in trouble and so was Desden. She was only vaguely aware of Kyle prying her fingers from the phone.

"You heard?" Desden was beside her, too.

Numbly she nodded her head.

"Mark figured all along that my boss was the leak. This only proves him right. I have a friend over at the Justice Department. I'll give him a call."

"Are you sure you can trust him?"

"Yes, and more importantly, Mark trusts him, too. Somehow I've got to warn Mark though. Do you have any idea where he planned to meet his cousin?"

Slowly she nodded her head. "There's a wall behind the cabin that was buried by the avalanche. I think they planned to meet there. I can get the snowmobiles and show you the way."

"It will be faster to go around by Isadora," Kyle interjected. "Mark borrowed my Durango and skis, which means that's the route he's taking. I can call the sheriff and have him meet you in Isadora or I can take you there myself."

"I can find it." Desden turned toward the door. "A couple of our agents have already followed that route. I'll take one of them with me. I'll feel better if you stay with Courtney." He turned to Kyle.

"I want to go." Courtney started after him.

"No. Both of you stay here." He pulled a wireless phone from his pocket and paused with his finger over the speed dial key, then evidently changed his mind. "No," he muttered. "I can't risk the wrong person hearing it ring." He stuffed it back in his pocket and left the room at a run.

FIFTEEN

By the time Courtney returned to the living room, Parley was ready to deliver his "message." He pulled a tattered copy of the *Ensign* from his pocket and began reading. What he lacked in reading skills, he compensated for with volume.

Amy's youngest brother crawled behind the Christmas tree and one of her teenage brothers nearly tipped the tree over trying to drag him out. The other two resorted to a face-pulling contest. The baby woke up and began to fuss. Both grandmothers hurried to his side. Lillian's father was asleep and snoring softly much to his wife's mortification. Courtney felt her nerves stretched to the breaking point. It was all she could do to remain seated. Each time her eyes met Kyle's he gave her a sympathetic smile, but she could tell he was worried, too.

At last Parley concluded his message and struggled to his feet. Jake and Luke both hurried to assist him. Since kneeling was impossible for the old man, they stood in a circle as the grandson mumbled a hasty prayer and offered a blessing on the family.

Liz swiftly took over, holding the old man's arm as she gently but purposefully propelled him toward the door. When he voiced a question about the dead cattle, she kissed his cheek and told him to give her love to Emma, then admonished the grandson to drive carefully. Parley was out the door before he knew what had happened.

"Why did that old bore have to come tonight?" Lillian sighed and leaned back against her husband.

"He means well," Liz spoke apologetically. "He's old and doesn't get around well anymore, but he likes to feel he's still a part of the community. I think that after what he saw on television, he was genuinely concerned about us."

"If you say so, Mom." Jake winked at Courtney, and she tried to pretend she was amused when at the moment, she wasn't interested in anything about their elderly neighbor. All she could think about was Mark.

"We could still sing a few Christmas carols and read the Christmas story," Liz encouraged. "That should restore our holiday mood." In minutes she had the group gathered around the piano and one familiar Christmas melody after another filled the air.

After a few futile attempts, Courtney concluded she couldn't sing tonight. She whispered in her mother's ear, then retired to the kitchen to prepare hot chocolate and arrange a tray of fruitcake and cookies. Like a shadow, Kyle followed, ostensibly to help. As they worked, a soft tap sounded on the kitchen door and Kyle hurried to answer it. Courtney turned in anticipation of seeing Mark and Desden. Instead Brent Glendowski, the agent who had accompanied Parley to the door earlier, stepped into the kitchen.

"Something funny is going on," he spoke to Kyle. "I think you'd better call the sheriff. The kid who was here earlier with the old man just came racing back to the house on foot. He said there's a badly injured man down by the gate. He's either unconscious or dead. The boy and his grandpa got him into their car. They were going to take him into town, but a phone in the guy's pocket started ringing. The kid answered it and a voice asked for her." He nodded toward Courtney, and set a small black cell phone on the kitchen counter.

"Me? Who was it?"

"The kid doesn't know. The caller hung up without saying anything more."

"I mean, who is the injured man?"

"The kid said he was here earlier tonight and from the description, he sounds like Draper."

"No!" Courtney gripped the edge of the cupboard until her knuckles turned white.

"Where are the rest of your men?" Kyle snapped the question as he grabbed for the phone on the wall.

The agent counted the others off on his fingers. "Bob Weldon is out on patrol; I tried to raise him on the walkie-talkie, but he didn't respond. Jim Lawson went with Draper. He didn't answer my call either. Cooper jumped on a snowmobile and headed toward the gate."

"What about the old man? Is he still with Draper?" Kyle paused with the phone in his hand. "Boulter will want all of the details."

"The boy said his grandfather is driving. He's on his way into Pine Creek. The old man sent the boy back to warn Miss Grant to be careful, but when I said I'd speak to her, the kid jumped on the snowmobile behind Cooper. They rushed off to see if they can catch up to the kid's grandfather."

Courtney's hand went to her mouth. If Desden wasn't already dead, he likely would be before old Parley Clagston drove ten miles. Between failing eyesight and rheumatoid arthritis, Parley had been refused a driver's license several years ago. Please, she prayed silently, *keep them safe. Don't let Desden die.*

She listened as if from a great distance to Kyle fill in the sheriff on the latest development. All she could focus on was that Desden had been injured and that he hadn't reached Mark to warn him. Kyle's words scarcely penetrated the thick fog pressing against her mind when he hung up the phone and began relaying the sheriff's instructions. He said the sheriff had already dispatched paramedics to intercept Parley. She vaguely understood that the family and their guests were to be informed of what had happened, then the men should divide into two groups. One group would patrol outside while the other remained inside. Every two hours the groups would trade assignments.

"The ranch hands all have Christmas off," she whispered.

"I know," Kyle spoke quietly as if he understood her fragile condition. "Boulter sent all of our men except me home tonight, too."

"I'd better call in." The agent reached for the phone. "The brass will want to know that Draper has lost contact and we have missing agents."

"No!" Courtney's senses screamed to alert. "There's a leak in your head office. I heard Desden say he suspects his boss has crossed the line."

"What?" The man stared at Courtney as if she'd lost her mind.

"It's true," Kyle seconded. "I heard him say it, too. If you attempt to call that Llewelyn guy, I'll place you under arrest even if you are a federal agent." His hand rested lightly on the service revolver at his hip. "I think we're on our own," he finished softly.

The agent bristled, then his shoulders slumped. "I may be new, but I've known from the start something about this case wasn't right. Draper would give us one set of orders, then Llewelyn would relay something different. I trust Draper, but I hardly know Llewelyn." He took a deep breath, then squared his shoulders and looked directly at Kyle. "It looks like for now, this case is under the sheriff's jurisdiction. You go tell the Grants what you have to, and I'll start patrolling the perimeter."

Courtney stayed behind while Kyle spoke to her family. An immediate uproar resulted in the other room, and she leaned her head against a cupboard door and prayed.

She jumped as the wall phone rang inches from her head.

"Hello," she gasped into the receiver before it could ring again.

"Miss Grant?" A woman's soft voice whispered into her ear and continued before she could respond. "Is Mark Stewart there?"

"No. Who's calling please?" There was silence on the other end of the line.

"It's really important that I speak to him." The woman's voice sounded more urgent.

"If you'd care to leave a message . . ." Courtney began, but the other woman cut her off.

"If you know where he is, get to him before Draper does and tell him to run. It's a trap. The only way he can save himself is to disappear again."

"Who are you?" Courtney demanded. "Why should I believe you?"

"Just tell him Venita said it was her fault and that she has no more illusions." The line went dead.

Venita was Mark's ex-wife. She was also Senator Perry's daughter. Cold chills slithered down Courtney's spine. She remembered all that Mark had said about the man he suspected of masterminding the drug cartel, the man with enough political influence to be privy to Justice Department secrets. Old Parley's words about the man who was about to announce his candidacy for president of the United States rang in her ears. With sudden conviction she knew Senator Roy Perry, Mark's former father-in-law, was the man Mark suspected of trying to kill him.

It made terrible sense. The senator wouldn't want anyone left alive who not only might send him to prison, but who, just by making the charge, could destroy his political career. The imminent announcement was the reason that eliminating Mark and his contact had turned critical. Only a man in his powerful position as chairman of the judicial committee could persuade federal law enforcement officials that he was the victim of an attempted political smear and that his disgruntled son-in-law who disappeared a year ago had a personal vendetta against him. The shooting of a rogue agent would appear justified.

But could she trust Venita? Was she working with her father? The moment Courtney attempted to warn Mark, would she be followed? Desden had received a call removing him from the case. There was a strong possibility his boss deliberately incited him to go after Mark, knowing Desden would not meekly return to Washington without warning his friend first. That was the trap Venita spoke of. Desden had been followed. If he'd told the agent who accompanied him where to find Mark and if that agent was taking orders from someone else . . .

Her attention focused on the pocket phone the agent had left lying on the kitchen counter, the one she assumed Parley's grandson had removed from the injured man's pocket. Picking it up, she flipped it open. Someone had turned it off; carefully she turned it back on. It looked like the one she'd seen Desden holding earlier. If it were, then it was a link to Mark.

She had no idea which numbers to press to reach Mark. Desden had considered placing a call too dangerous, but he had been expecting to receive a call from Mark. Leaving the phone turned on, she quickly closed it and thrust it into her shirt pocket. If Mark tried again to reach Desden, she would answer. She knew what she had to do. Desden hadn't reached Mark to warn him; she'd have to do it. But just in case Venita's call was meant to trick her into leading anyone to Mark, she'd have to be very careful. She'd also have to escape the house before Kyle came looking for her.

She dashed down the hall to her room for insulated pants and coat, then ducked into the garage. In seconds she had her Isuzu Rodeo started. She backed out, then paused to listen. The buzz of a snowmobile came from the trees behind the barn. Good! The agent who had volunteered to patrol the ranch was a long way from the lane leading to the road.

Courtney stopped at the shed next to the barn to retrieve her skis, then hurried back to her SUV. She hoped the roar of the agent's snowmobile would prevent him from hearing the Rodeo's engine. The thick walls of the house would keep the sound from carrying to her family.

She shifted gears and moved as quickly as she dared toward the county road. Even with snow tires and four-wheel drive she knew better than to risk driving so fast she might lose control on the slippery track. Minutes later she pulled onto the road, where she could increase her speed.

* * *

Mark reached the road half a mile below where he'd left the Durango. He was considering leaving the trees to move more swiftly along the obstacle-free path when he heard the growl of an engine. Concealing himself near the road, he waited. He didn't have long to wait. Desden's Explorer lurched around a bend and moved toward him.

Guiltily he remembered he'd been so emotionally involved with his meeting with Julie and Sam, he'd forgotten to call Desden. He hadn't meant to cause his friend to worry, and as fast as the utility was moving, Des must be plenty worried.

Just as he stepped from the trees, he realized two men were in the Explorer. An uneasy premonition had him shifting slightly so that a tree partly obscured him as the big four-wheel drive utility slid to a stop slightly past him. He recognized the agent, Jim Lawson, who stepped from the vehicle. Lawson took orders from Desden, but all of Mark's senses were screaming to use caution.

"Where's Draper?" he called. Something didn't feel right. He slid one hand into the pocket where he'd placed the Smith & Wesson beside the fliptop phone.

"He had a little accident. He sent us to get you." The agent moved closer and out of the corner of his eye Mark saw the other man slip out on the other side and make his way toward the back of the vehicle. He recognized him, too. Bob Weldon had been with the service since before his own time. He noted that a snowmobile took up most of the cargo space in the utility. A glint of metal warned him the other man was aiming a gun his direction.

Keeping his head concealed behind a thick screen of pine bows, he pulled out the phone and rapidly tapped a two button speed code. Holding the phone to his ear, he listened to the rings as he peered through the branches at the two agents. They'd stopped advancing toward him and seemed to be carrying on a whispered discussion.

"Come on, Des. Pick up the phone," he muttered under his breath.

Suddenly a tentative voice squeaked a high-pitched hello in his ear.

"Courtney?" No, it couldn't be Courtney. He pressed the off button. The voice had sounded like a kid, but how had a kid gotten a hold of Desden's phone and where was Desden? Courtney had mentioned that her sister-in-law's parents and younger brothers would be at the ranch for Christmas Eve dinner. Had one of Amy's young brothers somehow got his hands on Desden's phone? It wasn't like Des to be careless enough to allow that to happen.

"Stewart?" The man standing in the road called.

"Yeah," Mark responded while his mind spun with questions, and he began formulating a quick exit plan.

"Llewelyn sent us to bring you in. It'll be easier if you just walk over here."

"Easier for whom?" Mark laughed. "I'm sure you don't mean me." Crouching low, he let the skis carry him backward a few feet.

"No games, Stewart," one of the men shouted. "Llewelyn forwarded a full report to us. We know about the drugs and the dementia. You need a doctor."

Obviously someone had already begun damage control. If he were an addict or crazy and hated his former father-in-law, then his testimony could be easily dismissed. And if he died in a demented attack on two marshals, the proof to back his claims would die, too.

Estimating his chances of survival being slim to nothing if he surrendered to the two marshals, he opted for flight. Avoiding a sudden movement that would alert the other two men to his plans, he carefully shifted his position until he faced back the way he'd come. Remaining crouched, he slid silently behind another tree.

"Stewart, there's no reason for you to—"

"He's running!"

A shot whistled through the tree branches inches from his head. Digging in with his poles, Mark pushed off, retreating with zigzagging movements deeper into the trees. Another shot rang out, but it went wide of its mark. He didn't have much time to make good his escape. It wouldn't take the two men long to unload the snowmobile and come after him. If he could circle them, he might be able to reach the Durango before they called in backup help.

With long sweeping strides, he paralleled the road, pausing frequently to listen. The moon was up now and its brilliant light aided his ability to move through the trees where no trail existed. Unfortunately it would also highlight his trail for his pursuers.

He was close now. He pulled to a stop in a heavy stand of trees across the road from the hidden turnout where he'd parked earlier. Gently he parted the thick branches of a spruce tree. In the distance he heard the snowmobile start up and his pulse raced. The two agents were half a mile away, just beginning their chase. Even so he wouldn't cross the narrow open space until he felt satisfied it was safe to do so.

His eyes swept the road, noting the spot where he'd pulled the Durango through the trees concealing the entrance to the turnout where local fishermen had parked their trucks for years. Carefully he studied the trees. Everything appeared to be just as he'd left it. Moving further north he picked out the faint impressions left by skis where the turnout exited back onto the road. He frowned, thinking he hadn't covered his tracks as well as he'd thought when he'd left the clearing earlier.

Wait! There were too many tracks and they weren't his. The flat surface between the skis indicated a snowmobile had been in the clearing. He remembered the two masked riders who had tried to kill Courtney and him. They likely had found the Durango and were waiting beside it for his return.

A whisper of sound confirmed his suspicion. There was no possibility of using the big Dodge utility to effect his escape. He'd have to ski out, but he wasn't certain which way to go. He couldn't return to the ranch without knowing what had happened to Desden or whether a welcoming committee was waiting there for him. Besides he'd endangered Courtney and her family enough. That route was too dangerous.

He had no supplies with him. He'd starve to death—if he didn't freeze first—if he tried to hole up anywhere in the mountains or to make his way to a town well away from Isadora or Pine Creek. His only chance was to catch up with Julie and Sam.

A winter trek across the wilderness area was daunting. He wasn't in physical shape for such a trip, but it appeared to be the only choice open to him. If he didn't connect with Sam, he would likely die, but if he waited around here much longer, he would die for sure.

A sudden roar erupted from the trees across the road, causing him to sink more securely behind cover. He watched as a snowmobile burst from the trees and roared down the road. Hope flared for just a moment, then was deflated by the memory of two snowmobiles. Even if only one man had been left behind to watch for his return, in his weakened condition he couldn't risk a confrontation.

Neither could he continue to leave an easy trail. Quietly he backed away from the road and continued his journey north for another mile. This area was steep and rocky, ideal for his purpose. With great care he skirted the open area of an old slide beneath a towering ridge. It took more stamina than he could safely spare to work his way to the top of the slope while staying in the trees and avoiding rocks swept bare by the wind.

At last he halted beside a series of boulders and gasped for breath. His head pounded and his body ached, but he'd made it to the top. Below him he could hear the whine of engines and spotted the flicker of lights coming up the mountain. They were directly beneath the ridge. It was payback time. No, he chided himself. What he was about to do had nothing to do with revenge, only survival.

Taking several deep breaths, he began a slow journey along the ridge line. He didn't worry about whether or not he could be seen. The lights on the snowmobiles would make vision beyond their beams difficult and he was out of easy rifle range. Only night scopes in the hands of crack marksmen would present any real danger. Where the wind had curled a vast balloon of snow along the underside of the steep ridge was his goal.

This time when he stopped, he removed his skis and worked quickly to uncover the biggest rocks he could lift. One after another he pitched and dropped them over the edge. Some slipped through the snow's crust to quietly disappear. Some rolled a short distance before sinking into the fat balloon. Working his way to the drift he wished to dislodge, he poked and pushed with one of the skis. Starting an avalanche was turning out to be more difficult than he'd expected. Finally his efforts paid off. A massive chunk of rock-laden snow dropped silently to the field of snow below.

In seconds a ripple appeared across the surface of the snow. It gathered in intensity until a two-foot-high wave snaked across the mountain. Gathering momentum, it gathered rocks and trees, and the soft swish of rippling snow rose to a roar.

The men and machines were far enough to the side they would escape the brunt of the avalanche if they exercised reasonable care. He didn't want to kill the men following him, but he didn't mind giving them a good scare. What really mattered was wiping out his own trail and giving the appearance that he had perished in the slide. With that in mind, he brushed away footprints and staged ski tracks to the edge of the ridge, then gathering up the skis he made his way back to the tree line, stepping from one windswept rock to another where he could and wiping out tracks where he couldn't. When he deemed it safe to ski again, he snapped them back into place.

His sense of direction didn't fail him and he was soon back at the road, though several miles higher than before. He wouldn't attempt to return to the Durango. After ascertaining that the road was clear, he quickly crossed it. It was a short distance to the stream where he and his cousin used to fish. At this point the stream was at the bottom of a small gully and offered a steep descent to reach it.

Once more he removed the skis and strapped them to his back. As he scrambled down the almost perpendicular slope, he tried to plan his next step. He could cross the stream and follow it for several winding miles. Eventually it would lead to the old Isadora mine. He and Sam had camped not far from the mine numerous times in both summer and winter. He hoped he'd find him and Julie there tonight.

But he couldn't go there directly. First, he had to find a place where he could rest for a short time. His physical strength was spent. Second, he couldn't risk leading Perry's men to his cousin and his sister. He needed to find a place where he could watch his back trail until he could be certain he'd lost his pursuers.

SIXTEEN

Courtney could see colored lights sparkling in the distance before she reached Isadora. With a pang of regret she remembered it was Christmas Eve. Behind those lights families would be reading the Christmas story from Luke, children would be lying in bed straining to hear sleigh bells, and parents would be whispering as they assembled bikes and doll houses. She had a sudden vision of Mark and herself snuggling before the fireplace in his grandfather's cabin, reading the Christmas story from the Book of Mormon.

She shook her head to clear away her fanciful thoughts. The cabin was gone and if she didn't reach Mark in time . . . Kyle had probably reported to the sheriff by now that she'd left the ranch. Considering the sheriff might have a deputy in Isadora watching for her, she'd better avoid the town. Following rural roads, she made her way to the old county road leading to the saw mill and Isadora mine. The road was rough, but enough traffic had gone over it since the last snowfall to make it passable.

Anxiously she glanced at the dashboard clock. It was nearly eleven o'clock. It would take her another half hour to reach the saw mill. Once there, she'd put on her skis and ski the five or six miles over the crest and down into the canyon where she'd first met Mark.

The higher the Rodeo climbed, the more nervous Courtney became. She was making far better time than she'd expected because the road was a little too well-traveled. Mark was driving Kyle's Durango and she guessed he'd come this way. Mark's cousin might have come this way also. Desden hadn't made it this far, but his truck might have, she thought grimly. The road was too well packed for two vehicles traveling one way only. There was a possibility that Mark and his cousin were already on their way back and she'd missed them on her circuitous quest to bypass the main road, but some instinct told her Mark was still on the mountain, and that he needed help.

Her apprehension grew as she pulled into the mill yard. Hers wasn't the first vehicle there since the last storm. Deep ruts led from the road into the open area where lumber trucks and employee vehicles once parked. Slowly she drove in a circle hoping for a glimpse of the Durango, but whatever vehicles had packed the snow were gone now.

Deciding to leave her Rodeo behind a pile of scrap logs where it wouldn't be visible from the road, she pulled to the far end of the yard and lurched behind the rotting timber before turning off the engine. Pulling her flashlight from the glove box, she tucked it in her pocket beside the small telephone. She tugged a ski mask over her face, then fastened the hood of her parka. In minutes her skis were in place and she surveyed the area to get her bearings. Spotting the place where a logging road once snaked up the mountain and branched off to the homestead cabin, she began to move.

As she passed the mill shack something caught her eye, and she moved closer to take a look. A padlock dangled from one side of a broken hasp. Gingerly she eased the door open and peered inside. The moon which had been bright when she left the ranch had disappeared behind a cloud and she couldn't see anything. Deciding to risk a light she pulled the flashlight from her pocket and while partially shielding the lens, looked around the small room.

Camping gear and fuel cans met her eyes. The smell of wood smoke came from the pot-bellied stove in one corner and on an old desk were the remains of an interrupted meal and what looked to be a laptop computer. Two cots were covered with rolled-out sleeping bags. Hastily she closed the door and backed away. Someone was using the mill shack as a shelter and she had a pretty good idea who. Her heart pounded faster and she glanced nervously behind her.

She'd heard Mark and Desden discussing the likelihood that the two men who had burned the line shack and fired at Mark and herself were staying somewhere close by. Obviously she'd stumbled onto their hiding place, but it hadn't been that hard to find, so why hadn't the sheriff's men or the federal agents discovered their attackers' hiding place?

Digging in her ski poles, Courtney moved toward the logging road. She swooped around the first bend and nearly collided with a heavy utility van parked in the middle of the trail. Her heart pounded and she felt tension sizzle in her veins until she ascertained that it was empty and there was no sign of the men who must have left it there. She didn't recognize the van, but it was a fairly safe bet that it belonged to the two men camping at the mill. With their gear and van still here, those men had to be close by.

She debated for several seconds whether to check out the van or to put as much distance as possible between it and herself. She had a hunch Mark would have disabled it somehow. Nervously she glanced over her shoulder, then eased her way forward to check the doors and found them all locked. Giving another quick glance around the clearing, she knelt beside a back tire, removed her gloves so she could unscrew the cap from the valve stem, then pressed a fingernail against the pressure valve. The soft hiss of escaping air reached her ears.

After flattening one more tire, she stood and pulled her gloves back on. A flutter of lacy snowflakes touched her face and she looked uneasily toward the sky. The stars had disappeared and blackness was closing in. She needed to hurry before the snow became so thick she lost the track that led to the canyon and Mark.

With long, gliding strides, she followed the abandoned road through the trees. Though the snowfall was still light, she felt a sense of urgency. She couldn't see her watch without stopping to push back her glove, but she knew it had to be past midnight. Her parents would be worried and her brothers would be furious with her. Guiltily she wondered if she should stop and use the phone in her pocket to let them know she was all right. It would be the considerate thing to do, but she'd already wasted too much time checking the mill shack and flattening the van's tires. She needed to push on until she found Mark.

A light flashed in the distance through the trees. Courtney peered through the snow, straining to see it again. No, she must have been mistaken. There! She had seen a light! Stumbling to a stop, she swept her hood back from her head and listened. What began as a faint buzz was growing louder. A snowmobile, maybe more than one, was coming down the logging road toward her!

Kyle had mentioned loaning Mark his Durango and skis, but he hadn't said anything about a snowmobile. So unless that machine belonged to Mark's cousin, she was about to come face to face with the two men who had tried to kill Mark and her. She had to get off the road quickly. With a powerful dig of her ski poles, she shoved her way into the trees.

Her first instinct was to get as far from the road as possible as quickly as she could, but an unseen low tree branch sent her staggering to her knees. Her hand went to her forehead and she felt a goose egg rising. When she struggled back to her feet, she felt a twinge in one knee, and faced reality. It was too dark to move with any speed across rough terrain. She'd been lucky to sustain only minor injuries. A second accident might be much worse and she'd never find Mark.

Slowly she worked her way into a thick tangle of rocks and trees. From here she could watch the road. Even with the lightly falling snow, she could see fairly well. She'd been outside without a light long enough that her eyes had become accustomed to the meager light reflected off the white snow. The man or men on the snowmobile were following a headlight and would be almost blind beyond the beam of light it projected.

She crouched down behind a thick fir tree and flattened a branch so she could watch the road. Soon two lights appeared, one following the other. They were traveling faster than she would have considered safe for the conditions. The first rider shot past, leaving her with an impression of a dark-suited rider on a dark machine. The second machine carried two men, and her hand went to her mouth to prevent any sound from escaping. It was impossible to identify individuals, but both men's jackets appeared to be the same as those worn by the agents who had accompanied Desden to the ranch. She remembered the agent who had come to the house saying two agents were missing. Her mind immediately questioned their connection to the attack on Desden.

Dread enhanced her fear as the implications of the two agents being here sank into her mind. They were working with the men who had tried to kill Mark and her. They had turned on Desden, leaving him for dead. Was she too late? Had they already found Mark and Sam?

* * *

Black spots were dancing before Mark's eyes and his legs trembled as he finally finished constructing a small snow cave secluded in a tight copse of fir trees. He dragged himself inside and sank to the ground. For several minutes his breath came in painful gasps and he shuddered from fatigue more than the cold. Gradually he began to relax and strength returned to his body. He wanted to sleep, but didn't dare.

As his breathing became more normal his thoughts returned to Desden. He lifted the small phone from his pocket and stared at it thoughtfully. Did he dare risk a call? If one of Amy's brothers had somehow found the phone, surely Desden had recovered it by now. Holding his breath, he pressed the speed dial code.

* * *

When the sound of the machines faded in the distance without pausing and she knew the men riding them hadn't seen the marks in the snow where she'd left the road, Courtney picked her way back to it. Moving as swiftly as she dared, she headed north again. She was almost to the point where the logging road crossed a rocky ridge before sweeping down into the canyon when a faint sound reached her ears. Pausing, she swept back her hood again and listened. It came again and this time she grabbed one mitten with her teeth to jerk it off and dug into her pocket for the little telephone. Her hand shook as she punched the on button.

"This is Courtney," she whispered, though she felt relatively certain no one was near enough to overhear her.

"Courtney? Where's Desden?" Mark's voice was sharp in her ear. Hot tears pricked the back of her eyes. Mark was alive! Until this moment she hadn't realized how afraid she'd been that she wouldn't be able to warn him in time. Quickly she explained about the call Desden had received and the attack which followed.

"Is he going to be all right?" Mark's voice sounded worried.

"I don't know. I left the ranch while Kyle and the agent who told us about Desden were explaining what had happened to my family."

"Courtney, where are you?" Mark demanded to know above the rattle of static on the line.

"I left my Rodeo at the saw mill. I was skiing toward the homestead cabin to warn you. Right now I'm about a mile from the canyon rim."

"Go back to your truck and get out of here!"

"I can't." Her voice dropped lower and her eyes searched for movement beyond the curtain of falling snow. "Three men came down the trail on snowmobiles. They didn't see me, but they're between me and the saw mill. I can't go back."

He was quiet so long that a burst of static frightened her that the connection had been lost. Finally his voice came again. "You can't ski all the way back to the ranch in this storm. Besides, they'll be watching all of the routes back to the ranch, looking for me. If they were as far over as the logging road, they've probably booby-trapped the canyon entrance. The county road isn't safe either. There's a man posted there watching Kyle's truck." Static blocked out his voice for several seconds then he went on, "Do you know where the lower entrance to the mine is?"

"Yes." She couldn't help the quaver in her voice.

"Do you think you can find it in this storm?"

"Yes," she answered again though she wasn't at all certain she could make her way there across three miles of snow-covered wilderness. She'd only been to the long-abandoned mine entrance once. As teenagers she and her brothers had backpacked into the remote area for a three-day camping trip. She remembered how thoroughly concealed the cave-like entrance had been in a rocky cleft screened by willows.

"Meet me there." His voice dropped. "Be careful, and don't use the phone again unless it's an emergency. I don't know what kind of scanning equipment they might have."

She held the phone in her hand for several minutes after he hung up. At last the snow falling on her bare hand reminded her to put the phone away and start moving again. Looking back she could see where new snow had almost obliterated her tracks. She decided that was a positive sign. Reaching the mine would be difficult enough without having to worry about leaving a trail.

Not daring to go back to the point where the logging road was bisected by a trail leading in the general direction she wanted to go, she searched for an opening in the trees. Carefully she worked her way to a meadow she knew spread beneath a steep ridge. Once across the meadow, she could more easily ascend to the top of the ridge. Stooping low to avoid a branch, she burst onto the meadow and paused in horror. The meadow was gone. In its place and as far as she could see was a field of churned unstable snow left there by an avalanche. She couldn't possibly cross it.

With a sigh, she turned to the steep slope beside her. The trees were too close together for easy movement; she'd have to follow the edge of the slide and carefully stair-step her way to the top. The wind picked up, driving the snow in relentless swirls before her.

* * *

Mark slowed to catch his breath. The rest had helped, but he'd been moving steadily uphill since leaving the snow cave. He glanced uneasily to the west, picturing Courtney making her way up the west side of the slide he'd created. He wished he'd thought to warn her of that.

But for the snow, he would be able to see the main mine entrance from where he stood. He cocked his head and listened for any sound that shouldn't be there. When at last he was satisfied it was safe to proceed, he made a careful circuit of the mine before approaching the entrance.

Heavy planks covered the opening and a "No Trespassing" sign warned would-be explorers away. Undeterred, Mark removed his skis and hid them in one of the dilapidated buildings clustered around the mouth of the mine. The same building yielded a piece of metal pipe that had been flattened on one end. Picking it up, he weighed it in one hand. He would have preferred a crowbar, but this would have to do.

He felt more than saw the door open behind him. He raised the length of metal as he turned, ready to defend himself.

"It's me." He recognized his cousin's voice and checked the movement of his arm. "Sam!" he gasped, relief flooding through him. "How did you find me?"

"We heard shots, so I went to see if you were safe. I found where you hid your friend's truck. There's someone guarding it, so I figured you must not be dead. There's also an Explorer in the middle of the road about five miles down, and two more vehicles hidden at the saw mill, but not together. I looked for you there but when I didn't find you, I started back to our camp, thinking you would come to us if you needed help. That's when I saw three men on snowmobiles come out of the forest. They looked pretty angry, so I knew they hadn't found you although I wasn't close enough to hear their words. On the way back I found your snow cave."

"Is Julie with you?" Alarm colored his voice.

"No, but she's safe. I left her well hidden to wait for me. Don't worry, no one will find her. Come, we can be there in twenty minutes."

"I have to find Courtney." Quickly he explained how she had come to warn him that Desden's boss had betrayed him and sent agents to intercept him and keep him from making public any charges against Senator Perry. "We arranged to meet at the lower mine entrance. I have to go through the mine to reach her," he concluded.

Observing that the storm was too intense for travel over the mountain, Sam added, "I can see that your strength is nearly spent. But the tunnels wind for miles, and the mine has been closed a long time. Some of the tunnels may have collapsed or be dangerous by now. I'll tell you how to find Julie. Wait with her while I go after Miss Grant."

Mark understood Sam's caution and appreciated his offer, but he would not allow his cousin to risk his life on a trek over the mountain in an escalating snowstorm. It was too dangerous.

"The surface route is impassable by now," he stated flatly. "The storm has increased to the point that no one, not even you, can make it over the mountain to the lower entrance. The mine is the only way."

Sam reluctantly acknowledged that Mark was right. "I'll go with you then," he stated and Mark knew argument would be useless. Besides he might need Sam's help if Courtney was unable to reach the mine and they had to search for her.

It didn't take long to pry a plank loose with the bar Mark had found. Sam reached behind him to move the plank back into place, concealing their entry should anyone come looking for them. Then, hugging the cave-like wall, they began to walk down the tunnel. At first a glimmer of gray light crept through the planks to soften the darkness of the mine, but as they moved away from the entrance, the darkness deepened until touch was their only guide.

With nervous fingers Mark groped in his coat pocket for the flashlight he'd placed there earlier. His hand trembled as it closed around it. With childish relief he pulled the light free and fumbled for the button to click it on. His hands, made clumsy by the gloves he wore and the old fear clawing at his heart, lost their grip, and the flashlight clattered to the stone floor.

Panic gripped Mark with ferocious tenacity. Flattening both hands against the wall behind him, he leaned back, gasping for breath. Once more he was in that jungle prison without light or hope. Blackness, thick and tangible, opened its gaping mouth, threatening to swallow him whole.

Despair filled his soul. He couldn't escape the blackness. It roiled and twisted, drawing him down into nothingness. With stealthy fingers, it smothered and suffocated. It would be better to surrender quietly, let his mind take him deeper and deeper until the blackness was all that existed. All he had to do was let go.

A voice penetrated the blackness, compelling him to listen. *"Wo unto this people; wo unto the inhabitants of the whole earth except they shall repent."* The voice was Courtney's as she had read to him so

many long hours while he'd twisted in physical and emotional torment. He recognized the words of the Savior as they'd come
through the darkness covering the land at the time of his crucifix-
ion. *"For the devil laugheth, and his angels rejoice . . ."* A vision of
Roy Perry surrounded by the South American colonel, the cruel,
animal-like guards, the Dallas psychiatrist, the dead man in the
wrecked car, and dozens of faceless snowmobilers laughed and
smirked at him from the inky darkness.

He felt himself slipping. He couldn't hold on any longer. Then
Courtney's voice carried the Savior's words to him once more. *"Lift
up your head and be of good cheer; for behold the time is at hand, and
on this night shall the sign be given, and on the morrow come I into the
world, to show unto the world that I will fulfill all that which I have
caused to be spoken by the mouth of my holy prophets."*

A deafening noise crashed through his head erupting in spasms
of pain. Slowly he sank to the floor, holding his head. Vaguely he
became aware of Sam kneeling beside him, gripping his shoulder.
His cousin's voice slowly overcame the horrifying memories swim-
ming in his head.

"Are you ill?" Sam spoke softly.

"No," he gasped. "I dropped the flashlight."

"It's all right." He could hear the puzzlement in Sam's voice. "I
have another one. I only waited to turn it on until we were far
enough from the entrance that there would be no risk of any light
showing through the planks." He clicked his light on as though
demonstrating to a child that there was no need to fear the dark.

Mark leaned back against the rock wall and swallowed deep
gulping breaths. He knew now. He hadn't forgotten his God during those horrible days of fear and torture. Now he recalled regaining consciousness while still in the colonel's spacious office where
he'd been beaten. He'd lain still, pretending to be unconscious,
postponing further punishment. There had been another man
there, a gringo. He'd only seen the man's shoes and his impeccably
tailored pant legs, but he'd recognized the voice. He had listened,
stunned, as the man who had once been his father-in-law had
ordered the colonel to find out who Mark had given the report to.

"Punishment won't work on this one." The senator had nudged Mark's sore ribs with the toe of his custom-made shoes. "You have to find his weakness. My daughter claims that he cares more about his church than anything else. His church is too powerful back in my country for me to risk any attack on it there, but they send young people here as missionaries. He came to South America on one of those missions when he was only nineteen, so those kids just might be his weak spot. Threaten one of those missionaries each time he refuses to cooperate. If that truly is his weakness, he'll give us what we want rather than let anything happen to them."

The colonel was aghast. "We can't risk the diplomatic problems that attacking young Americans will bring!" he argued.

"I can't afford the risk of those papers surfacing at the wrong time," Perry responded in a threatening growl.

"If, as you say, his church is most important to him and he cares about these young people he doesn't even know, I will find out and make him talk. But if these young people mean nothing to him, I will not risk a confrontation with your government." The colonel reluctantly agreed, with a few stipulations, to Perry's plan.

There was no time to analyze what he should do. His strength was gone and he could no longer trust himself to remain silent. In his mind there had been only one choice. He had to fade so deep inside the blackness that the Church and all he valued in his relationship to God would disappear. He had to wipe from his mind all that mattered most to him in this world, including his cousin, so there would be no possibility he could betray Sam or the young men and women who came to this country to serve God.

Silently he'd prayed one last time, begging for the strength and the ability to fade deeper than he'd ever gone before. He thanked God for the military instructor who had drilled into him a technique few undercover intelligence agents were ever required to use. Briefly he'd considered the instructor's warning of the risk of total mental confusion and even death to those who went too far. He remembered thinking even as he locked the code phrase "Samuel the Lamanite," in his mind that only the Lord's call to "lift up his head" would ever bring him back all the way.

Tears ran freely down his face as he leaned his head back against the hard, stone wall of the mine. After all his enemies had done to him, he had emerged like a newborn infant into the world without memory of all he'd once held dear, but his Father had not forgotten him. He'd sent him the gospel once more.

His cousin found the dropped light and upon discovering that it still worked, pressed it into Mark's hand. After a couple of minutes Mark rose shakily to his feet and smiled sheepishly at his cousin.

"You must think I'm crazy." He ruefully clasped his cousin's arm, and his thoughts turned to his urgent need to reach Courtney. "We'd better get moving." As he moved forward with newly confident steps, he wondered how much of the feeling of lightness he felt was due to the small puddle of light preceding him down the tunnel and how much was due to his sense of reconciliation with God. A quiet assurance burned in his breast that the darkness would threaten him no more.

SEVENTEEN

Courtney fought the urge to sit down in the snow and bawl. Climbing up to the ridge had completely sapped her strength. Twice she'd felt the snow shift under her skis and she'd barely managed to pull herself free before being carried downhill by the unstable mass. Finally, fearing she might set off another avalanche, she moved further into the trees away from the still settling slide area.

At the top of the ridge she halted to catch her breath, but the wind screaming across the high flat area stole it from her. With near whiteout conditions, she feared she might lose her way as she continued doggedly in the direction she felt to be north. She prayed she wouldn't become confused when every direction appeared the same. Landmarks disappeared in the swirling whiteness as time and space took on an aura of unreality. When she felt the tips of her skis begin to slope downward, she slowed almost to a crawl. She didn't want to suddenly plunge over a cliff or fall in a crevice.

A dark shape loomed out of the swirling whiteness, then another. Surely they were trees. When she brushed by one close enough to touch it, she breathed a little easier. Once back in the trees, movement was more difficult, but there was some protection from the wind.

She remembered that she and her brothers had followed a game trail down the slope toward the mine. Finding the trail in this storm would be impossible. All she could hope for was that her instincts would carry her in the right direction, and she vowed to keep a constant prayer on her lips. She continued her downward trek for what seemed an interminably long time. Recalling every detail she could muster from that long-ago trip, she struggled to remember if there had been any cliffs or sudden drop-offs. She couldn't be sure, though the steep decline she followed seemed vaguely familiar.

Just when she was beginning to wonder if she were descending into the right valley, she ran into a thick stand of willows and breathed a little easier. Where there were willows, there could usually be found a stream. If this were the stream she sought, it would lead her right to the mine. Using the willows as a guide, she moved with sluggish steps in the direction she hoped would lead her to the spring near the mouth of the mine. In a matter of minutes, which felt like hours, she stumbled against a vertical rock face. Using her hands to feel her way, she soon found crumbling wood columns. With a gasp of relief she clutched at the wood pieces. She'd found the long-abandoned lower mine entrance!

Though it had once been boarded over, the boards had long since surrendered to the elements and now hung in broken disarray. Few people knew of the old mine tunnel, and the forest service had become lax in locating and sealing off some of the more remote abandoned mines in the mountainous area, including this one. The old prospector who first discovered silver in the mountain had worked this tunnel alone for several years, but with the advent of more modern machinery and the discovery that the greater deposit was several miles away, a larger, more easily accessible entry had been dug on the other side of the mountain.

Reaching down, she unclasped her skis and crawled through one of the many gaps in the boards, pulling her skis after her. She wasn't certain whether her instincts had proven true or whether she had been guided by a heavenly hand, but she certainly felt grateful to be out of the wind. Her legs refused to hold her any longer and she sank to the cold stone floor. Her breath came in aching sobs.

After resting a few minutes, she felt in her pocket for the flashlight she'd stuck there and aimed the beam around the narrow space. The light revealed an almost square room, and she remembered being told that the old prospector and his mule had slept inside the mine in this first chamber. As her beam worked its way around the small space, she saw where a tunnel branched off of the chamber. If she followed that tunnel, would she meet Mark? Of course, she might get lost if the tunnel branched in several directions and he'd never find her. It might be best to stay near the entrance where he'd promised to meet her.

Cold began to creep through her clothes and she shivered. As long as she'd been moving, the cold hadn't seemed as intense, but now it seemed to penetrate to her bones. In spite of her waterproof ski gear she felt damp and when she pulled off her ski mask there was no mistaking how wet her face and hair had become. She longed to sit down and rest, but she feared she would freeze to death if she didn't keep moving. Restlessly she prowled around the small space until her foot knocked against an old bucket. She sneezed as a cloud of dust rose to her nostrils. Whatever had once been in the bucket had been reduced long ago to lining for the nest of a family of mice.

As she stared at the pile of fluff with its tiny twigs and bits of fur an idea came to her mind. If she could find some dry wood, she could start a fire. Her father had insisted since she was a young girl that she and her brothers always carry small tin boxes of waterproof matches in their winter gear pockets along with a few pieces of hard candy and a pocketknife. These few emergency items had been zipped inside a pocket of her ski jacket so long she never consciously thought of them. She hesitated only a moment, questioning the advisability of building a fire. The mine entrance was difficult to see in bright daylight; with the blizzard raging outside, in addition to the protection of the thick willows, no one would see the light from a small fire. The alternative was to risk possibly fatal hypothermia. She had to make an attempt to get warm and dry.

She found a broken bench and hauled it to the spot she'd picked to build her fire. Obviously it wouldn't burn long or provide much heat. She needed something bigger. Turning to the entryway, she pulled off all the boards she could free with her hands. They were wet from the snow, but showed a few dry spots on one side. They might burn.

She needed a couple of logs, but where would she find them? The beam of her flashlight caught a supporting pillar and she shook her head. She was losing her mind to even consider it briefly. If she burned one of the supporting beams, she'd bring the mountain down on top of her head.

Once again catching the tunnel in the beam of her light, she considered following it for a short distance. Keeping the beam focused on the rough floor, she tentatively moved a few feet into the tunnel, then a few more. When she came to a branch in the tunnel, she debated going on or returning to the opening. She flashed the light down one tunnel, then the other. Something caught her eye and she moved tentatively toward a pile of rubble.

As she swept the beam of light over the rubble and up the sides of the tunnel, she could see where several beams had given way, sending a load of rock and dirt crashing to the floor. Keeping her light trained on dangling chunks of splintered beams, she backed up a couple of steps. Lowering the beam of light, she caught sight of a thick pole protruding from the rubble. It was exactly what she needed to build a fire. She wondered if she tugged it free, would it set off a chain reaction, bringing down the rest of the ceiling?

The beam of light fluttered and she realized she was shaking from the deep, jarring cold. Cold and fatigue added up to trouble, and if she hoped to survive until Mark arrived and then somehow flee across the frozen landscape to some place where they would be safe, she needed warmth and rest. Eyeing the mound of rocks and dirt that filled the tunnel, she guessed the rubble was all that kept the rest of the tunnel from collapsing. But she needed firewood. The chunks of wood protruding from the debris appeared to be her only source of dry wood. She would have to risk upsetting some delicate balance.

Carefully she inched toward the fallen timber. She could see at a glance that the broken beam was older than that in the other tunnel. Most of the supports she'd seen were milled, probably at the saw mill a few miles down the road from the main portion of the mine, and were as thick as railroad ties. These were tree trunks, hacked and hewn by an ax-wielding hand. They were smaller than their counterparts and not so even in circumference.

A feeling of reluctance came over her as she thought of placing her flashlight on the ground so she could use both hands to free one of the broken support beams. Since her ski parka sported a number of clips to which she could attach mittens or ski lift passes, she'd see if she could somehow hook the flashlight to her jacket. Her fingers ached and it took several minutes to attach the loop of her flashlight to one of the clips. She experimented with a couple of different positions before she was satisfied.

The dangling light cast weird shadows as she approached the rubble pile, but it was better than being entirely in the dark or possibly losing her precious light. She stooped to examine the log more closely, then began a careful excavation. An occasional creak or groan from over her head or from deep in the mountain kept her heart racing and her eyes frantically searching the darkness.

Estimating the log to be a little more than four feet long and nine or ten inches thick, she dug until she could twist it, gently easing it forward. As she worked the log free, her ear caught the sound of dirt and rocks trickling behind it. With only inches to go, an ominous groan sounded overhead. Acting from sheer terror, she grasped the log tightly, pulled it free, and fled down the tunnel with the trailing log thumping behind her. Monstrous shadows danced on the walls as the flashlight bounced against her leg and she ran faster.

Expecting rocks to rain on her head, she bolted for the main tunnel. If she dropped the log she could run faster, but she refused to give up her prize. Behind her she heard a loud crack followed by the slither of shifting rocks, and once more increased her speed. At last she stumbled into the chamber near the entrance and sagged to her knees, the log tightly clasped in her arms, and her head bowed. Holding her breath, she listened for the rumble of falling rock. All was silent.

* * *

Mark found the mine tunnel in surprisingly good shape, considering it had been closed four years ago. For the first couple of miles he and Sam followed the tracks once used by ore cars and made good time, but the tracks ended where the older portion of the mine began, and walking became more difficult. Both men had been in the mine numerous times as boys, mostly in the forbidden older end where they had explored the tunnels to their hearts' content while their grandfather thought they were camping or fishing.

The tunnel they followed twisted and turned, sometimes climbing sharply, then dipping as abruptly. It was narrower than the tunnel in the newer part of the mine, but the route leading to the lower entrance was easy to follow because it had been reinforced by new timbers thirty years ago to provide an escape route should disaster strike, trapping men in the far reaches of the mine. Even that long ago, some of the original tunnels were collapsing when the rough-hewn supports built by early miners were neither spaced correctly nor were they heavy enough.

Using the heavier support beams as a guide, Mark and Sam followed their flashlight beams into the labyrinth of tunnels. Occasionally one or the other would shine a light along a side tunnel filled with debris left from a collapsed ceiling, and they noted that far more of the mine was impassable now than when they'd explored it as curious youths. Occasional chunks of rock littered the tunnel they followed, reminding them that none of the tunnels were immune to cave-ins.

Once Sam stopped to shine his light on a puddle of ice. He raised his arm slowly, revealing a bulging wall of thick bluish-gray mud. Mark read the concern in his eyes and hoped they wouldn't find their way blocked, nor jar loose a wall in passing.

Five minutes later they rounded a corner and came face to face with a pile of rocks, completely filling the passage. Mark eyed the pile for several minutes then turned to Sam. "There's a little space at the top. We might be able to crawl over."

"I don't know. Wait here, I'll check it out." With careful movements Sam scaled the rocks until he could shine his flashlight into the narrow space. Turning back to Mark, he shook his head and climbed back down with infinite care. "There's a massive boulder sitting on top of the pile. It's probably all that's holding this whole section up. We can't get around it, and we can't risk moving it by doing any digging."

"All right, then, we'll find another route." Mark turned about, heading for the last side tunnel they'd passed. The old side tunnels twisted and turned, bisecting each other, and randomly reversing direction. Many were dead ends, but some looped around to join the main tunnel at another point.

Through trial and error and a great deal of backtracking, they moved steadily west but met with blocked tunnels or dead ends each time they thought themselves close to the main route. In frustration they paused where three tunnels branched.

Bracing his hands over his knees, Mark leaned forward, breathing heavily. He was exhausted. He questioned how long he could continue on, traveling on sheer determination alone. Somewhere he had to find the strength. Courtney needed him. He refused to consider she might not have made it to the mine entrance. He wished the little telephones they both carried could be used to let her know he was on his way and to check on her, but no signal could be sent from this far inside the mountain. He dropped his head, closed his eyes, and prayed.

Suddenly he lifted his head and sniffed. He could smell smoke. Turning his head, he could tell Sam had caught the faint odor as well.

"It's coming from this tunnel," Sam gestured toward the tunnel that seemed the least likely to lead them back to the main tunnel.

"I think we should follow it, but keep our eyes open for trouble," Mark spoke thoughtfully. Warily they advanced and as the tunnel wove its circuitous route, they paused frequently to listen and shielded their flashlight beams as they rounded corners. At last the tunnel ended in a junction with a slightly wider tunnel. Their lights picked out the wider beams and they knew they had succeeded in returning to the main route, but all the twists and turns had left them both uncertain of which direction to go.

"The smoke is coming from this way and there is a slight movement of air telling me we are near an entrance." Sam indicated with a nod of his head the direction he thought they should go.

A flicker of light ahead warned them they were approaching the source of the smoke. Turning off their flashlights, they cautiously continued on. The tunnel ended in a small chamber and Mark struggled with a sudden burst of emotion. Courtney lay curled on her side asleep on the hard ground beside a vigorously burning fire. Her ski mask lay inches from her fingers and her skis and poles leaned against the wall behind her. His first inclination was to rush to her side and wrap his arms around her, but empathy for her exhausted state told him not to awaken her.

"You need to sleep, too," Sam said softly. "When you have rested, we will begin the return journey."

When Mark would have protested, insisting that his cousin should rest, too, Sam just looked at him and Mark knew he was right. His body had not regained its strength. Without a short rest he would only hold them back. Wearily he moved closer to the fire and settled himself with his back to the stone wall. The warmth of the fire touched his face and he slept.

* * *

Courtney awoke knowing something had changed. Her fire had dwindled to ashes and charred chunks. Light made its way inside the cavern from the open entryway. A figure sat in the opening with his head bowed. She wasn't certain whether he was sleeping or lost in deep meditation. He didn't frighten her, though she suspected that when he turned around she would see a stranger's face.

The sound of heavy breathing behind her stiffened her spine and she turned warily, but relaxed with gentle joy as she recognized Mark. So the stranger was his cousin, Sam. They had come for her.

She lay still for several minutes watching Mark's dear face and her heart swelled with love. No matter what path he chose for the rest of his life, she would always love him. She had been wrong to desire marriage so much she'd been willing to settle for a man she didn't love with all her heart. Just as she'd learned she couldn't accept less than temple marriage, she knew she couldn't consider marriage without love. If Mark should choose to continue his dangerous career and live for months or years undercover, she would wait for him. She wasn't certain he loved her, but just as she sensed at some deep inner level that his faith in God ran deeper than he knew, she believed their being together was right. God had guided her through a terrifying journey during the night and a quiet peaceful stillness told her to have faith and he would guide her on this journey of her heart.

She turned her attention back to the man in the entryway and found he was watching her. He beckoned to her and she rose quietly and went to sit beside him. He didn't speak, yet she felt they were communicating as they surveyed the pristine whiteness spreading away in front of them. The storm had passed and the day promised to be bright and clear. No footprint or ski track indicated she had passed that way. No reminders of the dreadful hours she had toiled across a frozen wasteland remained. Peace filled her heart and she knew the man beside her felt it, too.

"You let me sleep too long," Mark's voice came from behind them.

Courtney scrambled to her feet and turned to face him. Her eyes widened at the light she saw in his eyes. Without being told, she knew he had all of his memory back. She took a step toward him and he met her with open arms. He simply held her, rocking slightly from side to side, as she struggled to control the tears that threatened to fall. Pulling back slightly, he kissed the tip of her nose, then settled a brief kiss on her lips.

"I let you sleep because you needed rest," Sam spoke solemnly. "The trip back will be arduous and we can't know what waits for us at the other end."

"I wish we could travel back over the mountain instead of going through it," Mark spoke wistfully as he moved nearer to the opening. For several seconds he surveyed the white landscape and Courtney's heart ached for him. She knew how terribly claustrophobic being inside the mine must have been for him. In his delirium back at the cabin he had told her of his fear of a great consuming darkness, and she knew of no place darker than a mine shaft deep in the bowels of a mountain. She took his hand and together they stepped outside. The wind had curled a drift around the opening to the mine, leaving an almost bare spot where they stood.

"The snow is at least four feet deep, in some places twice that, and we don't have our skis with us," Sam reminded Mark.

"You're right," Mark sighed, but he continued to stand looking toward the valley. The ringing of his phone startled them all.

Concern drew his brows together in concentration as he reached for the phone and clicked it on. "Stewart." He spoke his last name and wished he and Desden had arranged to use code.

"Thank God," Desden's voice whispered over the line, and Mark felt a moment's amusement at his agnostic friend's choice of words. "Can you talk?"

"Yes." His own voice was terse. "What happened? Are you all right?"

"Llewelyn ordered me off the case and sent someone after you. I was on my way to warn you—Lawson was with me—and when we stopped at the gate, I jumped out to open it, and Weldon jumped me. I fought with him, but Lawson clubbed me from behind. They left me in the snow, but some old man who had been visiting the Grants found me. I came to while he was barreling down the highway weaving from side to side. I nearly died of a heart attack then. The sheriff met us, and I made it to a medical clinic where the sheriff rousted some retired doctor out of bed to look after me. I'm fine, but what about you?"

"I'm safe at the moment, but it looks like I'll have to cross the mountains to get back to civilization. Perry's men have the roads out of here blocked."

"Sheriff Boulter and a couple of deputies left here at sunup to see if they can find you. They have warrants for Weldon and Lawson. There have been some national developments, too. I talked to our friend at the Justice Department. Llewelyn has been put on leave, and I'm back on the case. Boulter said if I managed to reach you to tell you they'd meet you at the mine entrance. Do you know where that is, and are you far from there?"

"Three or four miles," Mark drawled dryly.

"Another thing," Desden hesitated. "I hate to worry you, but Courtney disappeared last night. Her dad and brothers think she might have headed for your grandpa's old place. They've gone after her on snowmobiles."

"She's with me."

"With you? But how . . . ?"

"I'll explain later. Catch up to the Grants somehow and warn them not to climb the mountain beyond the cabin. I'm pretty certain there are explosives planted there."

He heard Courtney's sharp intake of breath and wished he could have spared her this new worry.

"Don't try to call again," Mark warned before turning off the phone. "The signal won't reach us where we're going. I'll contact you when it's safe to do so."

Courtney had heard enough to know her father and brothers were riding into danger and that her guess concerning Senator Perry had been correct. She reached for the phone in her own pocket and punched in the code for Luke's cell phone. She knew he would have it with him. She wasn't surprised when he didn't answer. The roar of the snowmobiles would drown out its ring. Instead she waited for the signal to leave an emergency message and briefly left a warning. Silently she prayed he would stop to check in with Mom or see if he had messages before starting up the canyon.

Mustering her courage, she turned back to the mine and picked up her skis. Resolutely she faced the gaping black tunnel. No words were spoken as Sam took the lead and Mark gathered up her poles.

EIGHTEEN

"We're almost out of the old tunnels," Mark encouraged softly as though he sensed her confusion. "We'll be able to move faster once we reach the newer part of the mine." Courtney wondered how he could begin to tell where they were. He'd explained about the different beams and why they had to follow one of the older, more dangerous tunnels to bypass a cave-in. It seemed to her they had been wandering for hours in a maze of crisscrossing tunnels, many of which were littered with fallen rock and patches of spongy mud.

Sam's flashlight abruptly flickered off, and Mark's followed, plunging them into a darkness that left Courtney with a rising sense of panic. She'd never known a darkness so complete that it felt thick and tangible. Sandwiched between the two men and carrying her skis, Courtney had left her flashlight in her pocket, thinking to save her batteries. Instinctively she groped for the light, but as her hand closed over the thick rubber casing she paused without turning it on. She sensed both men were listening intently and she strained to hear whatever had caught their attention. No sound reached her ears.

"There's someone coming," Sam warned in a barely audible whisper. "They're in the main tunnel, but once they reach the slide blocking it, they'll backtrack until they find this route around the blockage."

"It might be the sheriff," Courtney whispered.

"It might, but we won't take any chances," Mark said. "We'll stay in this tunnel until they pass by, then move as quickly as we can without lights, putting as much distance as possible between us before they begin backtracking."

"We need to move closer to where the trail branches or we'll lose precious time getting out of this tunnel when the time comes to hurry," Sam added.

"Take my hand," Mark whispered. Shifting her skis to her left hand, she fumbled with her right to find his hand.

"I've got the skis." Sam took them from her.

With her hand tightly clasped in Mark's, Courtney felt her way forward. Several times she stumbled over loose rocks on the floor, and she began to worry as she felt the hard rock wall give way to soft mud. Sam touched her shoulder and she stopped, her ears straining for any sound. A faint metallic clatter reached her ears and she jumped when a man's deep voice suddenly cursed from close by. Another voice warned the first to keep quiet.

"I don't take orders from you," the first voice snarled.

"Use your head," a third voice snapped. "If they hear us coming, they'll head out into the snow. By the time we return for the snowmobiles, they could be miles away."

"They're probably already dead. There's no way Mark Stewart or the Grant woman could have crossed this mountain last night," the first voice continued to grumble. Courtney stifled a gasp. How did they know she was here? Had they found her Rodeo and guessed she'd met up with Mark?

"I told you Walker got a call. His contact said Draper reached Stewart by cell phone this morning and that he overheard Draper talking to the girl's mother later. The guy who called Walker knows this country, and he says they're holed up at the far end of this mine. They're both alive and that Indian the boss has been looking for is with them."

"They won't be alive after I catch up to them. Three weeks in this . . ." His voice trailed off in a string of curses.

Once the voices faded completely away, Sam turned on a thin beam of light, then moved with quick sure steps toward the opening to the main tunnel. Before he reached it, he turned off his light again and returned Courtney's skis to her. He indicated she and Mark should wait while he checked the passage.

Sam was gone for what seemed like a long time, and when he returned he encouraged them to move with as much speed as possible. "They're digging!" he whispered. There was a controlled urgency in his voice that prompted unquestioning obedience to his whispered commands.

"Leave the skis behind," he told Courtney. They slid to the floor with a soft thump and she felt more than heard Mark lay her poles beside them before clasping her hand once more. He took off in long swinging strides before she could think about the sizable sum she'd paid for the practically new ski equipment she was abandoning or wonder how she would be able to move with any speed or agility once they left the mine. She had to practically run to keep up with him.

When they reached the main tunnel, they were able to trot side by side with Sam a short distance ahead, his flashlight casting a beacon for them to follow. The light concerned her and she worried that the men pursuing them might catch its glow. Hadn't Mark said they'd have to follow the tunnel in the dark? Now both Mark and Sam seemed more concerned with speed than stealth.

Mark caught her as she stumbled over a loose rock, but didn't allow her time to catch her breath before rushing her on. Something in the men's urgent manner communicated itself to her, and she hurried on without protest.

A loud crack echoed down the tunnel and the mountain shook, sending icy rivulets of terror down her spine. She'd heard the mountain crack and groan when she'd freed a log for her fire, but this time she knew it meant business. Some age-old instinct caused her to duck her head in a useless protective gesture. She thought she heard the echo of a scream as Mark shouted for her to run. The floor trembled beneath her feet, and she needed no further urging to break into a sprint. Mark lengthened his stride to a flat-out run, and she dug deep inside her waning stamina for the strength to keep pace. Sam's flashlight bobbed erratically as he dashed ahead.

Behind them a series of crashes and deep rolling thunder grew closer, heralding the domino effect of the collapsing tunnel. She recognized the point where the newer tunnel began, but she continued to run, expecting rocks to rain on her head at any second. She prayed as she ran that the newer shoring in this part of the mine would hold.

Her prayer seemed to be answered because Sam slowed his pace to a jog once they reached the tracks. Mark's breathing was labored and he staggered as thick choking dust caught up to them. She sneezed and felt herself stumble. Mark's arm came around her, and she wasn't sure who steadied whom as they struggled to keep pace with Sam.

Between the dust and their long run, her breath came in wheezing gasps and her chest felt ready to explode by the time she noticed the blackness around them thinning to gray, then gradually giving way to a blazing white beacon at the end of the tunnel.

Sunshine pouring through the mine entrance was like a glimpse of heaven to Mark. He'd managed to focus on moving and protecting Courtney after that first debilitating attack of claustrophobia when he first entered the mine during the night, but memories of the forbidding rock hole where he'd been imprisoned for ten months had continued to hover near the edges of his thoughts. At no time had he felt at ease with the rock walls and darkness. Now he longed to race through that distant opening to embrace the sky and the seemingly endless vistas of mountains and trees. He longed to roll in the snow like a child. Sam placed a hand on his arm.

"Wait here," he urged.

"I'll go with you."

"No, it's better for me to go alone. You should both rest while I see who is waiting."

Mark noticed Sam didn't say "if" someone was waiting. "Be careful," was all he said. It was hard admitting his weakened body could not keep pace with Sam and that his labored breathing would give away their approach if he accompanied him. He would be useless in a battle without first resting and regaining a small measure of strength. He glanced longingly toward the beckoning light, then eased his way to the hard ground. With a gentle tug, he encouraged Courtney to sit beside him.

Sam disappeared in seconds, but Mark knew he was following the side of the tunnel and avoiding the light as he worked his way forward. Leaning back against rock, Mark waited. Silently he acknowledged that waiting was perhaps the hardest fought battle. After a few minutes his breathing assumed a more regular cadence, and he noticed that Courtney was no longer gasping for breath either. The air wasn't as thick with dust here, and by sitting still, the weakness in his limbs lessened.

"Do you think they're all dead?" Courtney's voice held lingering threads of fear and revealed her exhaustion.

"Yes," he answered. "It's unlikely any of them were able to escape." He didn't elaborate, but even as he silently thanked God for his own escape and that of two people he held dear, he could take no satisfaction in the deaths of his enemies.

"How did Sam know the tunnel would collapse?" Courtney whispered again.

Recognizing the insecurity behind her question, he moved closer and wrapped his arms around her. In a moment of awe he recognized that he needed to hold her as much as she needed to be held. "We're safe here," he soothed, then went on to explain, "When we found the tunnel blocked, Sam climbed up the rocks to see if we could crawl over the top of the rubble. He found a large slab of rock wedged between the fallen debris and the ceiling. He figured it was the only support holding the sagging roof of that tunnel in place. Every support beam he could see was broken or cracked, and water was seeping around the rock. Wide cracks in the rock overhead showed its instability. It was only a matter of time until the water would cause the blockage to shift, and as it shifted, the big piece of stone supporting the ceiling would shift too."

"But how did he know it would happen right when those men reached it?"

"Sam has always had exceptional hearing. When he checked the tunnel to see if it was safe for us to leave our hiding place, he apparently heard the sound of digging. Instead of finding a way around the blocked tunnel, they were trying to dig their way through."

When Mark finished speaking, they sat in silence. Once he thought he heard a faint three-note whistle, but it wasn't the meadowlark trill that would signal all clear, so he continued to wait.

Feeling rested enough to go on, he chafed at the delay. He wanted to be on his way, to once more feel sunshine or cold blowing wind on his face. The sooner he escaped this mine, the better. But he wouldn't rest easy until Perry was arrested.

The sound of a rifle shot carried inside the mine, bringing him to his feet with heart pounding. Sam wasn't carrying a rifle!

Mark began to inch forward, the way his cousin had gone. He was rested now and he could wait no longer. Courtney began to follow.

"You better wait here," Mark whispered to her, but she tightened her grip on his hand.

"I'm not waiting alone," she protested. "If Sam has been hit, I can help him while you make certain the guy with the rifle doesn't get close enough to rush the opening."

Mark didn't waste time arguing. Staying close to the wall where the bright sunlight never touched, he led the way toward the entrance.

As he moved into the area where there was more light, he drew his gun and crept toward the opening. Hugging the wall, Courtney followed. Before reaching the wooden frame around the entrance, she could see Sam wasn't anywhere inside the mine. With his gun in one hand, Mark flattened himself against the wall and signaled for her to stop. Reluctantly she paused. She suspected Mark intended to leave the mine in search of Sam, and she didn't want to be left behind. But neither did she want to hamper him when he might need his attention focused on protecting himself and his cousin.

As Mark peered around the opening of the mine, she held her breath, tensed for the whistle of a bullet. When it didn't come, he crouched low and quickly disappeared. She held her hand over her mouth, fearing she might become ill as she waited, picturing Mark creeping behind the nearest building, then darting to the next. Seconds dragged into minutes and minutes seemed like hours.

She felt a presence seconds before a dark shape carrying a rifle silhouetted itself in the entry. Instinctively she shrank back against the wall.

"It's safe to come out," Sam spoke softly as if he understood a loud voice would shatter her fragile control. Recognizing his voice, she felt the relief wash over her in waves and her knees began to buckle. He reached to steady her.

"Mark?" She was ashamed of the way her voice wobbled and tears stung the back of her eyes.

"I'll take you to him."

"We heard a shot," she gasped. She squinted as Sam led her from the mine into the brilliant light reflecting off the snow.

"One man was waiting on the hill," Sam explained, speaking matter-of-factly as they walked. "He saw me leave the mine. When he raised his rifle, my wife shot him."

"Your wife?" She hadn't given a thought to whether or not Sam was married, and it hadn't occurred to her that he wouldn't come alone to meet Mark. Her mind was still grappling with this information when they stepped from behind a building and she saw Mark.

He was standing at the top of a small rise in a well-trampled clearing. In his arms was a petite figure with long, straight black hair, spilling down her back. Her arms were clasped around his waist, and her face was pressed against the front of his coat. Too stunned to think or even feel, Courtney stood paralyzed, forgetting to breathe.

"Come, you must meet my wife." Sam's words made no sense. The woman couldn't be Sam's wife; she looked like Venita, Mark's ex-wife. And if she were Sam's wife, why was Mark holding her?

"Courtney." Mark raised his head and smiled as she approached slowly and reluctantly. Releasing the woman, he hurried toward her. "I want you to meet someone I thought I had lost." He took her hand and pulled her toward the other woman, while Courtney felt like she was walking on shattering glass. She closed her eyes to ward off the pain.

"This is Julie," Mark's voice reached past her numbed senses. "My sister." Her eyes flew open and she looked at the woman smiling tentatively at her. She wasn't Venita. She could see that now. The similarities were only superficial. But how could she be Julie?

Sam stepped to the dark-haired woman's side, and his arm circled her shoulders as he briefly explained why Mark had believed his sister had died in the accident that had claimed their parents and how he had waited for her to grow up, then married her.

"You should have stayed where you were safe." Sam lightly brushed his wife's cheek with two fingers in an affectionate gesture.

"I heard snowmobiles minutes after the sun touched the mountain peaks. Since you hadn't returned, I was afraid that you needed help," Julie explained to her husband. "I stayed far back in the trees and looked for a place where I could watch the snowmobiles. Three men with rifles, picks, and lanterns entered the mine; a fourth hid himself and stood watch. I became worried, and then angry, because I knew they were looking for you and Mark, but I didn't know what to do, so I waited."

"Did you really shoot the man they left to guard the mine entrance?" Courtney couldn't believe the tiny, feminine girl with wide, innocent eyes could have done so.

"He would have shot Sam," she said as though no other explanation was necessary.

"He isn't dead," Sam added. "I tied him up and left him in one of the sheds. He's in no danger of bleeding to death, but he will need to have his shoulder . . ." He broke off as the pulsating throb of a helicopter's blades reached them.

Mark grabbed Courtney's hand and jerked her toward a thick stand of pine. Floundering in thigh-high snow, she feared they could not reach safety before this new threat arrived over them. Mark half-pushed, half-shoved her into a shallow depression against the trunk of a twisted tree. Broad, full pine boughs laden with snow drooped in front of them, offering a hidden vantage point from which they watched the helicopter stir up a flurry of snow as it settled in the wide space in front of the mine buildings.

Remembering Julie and Sam, she looked around anxiously. She couldn't see them anywhere, which was probably a good sign.

Turning her eyes back to the clearing, she thought the people in the chopper must be waiting for the whirlwind of snow to settle before venturing out. She hoped the propeller-driven storm would aid in hiding the footprints she and the others had left in the snow. As the snow settled, a large, familiar "3" became visible on the side of the helicopter. Then the door on the chopper opened just as an extended cab pickup truck with a sheriff's department logo on the door pulled into the clearing. It was followed by a heavy utility bearing the same logo.

Courtney's father was the first person out of the chopper. Jake and Kyle, both scowling ominously, scrambled out behind him, but she only had eyes for her father. In seconds she was lunging through the snow to meet him. Her heart swelled with gratitude that he'd received the message in time to keep him from proceeding up the homestead canyon. He saw her coming and rushed toward her. When they met he swept her into his arms and wrapped her in a fierce bear hug. Laughing and crying, she hugged him back.

Over his shoulder she saw Sheriff Boulter, four deputies, one of the agents who had been at the ranch, and Desden Draper with his arm in a sling and a new bandage on his head, moving toward them from the Sheriff's Department vehicles. A slight movement behind the utility caught her attention. It took only a second to recognize the bright rays of sunlight reflecting off the barrel of a gun aimed up the hill behind her. She turned to scream a warning to the three people still picking their way down the slope.

Noise exploded around her. Shots rang through the still mountain air, men were yelling, and her father was shouting for her to get down. His hand landed roughly in the middle of her back, and he shoved her face first into the snow. A shotgun blast boomed from somewhere nearby. Then for the space of a heartbeat all was silent.

Voices, all talking at once, floated over her head. Feet rushed past.

"Let me up," she panted as she pushed at her father's broad chest. Slowly he released her and helped her to her feet. Her eyes flew to where she'd last seen Mark. There was no sign of him, only a cluster of men, some standing, some kneeling, gathered around something in the snow. Bright splotches of red dotted the pristine whiteness around them.

"Mark!" she screamed as she ran toward the circle of people. A deputy with a walkie-talkie in his hand stepped out of her way. One of the kneeling figures turned as she reached the group. It was Mark and the look of agony on his face stopped her. Needing to know he was truly unharmed, she reached hesitantly to clutch his shoulder. As she did, she looked down at the figure lying in the snow. Julie lay staring up into Sam's eyes with more love and trust than Courtney had ever before witnessed. A shudder trembled through her slight form and her eyes drifted shut.

"Julie!" Sam's anguished whisper reached Courtney's ears, and she felt an ache in her own heart.

"Mark!"

Courtney raised startled eyes to his face as another woman's voice called his name. Turning toward the voice, she saw a woman striding as rapidly as the deep snow permitted toward them. This time there was no mistaking Venita Perry.

Mark stood to face her and Courtney couldn't read the enigmatic expression on his face. Was he pleased to see his former wife? Or did he resent the intrusion of a reporter, especially this one who could be expected to be sympathetic to the man trying to kill him?

"The helicopter is yours if you want it," Venita offered abruptly. "The deputy that fired at you is dead, but you have a chance to save this woman. My pilot can have her in Denver in less than an hour." For the first time Courtney became aware of a second cluster of figures gathered around a still form beside the sheriff's department van.

Mark looked down at Julie, then back at Venita, his face reflecting his doubts. "She isn't just a woman," he spoke quietly. "She's my sister, Julie." Venita's face blanched.

"Go on, take it." Venita's voice suddenly broke. "Daddy doesn't know I'm here, and even if he did, I owe you one."

"You don't owe me anything." Mark's voice carried a note of sadness. "I never blamed you." They both seemed oblivious to Courtney standing there beside Mark, and she wondered if she should leave them to talk privately, but as she loosened her grip on his arm, he reached for her hand and held on as though she were some kind of lifeline.

"You should have blamed me." A strange note of bitterness crept into Venita's voice. "None of this had to happen. It was from me Daddy discovered that you often made copies of your reports and sent them to a friend for safekeeping. I learned a long time ago that he planned to turn this mountain into a world-class ski resort and that he had some scheme in mind to close the mine, then acquire your grandfather's property through our marriage. He also thought he could use you through your career to gain an advantage over his political enemies. That's when I insisted on a divorce.

"I thought that was all there was to it, until you, along with all of your family, supposedly died less than a week after a sensational trial pointed to the involvement of a highly placed politician. Dad seemed to take your death hard, and I thought he was concerned that because of your death the mastermind behind the scheme would never be known. That's when I assured him you wouldn't have left that possibility to chance. I told him about your habit of keeping duplicate files and that your secret contact would eventually produce the proof to send the man to prison. I regretted your death and was suspicious that you had been murdered, so I conducted my own investigation."

"You didn't like what you found," Mark stated evenly. It wasn't a question, only a statement of fact. She grimaced.

"I thought you were dead and that exposing my father's underworld connections would only destroy my family." It was as close as she could come to justifying her silence.

He reached out with both hands to grasp her shoulders, his voice harsh, "Will you still offer me the chopper if I tell you that as soon as I leave here I intend to send your father to prison for the rest of his life?"

"Take Julie! Don't let her bleed to death!" Venita twisted away from his grasp and stumbled toward the sheriff's truck.

"Get Julie in the news chopper," he ordered briskly and several men leaped to do his bidding. Sam followed Julie aboard and just before he joined them, Mark pulled Courtney aside to brush his lips against hers briefly, then he was gone.

She stood rooted to the spot staring at the sky long after the aircraft disappeared from sight. Finally her father placed his arm around her and led her to the sheriff's truck. Desden huddled in one corner of the backseat looking as sick and miserable as she felt. Climbing in beside him, she remembered the sniper who had been left tied up in one of the sheds. She explained to Desden, and he relayed the information to the sheriff.

While two deputies ran to find the prisoner, she leaned her forehead against the cold window glass and watched two deputies load the blanket-wrapped body of the dead deputy in the other vehicle. She didn't even know which deputy had died and she wasn't sure she wanted to know. He had shot Julie, tried to shoot Mark, and had been a conspirator in all the attempts on both their lives. She knew all of Sheriff Boulter's deputies, and she wasn't sure she could handle knowing which one had betrayed her. She'd guessed earlier that there was a leak in the sheriff's office. If she'd shared her suspicion with Mark and Sam, perhaps Julie would be safe and this whole tragedy could have been avoided.

Courtney glanced ahead to where Venita huddled in the front passenger seat and remembered her words of self-condemnation She didn't blame Venita, and she wouldn't blame herself either. The blame belonged to the evil man who let greed and his craze for power destroy all who got in his way. She wondered if Venita would be able to tell this story to a sensation-hungry world. She found it in her heart to feel compassion for the other woman.

"He's just a kid," she heard someone standing nearby say.

"It wasn't a kid who did what he did," someone else said.

"Makes it hard when it's one of our own."

She stared at the blanket-draped figure lying motionless in the other vehicle. Of all Sheriff Boulter's deputies, the only one that could be considered a kid . . .

"Kyle!" She practically screamed as she turned to Desden. "Where's Kyle?"

"Kyle?" Desden looked around uncertainly. "Uh, I'm not sure."

"He found his skis where Mark hid them and went looking for his truck." Her father slid in beside her and closed the door. "He'll be all right, just needs a little time alone."

"He's a good cop," Desden mumbled. "It was good thinking to get that news chopper to find you and your sons, then bring you on up here." Desden was speaking over her head to her father.

"Good thing he came on the chopper and was standing behind us when you screamed." Her father patted her arm. "He was the only one in a position to see Franklyn pointing that gun barrel up the hill."

Franklyn? Hal Franklyn? She felt sick. He'd been right there beside her ever since she and Mark had returned from the cabin. She'd thought he was a friend shielding her from danger. Instead of protecting her, he'd been using her to get close to Mark.

"It's tough for any officer to have to shoot someone, but when that someone is a fellow officer . . ." Desden's voice trailed off. He shook his head sadly, and Courtney knew he was thinking of his own men buried inside the mine. Her heart ached for Kyle. Having once read his school essays, she knew of his personal reverence for life and how deeply being required to take a life would hurt him. Her own gratitude for his quick action knew no bounds. If not for Kyle, Mark would be dead.

Courtney found her legs would scarcely hold her as she stumbled into the ranch house a few hours later. Her family surrounded her, smothering her in hugs and questions.

"Can we open presents now?" Amy's youngest brother shouted and Courtney remembered with a kind of shock that it was Christmas. She looked around at the glowing tree and the mounds of untouched gifts. Delicious aromas drifted from the kitchen, and she struggled to contain the emotions threatening to shatter her slender control.

"Please, don't wait for me." She turned to plead with her mother. "I'm so tired." Her mother understood without further explanation. In minutes Courtney was settled in bed with an empty glass and a half-eaten turkey sandwich on the stand beside her and a heating pad at her feet. While the rest of the family retired to the living room for a much-delayed Christmas, she prayed that Julie would live and Mark would be safe. Slowly she drifted into a restless sleep.

* * *

"Courtney," her mother spoke softly and gave her shoulder a slight shake. Groggily she opened her eyes.

"It's Mark." Her mother smiled. "He's on the phone, and I thought you would want me to wake you."

Suddenly wide awake, she stumbled from bed and staggered into the hall to grasp the phone.

"Mark?"

"I'm okay, how about you?" His voice soothed and reassured.

"Is Julie going to be all right?" She ignored his question.

"Yes, she was in surgery almost two hours, but she's in a private room now and the doctor thinks she'll recover fully. No one got a chance to tell you that she's pregnant, but that added to our concern for her. The doctor says the shock could still bring on a miscarriage, but he doesn't think it will happen. Julie's strong and it seems her baby is, too."

They talked about Julie for several minutes, then he spoke of the file he still had to recover.

"I won't call again until this is over," he warned. "I'm leaving Denver tonight, and it's best that you not know where I'll be going. Perry knows by now that his men have failed to stop me. He'll send others, but this time I have backup I trust, and there are no blank spaces in my memory."

She wanted to ask if he'd be coming back. Instead, she said, "Please be careful. You'll be constantly in my prayers."

"And you in mine." His voice dropped a register. "I know now that God never abandoned me for a minute, but there are things I still need to work out. I'll be in touch as soon as I am able. Oh—and Courtney?"

"Yes?" she whispered, her heart aching for a man who was only promising to get in touch with her when he felt it safe to do so.

"I feel in my heart that next Christmas will be better—for both of us."

She gathered her courage to speak what was in her heart. "It will be if you are with me," she said softly.

"Merry Christmas—until then."

"Merry Christmas," she whispered back as he gently broke the connection.

NINETEEN

Mark stood at the window of the empty banquet room, not seeing the sturdy pansies and crocuses making their debut below. He didn't want to be here. The faraway Colorado Rockies seemed to call to him, and he thought of the woman he hadn't seen for three months, but whose image never left his mind. Footsteps, light and quick, could be heard in the corridor. He didn't turn until they paused behind him.

"Hello, Mark." Venita's voice was soft, hesitant.

"Why did you ask to see me?" He skipped the pleasantries, but didn't fail to notice that she had lost weight and her eyes were rimmed with red. Her hair lacked its usual luster, and the navy skirt and blazer she wore appeared uncharacteristically conservative and dull for the woman who had once been his wife. It wasn't the first time she'd contacted him to plead for her father since his return to Washington, but it was the first time they'd met face-to-face. Even though he'd be forever grateful for her generosity that probably saved Julie's life and that of her baby, he wouldn't have agreed to meet her today if Desden hadn't insisted.

He had no desire to hurt Venita, but neither did he have any desire to eat lunch with her and listen to her try to justify the actions of a man who had no scruples, to whom power and prestige were everything, no matter how much his daughter loved him. When the maitre d' offered to seat him, he'd impulsively requested permission to wait in the banquet room for his lunch partner's arrival.

Marshals would have placed Senator Perry under arrest by now. He had hired an army of attorneys to stall his being sent to prison to await trial. An intricate plan to remove evidence from the Justice Department had been anticipated by Draper, and two days ago the only survivor of Perry's team in the Colorado mountains, one of the two mysterious men on snowmobiles who had attempted to kill him and Courtney, had negotiated a plea bargain. In exchange for his testimony against Perry, Walker would plead guilty to reduced charges.

Early this morning a federal judge had ordered that Perry be picked up and held without bail. He'd set a trial date for late September.

"Would you like to sit down? I reserved a table." Venita sounded both tired and resigned. For just a moment he wondered at the irony of perhaps the biggest story of her career landing squarely in her lap, yet not one word had aired under her byline concerning her father's involvement.

"I'm not hungry," he demurred. "But if you . . ."

"No, this is more private here." She stared through the glass windows of the balcony as he had done earlier. For a woman who made her living talking, what she had to say now came with great difficulty. Finally she said the words baldly, without preamble, "Daddy killed himself this morning."

Mark froze, unsure he'd heard her right, then found himself drowning in a storm of feelings. There was anger that the selfish old man had cheated justice. He wouldn't have to face the collapse of his empire, endure the scorn of either his contemporaries or his constituents, nor would he have to spend one night locked in a cell. He wouldn't have to pay for all the misery and heartache he'd dealt others.

His eyes traveled slowly over Venita's face and his heart softened. She'd loved her father, and for her there was no consolation that he'd gone to a better place. Her idol was gone. He hadn't only died; he'd left a legacy that mocked the memories she should have been able to treasure. The first tears he'd ever seen her shed slipped down her cheeks. He opened his arms and held her as she sobbed. Her tears seemed to wash away some of his anger.

After a few minutes her tears subsided, and she groped in her bag for a tissue. When she'd wiped her eyes and patted the wet spot on his jacket, she looked up at him, her green eyes shimmering wetly and he was struck by a resemblance to Julie he'd never consciously noticed before. Perhaps she, too, had a mixture of European and Lamanite ancestors.

"Exposing Daddy's crimes will accomplish nothing now," Venita spoke earnestly. "Dragging his name through the mud will only hurt Mother and my sisters. I know there are others involved who will be prosecuted and Daddy's name will come up, but I can lessen the pain for both my family and the people back home he betrayed. I've already released a statement to the press saying Daddy had cancer and that the pain had become unbearable. Please don't be angry because of what I've done."

"You know, don't you, that both of your sisters' husbands were involved? Your family won't escape scrutiny no matter what story you tell." He took no satisfaction in the pain in her eyes. He could only admire the courage that kept her fighting.

She made no excuses, but her eyes told him she needed some kind of forgiveness from him. It was time to let all the anger and bitterness go. Roy Perry would face a worthier judge now than he would have ever faced in any earthly courtroom.

"I told you I don't blame you for anything," he spoke gently. "I admire you and your talent. I always have. If there were any way to spare you the pain your father has brought you, I would do it, but I don't doubt for one minute that you will make it."

"Thank you," she whispered. "Sometimes I wish I had tried harder to be the kind of wife you wanted."

"We both know our marriage was never meant to be, but I think we can take comfort that we didn't fail entirely. Respect remains." He brushed her cheek with his finger.

"Yes, respect, and I hope friendship," she echoed. "But not the kind of love and shared values you once told me would forge a union that would endure through all eternity. At this moment I find myself wishing I could believe in that kind of love, but in all honesty, I don't believe it exists. At least it doesn't exist for me . . . though it might for you if you return to Colorado."

Mark smiled. Suddenly he felt as though a load had been removed from his shoulders. He had a life and dreams he wished to claim. He'd still have to testify at some of the trials of other participants named in the indictment, particularly the doctor who had treated him in Dallas, but he wouldn't have to stay in Washington. He could go home. A rush of warmth filled his heart. Venita, too, needed to put the past behind her. If lending his validation to her plan to protect her family in some small way by lying about her father's reason for taking his life would help her, he wouldn't dispute her claim. The truth would eventually emerge, but hopefully by that time, Venita and her family would have found their own peace with the past.

* * *

Feeling as restless as her students, Courtney checked her watch. Ten more minutes until the bell. She wasn't certain whether the flurry of snow outside her classroom window after two weeks of spring weather was the reason she found focusing on verbs a chore, or if the snow brought with it too many memories.

Mark hadn't called since Christmas, and she'd caught the pitying glances her mother and sisters-in-law gave her when they thought she didn't see, but somewhere deep inside she knew that one day Mark would return. He'd promised that when the Perry case was settled he would be in touch. Implicit in that promise had been so much more. Perhaps more than by any words Mark had spoken, she had been sustained by a deep spiritual awareness that her Heavenly Father approved of the hope she sheltered in her heart.

She'd followed the progression of the case in the papers and been surprised that so little of the story had been told. She knew the Brewster family and her former fiancé had been questioned by a grand jury concerning their connection to Perry's schemes and that the Brewsters were facing financial difficulties. The company Greg worked for had filed bankruptcy, leaving him unemployed. His wife of only four months was said to be seeking a divorce, but Courtney took no satisfaction in Greg's troubles. She only wished Perry's trial would begin soon.

The bell finally rang and her students raced for the door. Gathering up her purse and a portfolio of papers to grade, she followed them at a slower pace. As she reached for the front door of the school, a hand pushed it open and a voice said, "Thank goodness. I was beginning to think that bell would never ring."

She looked up into Mark's smiling face and felt her heart turn a quick somersault. He'd been attractive when she'd first seen him in spite of his months of malnutrition and a thick stubble of whiskers on his face. Now with his hair styled, his mustache neatly trimmed, and an additional fifteen or twenty pounds filling out his frame, he took her breath away.

Taking her hand, he led her down the steps. Instead of turning toward the faculty parking lot, he began to walk. Huge fat snow flakes fluttered lazily to the ground around them. She didn't know what to say. There was so much she longed to ask, so much she wanted to share, she didn't know where to begin. Strangely, it was enough to walk beside him with her hand in his.

At last he stopped where a small footbridge crossed a tiny stream swollen with early spring runoff. He released her hand to clasp her shoulders, turning her to face him.

"It's been so long," he whispered. "And you're as beautiful as my memory kept telling me you were."

"I'm not beautiful," she denied his words. "You're the one—"

"You are beautiful," he insisted. "I once thought that when a woman was referred to as being beautiful on the inside, it was a subtle hint that she didn't look like much on the outside, but she was nice. Now I know a woman can truly be beautiful any way you look at her, both inside and outside." He grinned in a mischievous way she'd never seen before. "And I can assure you, you're more than pleasant to look at."

"I missed you," Courtney admitted with a blush as she brushed aside his compliment.

"I didn't call," he told her, "because there was so much I wanted to say, and there was too much to resolve before facing you. My memory returned completely that night we were in the mine. I wanted to tell you what I learned, but I wanted to discuss it first with the man who was my bishop when I lived in Washington before. He's now a stake president, and he arranged for me to spend some time with a visiting authority from Salt Lake."

He paused, and she waited for him to continue. The words began to spill out, and he recounted his nightmare imprisonment and the terrible choice he'd been forced to make. She felt a mounting sense of horror as he recounted the threats made by Senator Perry that drove him to push the fade to black concept he'd learned in the military to a dangerous level he might have never escaped. A sense of wonder filled her heart as she realized the depth of faith it took for him to do what he had done. His faith in a loving Heavenly Father was the only thing his captors had been unable to strip from him. Prayer had been his only comfort. Yet he had voluntarily risked all that, knowing his mind could be permanently shattered, to protect Sam and those who carried the gospel to the countrymen of his tormenters.

"God didn't abandon me even when I struggled through the deepest darkness. He sent me to you and allowed you to show me the light," he ended his story.

"It wasn't me," she smiled and found speaking difficult. A lump had grown in her throat, inhibiting the words she wanted to say. "When I was in Honduras, many of the people we taught told me the Book of Mormon sounded familiar to them and I knew the Holy Ghost was stirring memories of their premortal life. I think the same thing happened to you. You chose triggers that would penetrate the deepest well of mental blackness you could sink into, then trusted God to send someone to share the gospel with you once more."

"I don't believe he sent just anyone to bring the gospel back to me," Mark's voice dropped to a conspiratorial whisper. "He sent you because he knew I not only needed the gospel in my life, but I need you beside me throughout this life and forever. I love you, Courtney. Will you share forever with me?"

"Oh, Mark," she whispered, trembling with joy. "Nothing could make me happier." Leaning into him she met his lips with her own, becoming totally oblivious to the falling snow and the honking horn of a car full of students on their way home from school.

"You should know that before coming to you, I had a talk with my bishop concerning my marriage to Venita and the divorce we obtained. I didn't want anything to keep us from starting our marriage with eternal vows in the temple. I also needed to make certain I could support a wife and family, so I applied for Kyle's job with Sheriff Boulter, but if your dad agrees I'd like to buy a partnership with him and your brothers."

"Part of the ranch should have been yours." She knew that if his grandfather had known he was alive, the old man would have left the ranch in his care instead of selling it to her father.

"Grandfather sent all of the money your father paid him for the ranch to Sam. Knowing Julie and I were alive, Sam never touched the money, but saved it for us. I'd like to invest my share of that money in the Grant ranch."

"Kyle?" She remembered the other part of Mark's statement. "Is he leaving?"

"Desden offered him a deputy marshal position and he accepted," Mark explained, then with a rueful smile he continued. "Des said to tell you if you decide to accept my offer, he'll venture out here to wish us well at the reception, but other than that we'll have to go east to visit him. He says the West isn't good for his health; he suffered more injuries and uncomfortable weather conditions here in two weeks than he'd gone through in all his previous years."

Courtney laughed. A snowflake landed on Mark's mouth, and standing on her toes, she kissed it away. His arms tightened around her and she felt her heart begin a familiar rhythmic beat. Mark raised his head and listened as though he, too, heard the beat. It came softly through the falling snow, not a pounding, angry beat, but a sweet promise of peace and love carried by the pulse of native drums. Mark clasped Courtney's hand and looked into her eyes. A silent promise passed between them as Mark quietly spoke the final line of the song that had brought them together: "Giv'n this land if we live righteously." And in her heart she knew God promised so much more to those who hold his gospel most dear.

ABOUT THE AUTHOR

Jennie Hansen attended Ricks College and graduated from Westminster College in Salt Lake City, Utah. She has been a newspaper reporter, editor, and librarian, and is presently a circulation specialist for the Salt Lake City library system.

Her church service has included teaching in all auxiliaries and serving in stake and ward Primary presidencies. She has also served as a den mother, stake public affairs coordinator, and ward chorister. Currently she is the education counselor in her ward Relief Society.

Jennie and her husband, Boyd, live in Salt Lake County. All five of their children and their spouses live nearby, which means that she gets to see her four grandsons often.

All I Hold Dear is Jennie's seventh book for the LDS market.

Jennie enjoys hearing from her readers. You can write to her in care of Covenant Communications, P.O. Box 416, American Fork, UT 84003-0416.

RUN Away HOME

"HE BLAMES YOU, YOU KNOW."

"I don't care. He deserves everything he got and then some." Megan crossed her legs and leaned back in her chair. She was glad the trial was over. In her work as a television investigative reporter, Megan found that every abuse story she covered stirred painful memories.

"Well, it was a great story, but I wouldn't want to be in your shoes when that guy finally gets out!" said her boss, Prescot.

"I'm not scared. Jasper talks a tougher game than he plays. He's really a sniveling coward." It wasn't the first time she'd met a man like Jasper. In her work Megan had met a lot of Jaspers, men who fed off the vulnerability of those smaller and weaker than themselves.

"Maybe. I'll admit it doesn't take much courage to cripple and starve children, then make them the focus of a solicitation scheme. After all, most people are only too willing to give to hungry, homeless children. But he won't forget he might have gotten away with it if you hadn't poked your pretty little nose into his scam and made it the highlight of the six o'clock news."

"What are you complaining about? I thought that's what you paid me for. I thought I was supposed to make certain your news team has—and I quote—'relevant, local, hard news' for your six and ten o'clock shows."

"Right—that's what I pay you for. What I don't pay you for is to do the prosecuting attorney's job for him. You could have gotten several exclusives out of the material you gift wrapped and handed to the prosecutor."

"But he wasn't even looking for a previous pattern of abuse. He might not have gotten a conviction without the testimony of Jasper's ex-girlfriend." Leave it to Prescot to be more concerned about the station's ratings than whether or not justice was served.

"I know. I know. You consider him an incompetent boob, and it isn't just him, is it? You don't have a very high opinion of men in general. Come to think of it, I don't think you like women much either, judging by the way you exposed that Bradshaw woman and her Women's Clinic last fall."

"Battered and neglected women and children have enough strikes against them without allowing scavengers to manipulate them and siphon off the already insufficient funds available to the few protective service programs out there," Megan said.

"Try to remember you work for Channel Two, not the social services department!" Prescot leaned across his wide desk, a stubby highlighting pen gripped in his thick fist. His round face was serious as he shook the pen at her for emphasis. "Maybe I've assigned you too many family problem stories. You take them too personally. That kind of emotional involvement can affect your work."

"Am I being complimented or reprimanded?"

"Complimented, I guess," Prescot chuckled. "You're tough and bright, the best reporter to come this way in a long time. I'll admit you're as good in the field as you are on that computer in there. I like you, but I don't understand you. A woman who looks like you should be in front of the camera, breaking your own stories on the air."

Bristling at his personal tone, Megan said dryly, "As you've mentioned before. But I don't want to read the news. I want to investigate and write it.

She stood up. "See you Monday, Prescot." She waggled two fingers at him and started toward the door.

"Not so fast. I called you in here for more than to compliment you on a story. It's come to my attention that you haven't taken any vacation time for more than two years. Personnel frowns on that. You do recall paid vacation is one of the benefits listed in your contract, don't you? I'll see you the first of September, not Monday." Holding up one hand to prevent being interrupted, he added, "That's an order."

Megan left Prescot's office with mixed feelings. What was she going to do with six weeks free of pressure and deadlines? She couldn't remember a time when she hadn't had to work.

Just as she reached for a tray of computer disks, two strong, male arms wrapped firmly around her. Megan instantly went rigid although not a flicker of emotion crossed her perfectly made-up features.

"Megan, I'm sorry. I should have known better." The arms holding her relaxed their grip and slowly turned her about. Warm brown eyes met hers in a questioning look before A.J., the cameraman, stepped back. Glancing at the items in her hands, he raised one eyebrow quizzically. "Surely the old ogre didn't fire you? After the journalistic coup you just pulled off, he's probably promoting you to the upper echelons and moving you into your own swank office!"

"Don't be silly, A.J. He just ordered me to use up my vacation time—beginning right now."

"Now that sounds like a cause to celebrate. Come, your chariot awaits. Let me just carry these things for you. Wave good-bye to the nice people." Taking her arm, he hustled her swiftly toward the door.

"A.J."

"Uh-uh. Don't stop to think. Don't pause to give Mr. P. time to reconsider. Just vamoose!"

"Really," she tried to protest as the laughing man ushered her through the door and into the elevator. "I can find my own way to my car." She put up with more nonsense from A.J. than she ever had from anyone else. Unlike most men who tried to get close to her, he didn't really frighten her. Sometimes he made her uneasy, but down deep she sensed a kindred vulnerability she couldn't brush off.

"Great! You can drop me off at my apartment on your way. I could even invite you up to see my etchings," he added with an exaggerated leer.

"In your dreams!" Megan's laughter floated across the parking garage as she unlocked the doors of her practical, navy blue Ford Escort.

"How about dinner tonight?"

"You never give up, do you? You know I don't date." The little car accelerated sharply away from a traffic light.

"Why not?"

"You're about the only friend I've got; I can't risk losing a friend by dating him."

"Why can't friends have dinner together?"

"Too dangerous. I don't want any entanglements. Entanglements have a bad way of starting over dinner for two."

"Where did you pick up that brilliant bit of philosophy? It sure wasn't from experience. I'll bet you could count on one hand the number of guys who have taken you to dinner."

Megan's face took on a shrouded look. A little white line formed at the corner of her mouth.

He knew she was hurt. "Oh, Megan. I'm sorry. Look, I know perfectly well you could have all the dates you wanted, but you just don't want to let any man in your life. That's the whole problem. Somebody hurt you so badly there's no way you'll even give the rest of us poor slobs a chance!"

The car lurched to an abrupt stop as Megan narrowly missed running a red light.

"Oh, great! Me and my big mouth! This is neither the time nor the place. You concentrate on driving, and I'll concentrate on keeping my mouth shut. Deal?"

"Deal."

He wasn't getting anywhere. What was he going to have to do to get Megan to confide in him? He'd like to build a more personal relationship, but there didn't seem to be any way past the barrier Megan erected every time he tried.

A few minutes later, Megan pulled up to the curb outside A.J.'s apartment building.

"Thanks for the lift."

"See you around!"

"Sooner than you think!" A.J. winked.

Megan shook her head as A.J. walked away, then pulled out during a break in traffic.

She wished she could be head over heels in love with the guy. He was fun, intelligent, and talented, and most importantly, Jason liked him.

"Mom, you left my uniform in the dryer too long again. It's all wrinkly."

"Just put it back in with a damp towel for ten minutes, Jason. It'll be okay."

"Are we going to stop at McDonald's on the way to my game?"

"No, you know your coach said to eat after, not before games. Get a glass of orange juice. That should hold you."

"Aw, Mom!"

In less than a minute Megan heard the refrigerator door slam and the unmistakable sound of a chair being dragged across the kitchen floor. Smiling, she stepped out of her skirt. After snapping it in place on the hanger that already held its matching jacket, she hung it in its place in the large walk-in closet covering one end of her bedroom. Moments later the sharp sting of warm water struck her bare skin. Ten minutes later, she was dressed in pale green linen pants and a neat, white pullover. With her beige-pink polished toes peeping through white sandals, she sat before her make-up mirror to urge her short, sleek curls into their usual flawless, sunny cap.

"Mom, aren't you ready yet?" Jason tapped on his mother's bedroom door before strolling in.

"I'll just be a moment. Do you have your glove?"

"A.J. has it. Come on. We get to ride in A.J.'s car with the top down."

"A.J.?"

"He came to see me pitch. Hurry, Mom. I can't be late. Coach Jensen said if anybody is late they have to sit out the first inning. If I'm not there, he'll let Monica pitch. Then we'll lose."

Taking one more glance in the mirror, Megan stood up. "All right. I'm ready, but we're not riding with A.J. We'll take our own car."

"But Mom, I never get to ride in A.J.'s car. Please . . ." The argument continued as Megan locked the door and approached the startlingly red Ferrari blocking her driveway.

"Please," A.J.'s voice joined her son's. "Besides, if we sit here arguing Jason will be late, and you know what that means!"

"Oh, all right!" Megan agreed reluctantly and pulled a green silk scarf from her handbag. "But you guys know I hate convertibles!"

When they reached the park, Jason scampered out of the car and raced to the home dugout, yelling over his shoulder, "Thanks, A.J. That was cool!"

"Whew! Guess we'd better find seats." A.J. lightly brushed his knuckles across Megan's cheek before opening his door. The unexpected touch sent a shiver down her spine. She jumped out of the car before he could reach her side.

"You find seats. I'll be back in a minute." Needing an excuse to escape his presence for a moment, she hurried to the ladies' room to straighten her hair. "Why can't he leave me alone?" she muttered crossly to herself as she tucked a curl behind her ear and lifted the crown, which had been flattened by her scarf. "I can't give him what he wants." Giving herself one final glimpse in the mirror, she left to rejoin A.J.

"Batter up!"

"Perfect timing, they're just starting." A.J. patted the space beside him. She knew he noticed the careful space she left between them on the bleacher bench. To her relief he didn't comment.

"Your right fielder is too deep!" A.J. yelled at the coach a few minutes later. "Bring her in! Jason, watch the way that batter is choking up on the bat! Keep an eye on first base!" Megan smiled in amusement. Their position behind the backstop didn't deter A.J. When Jason hit a line drive and managed to make it all the way to second base, she found herself standing and clapping too. "He's safe!" A.J. roared.

"Safe!" bellowed the umpire as Jason's teammate Monica slid into home. Dusting off the seat of her pants she swaggered, red pigtails dancing, toward the Blue Jays' dugout while the Lobos' coach screamed insults at the catcher for letting a girl get past him. Megan smiled at Monica, who waved at her. It irritated Megan the way the Lobos' coach ordered his team around as though he were a Marine drill sergeant.

"If Jason ever had a coach like that oaf, I'd pull him out of Little League," Megan whispered to A.J.

"Aw come on, Megan," A.J. argued. "You won't punish Jason because he draws a bad coach once in a while, will you?"

Megan shaded her eyes with one hand against the glare of the late afternoon sun before she answered with fierce intensity. "He's my son. I won't let anyone treat him that way."

"You can't always fight his battles for him, Megan. Too much protection hurts more than it helps."

"I won't let him be abused!" No way would Megan sit by and see Jason burdened with physical or emotional scars.

"Okay, don't get upset. Let's just watch the game."

"Pass the chicken, champ!"

"Sure, A.J." Jason wiped his fingers on the grass before handing the paper bucket to A.J. The three sat on A.J.'s car blanket in a shady spot in the park.

"See, this isn't so bad, is it, Megan? We're having dinner together, and it doesn't hurt a bit." His brown eyes laughed into her blue ones.

"You've got to be kidding! I'm sitting on the ground like some kind of contortionist, trying to keep grass and dirt out of my plate, getting grease all over my fingers, and you think we're having fun?"

"At least you can't call this getting involved."

"Mom, we can go now if you want to."

A.J.'s mouth tightened as he caught the look of concern in the boy's eyes. He'd noticed the uncanny way Jason immediately zeroed in on any hint of physical discomfort from Megan. Mother and son were close, but Jason assumed an adult responsibility at times that left A.J. uncomfortable.

"No, I'm all right," Megan reassured Jason. "Eat your chicken. We're celebrating, remember? It's not every day the Blue Jays beat the Lobos!"

"How about those Blue Jays!" A.J. pretended to slug Jason's shoulder. After a brief tussle, Jason sat quietly staring into the distance. Turning thoughtfully to the man beside him he asked, "Are you my dad, A.J.?"

"What—?" A.J. coughed as the soft drink he was attempting to swallow seemed to get caught in his throat.

"Jason! You know he isn't your father!" Megan turned embarrassed eyes briefly to A.J. before giving her attention back to her son. "Whatever made you ask that?"

"Well then, are you my uncle, A.J.?" the boy persisted.

"Jason!"

Jason hung his head sheepishly. "Monica said when dads don't live with moms, then uncles come to visit, and A.J. is the only man who ever comes to visit us." He looked challengingly at his mother.

"Oh, Jason!" Megan's cheeks flared red.

"I don't believe it. The unflappable Megan Nordfelt is embarrassed!" A.J.'s laughter rumbled from deep within him, making her even more mortified, and A.J. found his laughter met with a stony glare.

Jason looked contrite. "I'm sorry, Mom. I didn't really think A.J.

was my dad. I just thought he might be an uncle, and if he were, he could tell me about my dad."

A.J.'s laughter disappeared. He sat very still.

"Jason, I've always answered your questions about your father." She avoided thinking about the past as much as possible, but long ago she had determined to be honest with Jason about his father. She'd always known a time would come when her child would want to know his father's name and possibly contact him. She hoped that time hadn't come. She wasn't ready. Why was Jason asking these questions now? Puzzled, she faced her son. "What do you want to know that I haven't told you already?"

"Oh, just stuff." The boy paused, digging one sneakered heel back and forth in the grass.

Megan put her arms around the troubled boy. "He's just like a bigger you." She tried to smile.

"Mom, you told me he looks like me, only bigger, and I know he had to go away to a far-off country, and you were too young, so he doesn't know about me. But you said you didn't know if he likes sports or what position he played when he played Little League. Maybe he didn't even play Little League."

"You're right," Megan whispered. She felt a haunting sadness. "I don't know about things like that. I just know he's big and strong and very kind . . . and he likes to climb mountains. That's a sport, isn't it?"

"Really, Mom? He climbs mountains?"

"Oh, yes. He's a very good mountain climber."

"Gosh, Mom. You never told me that before."

"I guess I didn't."

"I wish I could meet him."

"Someday, son." Her arm went around his shoulders to pull him closer for a quick hug.

"It's not really fair, Mom. Other guys live in the same house as their dads. Even Monica's uncle lives at her house, and he's cool and really funny."

The word "uncle" reminded Megan of A.J.'s presence. Abruptly she lifted her chin to find herself staring directly into A.J.'s face. For long seconds their eyes held. A.J. was the first to look away.

"Perhaps we should get this young man home." A.J. rose to his feet and began gathering up the remains of their impromptu picnic. Megan helped him. Her movements felt jerky and uncoordinated. She wished A.J. hadn't been a witness to the things she'd told Jason.

The pinks and golds of sunset had faded away, and the first early stars of evening were coming out when Megan found herself alone with A.J. on her small patio. They watched silently as gray shadows turned inky black.

"Are the things you told Jason about his father true?" A.J. put the question to Megan abruptly. After taking Megan and Jason home, he had stayed until Jason was in bed, blandly ignoring Megan's hints that he should leave. Shadows lengthened as day turned to night. She welcomed the protection of shadows.

"I've never lied to Jason," Megan bristled, "about his father or anything else."

Staring at the deepening night sky, she observed how the stars looked remotely like chips of ice on warm, black velvet spread across the vast sky.

"Was he really kind to you? Jason's father?"

"He saved my life." She wished A.J. would go away. She didn't want to remember.

"I thought he hurt you badly."

"Why would you think that?" Pain was creeping in, but not the kind of pain A.J. referred to.

"I don't know. Some man hurt you. I assumed it was Jason's father."

"You assume a lot." The pain was there, deep and dark.

"Do you still love him?" The words were barely a whisper.

"It's really none of your business, but no, I don't. I never did." In the back of her mind a nagging doubt questioned whether she was really telling the truth. "As I'm sure you've guessed, we hardly knew each other. He rescued me when I was hurt and frightened, then he married me."

"Does he know about Jason?"

Megan couldn't answer. He was twisting her soul.

"Why didn't you tell him?"

"How do you know I didn't?"

"I just know."

"It didn't seem right."

"I don't understand."

"You don't need to understand." She fought to maintain her smooth, cool facade. She could feel great cracks spreading across her protective shell. "Please go, A.J. I'm really tired, and it's all really none of your concern."

"It's more my concern than you realize. But okay, I'll go. Just answer one more question. Are you still married?"

Megan didn't bother to respond.

Without a word A.J. understood that she had no intention of discussing her private life with him or anyone else. He stood, his fists clenched then unclenching, his mind six hundred miles and ten years away. For a long time he watched the silent woman cloaked in a distant sadness. She was the most self-contained, closed person he had ever met. Only where her son and her work were concerned did she ever exhibit passion and vitality. Even there, something was missing. Grimly his lips tightened and his knuckles whitened. It was time to wake the sleeping princess.

Turning on his heel he abruptly walked away.

Megan listened to the red sports car roar to life. Leaning back in her chair, she surveyed the brilliant stars glittering in their rich heavenly setting above her, but in her mind's eye she saw only the intense shine of two eyes that had once gazed down into hers, full of promises. She remembered reaching for those stars, only to find her hands were left holding ashes. Shivering in spite of the warm summer evening, Megan rose to her feet and hurried inside, locking the patio door behind her.

Run Away Home
is available at all LDS Bookstores